# Succulent Tales

Pat

Thank you for
making me a part of your
TLC celebrates

Enjoy the sexy poem
and good foods

Valerie J Reese

June 2007

apples

# Succulent Tales

## A COOKBOOK OF SENSUAL PLEASURES

Valinda Johnson Brown

ILLUSTRATED BY John T. Scott

CITADEL PRESS
KENSINGTON PUBLISHING CORP.
www.kensingtonbooks.com

CITADEL PRESS BOOKS are published by

Kensington Publishing Corp.
850 Third Avenue
New York, NY 10022

All Kensington titles, imprints, and distributed lines are available at special quantity discounts for bulk purchases for sales promotions, premiums, fund-raising, educational, or institutional use. Special book excerpts or customized printings can also be created to fit specific needs. For details, write or phone the office of the Kensington special sales manager: Kensington Publishing Corp., 850 Third Avenue, New York, NY 10022, attn: Special Sales Department; phone 1-800-221-2647.

First printing: September 2006

10 9 8 7 6 5 4 3 2 1

Printed in the United States of America

Library of Congress Control Number: 2006926712

ISBN 0-8065-2733-1

# Contents

# Foreword

Kalamu ya Salaam

WE COME FROM THE SOUTH, FROM THE SUN. A PLACE WHERE FOOD WAS available winter, spring, summer, and fall. Fruit and vegetables, fish, fowl, and red meat available year-round.

Once, when I was in Tanzania, I saw so many varieties of bananas I could have eaten a different kind each day of the week. Really loved those small orange ones! The nearby emerald Indian Ocean provided a bountiful harvest. I had barbecued fish, fresh from the dockside of Dar Es Salaam.

In Ghana, I saw a young sister sporting a carrot top—not dyed hair but a tray of tender young orange tubers. Somehow it had never occurred to me that I would see carrots in Ghana, but I did, beautifully ported atop the bushy crown of a smiling chocolate-colored sister. There I tried the chewy spiciness of smoked fish.

And don't get me started about the Caribbean and South America, about the delectable herbs, spices, and vegetables of Jamaica, the succulent citrus and sweet fruit Garden of Eden that is Surinam, the callaloo of Trinidad, the curried crabs of Tobago. Which is to say, by the time our people got to America, we had traveled through continents and islands, tasting and bringing with us all kinds of culinary dishes and cooking routines.

After centuries of culinary investigation, we know fried, we know baked. We know fricaseed, we know barbecued. We know that gumbo is more tasty than soup. We know swamp water (tea and lemonade combined), we know ginger beer, sorrel, and sarsaparilla. We know that every flavor has a multitude of complements. You can put nuts in salads, fruit with your fish. And on and on.

Cooking is not just about rotely obeying a recipe, but rather, at its most high, cooking is about using a recipe as a starting point while following one's tongue and one's muse. The admonition "don't play with your food" does not apply to creative cooks. Even if the meal is but a simple platter of red beans and brown rice, it should be prepared with care and be a pleasure to consume.

Good food should make you shake your head and wiggle your toes, should make you literally dance as you chew. Plus, as anyone who has seen black dance can testify, our stepping is a sensual celebration of sex. No doubt. Which, all taken together, brings us to Valinda Johnson Brown's hot cookbook, "Succulent Tales: A Cookbook of Sensual Pleasures." Ms. Brown's cookbook celebrates both food and sex, and offers recipes for life based on the philosophy of enjoying life through the art of cooking and the art of loving. This cookbook is about what one does when one appreciates life.

A person who has not cooked for someone whom they love has not yet fully expressed their love. If you have a passion for someone, prepare them a dish. If you don't know how—how to cook, how to love—here is a book to get you started. Good food. Good sex. The essence of life. Enjoy.

# Introduction

I WATCHED HIM DRIZZLE PURE VIRGIN OLIVE OIL ON HER NAKED BODY and massage her gently while he held her and separated her slender legs. He glanced at me as he laid thyme in her. He opened the oven door. It was hot. We drank red wine as we stood patiently at the stove, absorbing heat from every which way while we inhaled the aroma of the slow-roasting goose. I sat at his table. Brownstone flatware, hand-painted glass goblets, and a small bouquet of pink peonies adorned his dining room table.

He placed my plate before me. He pulled his chair close to me. He sat so close, his leg touched mine. The goose was cooked. We began our intimate dinner of crispy roast goose, sweet potato pecan yams, buttery French beans, and good bread. He offered to slice my goose. I obliged. He offered to serve me the tender meat. I obliged. He offered to give me more sauce. I obliged. No longer could I separate food from erotica. And no longer did we. That was the beginning.

I HAD NEVER eaten food like roast goose or turtle soup before I met my husband, Ed Brown. Nor had I experienced the tasting and eating of food with such erotic pleasure. But that evening, during our early courtship, he invited me to his home for supper, and I saw him tenderly massage that goose for the oven and orchestrate the slicing and offering of the meat to me. I discovered that evening that eating food sustains more than the body; it sustains the spirit and gives birth to dreams of erotica. And this is what *Succulent Tales: A Cookbook of Sensual Pleasures* is all about—delicious recipes accompanied by poems and prose that capture the sensuality of food and inspire tender moments of love.

We are multisensory beings, but we use only a fraction of our gift to allow love and beauty to enrich our lives. We should make full use of our senses of taste, smell, sight, and sound to extract all the beauty created when we are giving and sharing good food and company. When we are graced at the table, we should not only fill our bellies—but we should feed our souls. How do you do that? You must invite love to the table. Be it love for whom you cook, love for the celebration, love for the meal's creation, love for the foods selected—no matter what, love must be the main ingredient.

This love is the reason why food is such a visceral part of my life and my writing. I offer other reasons too, for I have given some thought as to how I became a writer of food erotica, and I want to share my experiences and my process with others who want to follow their passion.

Without the generous heart, warm affection, and masterful cookery of Ed, I would not be who I am today. Ed's love of food and his remarkable Creole cooking that he fed and taught me, threw me over the edge—like his Louisiana gumbo, which inspired me to write the following piece entitled "Sea of Indulgence":

> *A climax of intense acceleration endures*
> *when you eat his gumbo. First, you*
> *climax, then serenity enters. But*
> *it's not anticlimactic—you come and*
> *come again with each mouthful.*

This gumbo, his gumbo, always makes my libido blossom.

With a degree in journalism, a completion of cooking school, and years' shared experience of love and food with Ed, cooking and writing about food became a natural progression. When I was asked to write restaurant reviews as a student at Peter Kump's New York Cooking School, it was not an assignment, it was an orgy. I instinctively gave the foods voices and personalities that enabled me to describe the dining experience more intimately, both as a student and later as a freelance food writer for *The Atlanta Journal-Constitution*.

Learning proprioceptive writing, taught to me by Atlanta playwright Sandra Deer, became the vehicle by which I often used to write food erotica. This practice is the process of listening to one's thoughts and writing them freely without self-criticism.

Using this technique to write my poems and create my recipes, I would

prepare a dish, sit at my kitchen table, light a candle and, most times, play
John Coltrane's "Love Supreme." I would reflect on the preparation of the
food, inhale its aroma, and gaze at its sight. Then I would taste. I now had all
I needed to write because I also had my imagination and memories of sensual encounters that I would interweave into the delight of the moment. So
I would take pen to paper and write freely to create the food's sexual persona
and my erotic fantasy.

It was in the coming together of love experienced, good food shared, and
sex enjoyed that I began to write *Succulent Tales*. The initial writing came
when Ed prepared shrimp étouffée. With the first mouthful of this spicy
dish, I had the strong desire to seduce this Louisiana cook. I reached across
the kitchen table, pushed away the vase of flowers, grabbed Ed, held his
head to mine, and gave him a full-bodied wet kiss. That moment of lustful
celebration was so delightful and so sensual that I had to find a way to doc-
ument that wild fling. So I wrote a light-hearted tale of this experience and
called it "Reckless Love Affairs":

> That's why I jumped over the table. I was out of control when I
> wrapped my body around his chest. I admit it. But after eating the
> shrimp étouffée, I had to seduce somebody . . . don't you see.

I shared the piece with my dear friends, George Howell and Mtamanika
Youngblood. They came up with the idea of a book of erotic food writings,
and they were the force behind this project. George and Mtamanika inspired my confidence in this project and were my most ardent cheerleaders
and critics throughout.

Once the idea for *Succulent Tales* was planted in my head and my heart, I
began to develop recipes and search for foods I believed were nakedly attractive—for example, the Yellowtail Snapper of "I Miss You." The snapper itself, with its yellow streak down the sides of its pink scales, offered up an
innately seductive sight. Not much else is needed to make this dish more appealing, but I do seek to maximize the moment of total sensual bliss in each
food experience. So I decided to stuff it with a spicy crabmeat dressing.
Upon eating nearly half of this most fortunate choice, I realized how much I
was going to miss it when I ate the last morsel, and I wrote:

> *Even now as I eat you*
> *I miss you*

*and know that it can end*
*Bite by bite*
*you disappear*
*to leave me alone*

I devoured the snapper almost whole and became drunk from its absence and missed it with each bite.

I would also seek out sensual encounters in the shopping for fresh ingredients, in the preparation of meals, and in the drama of food consumed. If any part of the process tripped my senses to one of erotic pleasure, I stepped into it and let myself become absorbed in the brief passion passing. I then began to write those feelings down with the pen of a food seductress. It was like falling in love every day—exhausting and exuberating.

Although the theme of aphrodisiacs bounced around in my mind occasionally while writing this book, foods were not selected based on any erotic qualities particular to the foods. What I sought was the sprouting of sensuality with the combination of food and love on whatever unforgettable, erotic spark had introduced itself. Therefore, selections for the book were based on the ability of the food to seduce through its aroma, its sight, its taste, or its erotic persona with my appreciation or with the sharing of foods with my husband, family, and friends. The opportunity to seduce was wide open. However, if it could not awaken passion, it did not make the cut.

Use this cookbook with the poems, stories, and recipes as a script to act out your sensual life of food and love. Make erotic pleasures your own so that they become second nature and spontaneously tasty for you and your lover. This I offer as a preliminary guide to study, in hopes that you will broaden your imagination and enjoy the art of food erotica. With love and respect from your lover with whom you share your table and with the love transmitted through the foods enjoyed, you can stimulate your imagination and assist in the deliverance of dreams heretofore deferred.

The pursuit of pleasure between lovers should know no shame. As you read and cook from this book, dispel all inhibitions. Liberate your imagination when you are planning a seduction. Always keep an attractive, clean, and uncluttered space during the course of a romantic evening, as it's a must in creating a sensual setting. Always cook with the freshest ingredients. Do not sacrifice quality. Half the effort of creating tasty morsels is cooking with the best ingredients. It's simple. If it starts well, more likely it ends well.

After you've mastered a recipe, make it your own, that is, add or subtract whatever you wish that makes it tastier to you. Stories embellish eroticism, so read the poetry to your lover. Make it a prelude to a kiss. I offer *Succulent Tales: A Cookbook of Sensual Pleasures* as a stimulus to the creation of a world of food erotica in your lives.

# Acknowledgments

I GIVE THANKS TO THE ONE WHO LOVED ME FIRST AND BEST, MY husband, Ed Brown, who opened my life to the passions of food and love; my most loyal and best friends, Mtamanika Youngblood and George Howell whose idea it was to create this work and who assisted me with their suggestions, editing, and critiquing to its completion; Sandra Deer's friendship and teaching of Proprioceptive Writing that became a vehicle to produce this work and the Atlanta proprioceptive writers for their support and encouragement throughout the years; Kalamu ya Salaam's early inspiration and acknowledgment of my work's potential and clear and focused advice all along the way; John T. Scott's generous acceptance to be a part of this project and his extraordinary body of the most beautiful and creative art in the world; Sandra Locklin's giving of her outstanding organizational skills and everlasting friendship; Dot Greer's lifelong friendship, encouragement, and financial support; Patrise Perkins-Hooker, Harriett Thomas, Sepati Mogotsi, Palesa Mohajane, Jeanette Foreman, and Rabiyah Crichton for their friendship, loyalty, and willingness to listen whenever I spoke of my work; Val Suber and Diann Kayah for their friendship and daily advice of the book's work-in-progress and, their patience to hear me out; Mary Erickson's friendship and her honest and precise copyediting; Ekwueme Michael Thelwell's eloquent embrace of my work; Nora Harlow, who first said to me, "You've got to get this out there"; Kay Goldstein's and Susan Puckett's generosity; Zeb and Bobbi Blackman's support; Michael Johnson, my son, who smiled encouragingly whenever I spoke of my work and never doubted its success; Beatrice Ross and Sylvia Andrews, my sisters, and Elliott, Perry, and Bernard Warbington, my brothers, and Alveno Ross, my brother-in-law, for their love and constant support; Felicia, Charlotte, and Deborah, my nieces, who were always encouraging and excited about my work. Rebecca Lillian Hart Warbington and William Henry Warbington, my parents, for their love and faith in whatever I did and their good Southern cooking; Alexis, Aliyah, and Tyler, my grandchildren, who visit me every other weekend to reorganize my work space so that they can write their own stories while eating cake and popcorn and drinking hot chocolate; Nika, my goddaughter, who took cooking lessons from me at the age of ten and has been building her culinary repertoire ever since; Daryl Evans and Nancy and Cary Smith, who first gave me a chef job; Oprah Winfrey's inspiration over the airwaves and her philosophy that you can, you will, you must follow your passion; Emeril Lagasse's kicking-it-up-a-notch food philosophy; Gabriel Garcia Marquez's and Toni Morrison's magical literary body of work; Eric Waters and Bruce Morton, photographers and nature purists; Marie Brown, my agent, who worked tirelessly to get this book published "well" and along the way offered her intellect and her thoughtful suggestions to improve *Succulent Tales;* my initial editor, Bob Shuman, who saw the potential of this book from the beginning and offered ideas on how to make it better; and my editor, Danielle Chiotti, who gave persistent precise yet tenderly thoughtful suggestions to create a more beautifully structured *Succulent Tales.*

# Succulent Tales

apples

# CHAPTER ONE

## *Succulent Soups*

*I close my eyes and see you coming. . . . I say this for I dearly
need you to know how dreadful it is for me after having you,
how not having you affects me most drastically and most dearly.
Please be aware, though, that I am not crazy.*

—SHRIMP BISQUE, "GOOD STUFF"

**RECIPES**

"A Sea of Indulgence" / Ed's Gumbo

"All I Want" / Brie and Smoked Salmon Soup

"I Love To" / Crawfish and Corn Bisque

"Good Stuff" / Shrimp Bisque

"Naked" / Sweet Corn Soup and Roasted Red Pepper Soup

"Your Musk Entered the Room" / Wild Mushroom Soup

"You" / Potato Leek Soup

"No Strings Attached" / Spinach Soup

"I Love All of You" / Tomato Basil Soup

"If Something Goes Wrong" / French Onion Soup

"A Swift Soft Sphere" / Butternut Squash Soup

"My Dear Baby" / Roasted Peppers and Pear Soup

"Ed Fed Me First" / Ed's Turtle Soup

"Dark and Succulent" / Duck and Andouille Sausage Gumbo

"My Morning Glory" / Roasted Sweet Potato Soup with
   Andouille Sausage

1

# A Sea of Indulgence

I take one spoonful of his gumbo and my libido blossoms. A mist of moist morning dew gathers in the domain of my passion, creating magnetism between my legs, making my knees leap inward to touch, to be touched, to come within, to hold that moment. Its dark brown filé sauce is potent as I get deeper into its delicious taste. A climax of intense acceleration endures when I eat his gumbo. First, I climax; then serenity enters. But it's not anticlimactic; I come and come again with each mouthful.

The dried sassafras leaf, ground to a Creole seasoning of filé powder, is the maestro of the dish and sets the stage for seduction. It lures me with its mahogany roux, tempting me to come closer to savor its aroma and experience its hot spicy bite. I'm captured! Like a New Orleans spell, I am now in its orbit—drunk from its captivating essence and ready to be taken.

Quivering with anticipation, I extend my hand to the bowl and dip my spoon into the rich broth, extracting slivers of thin crabmeat, curled around pink shrimp, entwined amidst white rice, red tomatoes, green onions, garlic, and okra sailing like conquering voyagers in a sea of indulgence.

I separate my lips . . . it enters my mouth . . . my pulse quickens . . . my eyes close. Fire, steam, then smoke race from every pore of my body. Effervescent spirits rush into me as I am propelled into a spiral of no return. That is, until the next spoonful.

## Ed's Gumbo

Sometimes in our lives, we might be lucky enough to get a lover who exudes sexual fumes by his mere presence, creating heat in all of your cleavages, even in your dreams. That's when you know you're in a sea of indulgence. Outrageous lust as powerful as this comes only at night, and maybe that's why Ed refuses to make his gumbo during the daylight hours. He conjures it up late when I'm asleep, causing rapturous dreams of intense moans and yearnings of seduction as I reach for him and his pot of gumbo. Yes, with aromatic dried sassafras leaves of filé powder steaming from the pot of queenly crabmeat and strutting shrimp, and break-dancing with onions, garlic, okra, and tomatoes, Ed maketh me lie down in his pasture always, even in my dreams.

2 quarts fish stock (see appendix A), in all, or store-bought
    low-sodium fish broth

6 blue crabs, precooked (break in half)

3 tablespoons oil

3 large onions, chopped

5 garlic cloves, minced

1 16-ounce pack frozen sliced okra

1 28-ounce can Italian plum tomatoes with juice

1 tablespoon Creole seasoning

6 tablespoons oil

6 tablespoons flour

2 cups stock

1 5-ounce bag dried shrimp

5 bay leaves

2 cups chopped green onions

1 cup chopped fresh parsley

3 teaspoons dry thyme

16 ounces crabmeat

2 teaspoons salt

1 teaspoon pepper

3 teaspoons gumbo filé

1 teaspoon Creole seasoning

2 pounds, medium-large shrimp, peeled and deveined

Salt and pepper to taste

5 cups cooked long-grain white rice

1. Prepare fish stock in a large pot, cooking about 20 minutes. Add precooked blue crabs broken in half and cook another 20 minutes. Strain stock and set aside. Remove crabs and set aside. Discard the remains.

2. Heat oil in a large heavy-duty pot, and sauté onions and garlic until translucent, about 3 minutes. Add okra and cook until tender, about 20 minutes, stirring and scraping the bottom of the pot constantly. Add tomatoes (squeeze and break tomatoes by hand over the pot). Add 1

tablespoon Creole seasoning and stir. Cook about 30 minutes over low heat, stirring constantly.

3.  In another large skillet (preferably cast iron) make a dark roux (see appendix A). Pour 6 tablespoons oil into skillet over medium-high heat and cook until oil smokes slightly. Stir in flour with a wooden spoon. Stir constantly about 20 minutes or until roux is a deep dark black-brown. Be careful not to burn. Carefully add 2 cups of the stock and continue to stir. Once completely mixed, pour into pot of onions, okra, and tomato mixture and stir.

4.  Add remaining stock and bring to a boil; then simmer. Add crabs broken in half.

5.  Add dried shrimp, bay leaves, green onions, parsley, and thyme. Simmer 30 minutes, uncovered. Stir occasionally.

6.  Add crabmeat, salt, and pepper. Continue to cook. Cover pot and simmer 30 minutes. Add filé powder to pot and whisk quickly. Sprinkle 1 teaspoon of Creole seasoning on shrimp. Add shrimp to pot and stir. Cover and simmer 10 minutes. Remove from heat and discard bay leaves. Salt and pepper to taste.

Makes 10 servings.

*Notes:* 1. Ladle gumbo into bowl. Place about ½ cup cooked rice in center of bowl.

2. I use Tony Chachere's Creole seasoning (see appendix B).

# *All I Want*

*All I want is something in my mouth*
*to saturate it with the yearning that I desire*
*that which forsakes me now*
*that which eludes me now*
*the fullness of love*
*the fullness of loving and loving and loving and releasing*
*for now*
*can this Brie and smoked salmon soup saturate the depth of*
    *my yearning*
*can it whet my appetite*
*with sensations I live for*
*as I continue dreaming the dreams*
*dreams of wanting, aching, yearning for*
*the penetration*
*it eludes me and I ache for it*
*as I wish, pray, plead for it*
*the penetration*
*the full penetration*
*but can this soup master this tale*
*can this soup saturate the craving*
*can it coat the pain*
*ease the longing*
*stop the dreams*
*change the course?*
*You silly girl*
*it's just soup*
*try the stuffed leg of lamb.*

# Brie and Smoked Salmon Soup

During the 1996 Atlanta Olympics, I had the opportunity to view "Rings: Five Passions in World Art," a traveling art exhibit of masterworks spanning seven millennia, at the High Museum of Art in Atlanta. The works covered the subjects of love, anguish, awe, triumph, and joy. Of course, for me it was the love that got me at hello. After being completely drenched by Rodin's "The Kiss" and Khajuraho's "Lovers" and Vecellio's "Venus and Adonis," I felt a need to receive deep love immediately. At the reception of the exhibit, Ed and I shared in the consumption of the Brie, smoked salmon, and wine. But while Ed, as a member of the High, stayed upstairs at the reception to greet and meet, I went downstairs to the museum's coffeehouse and wrote "All I Want." Then we went home for further elaborations on "Rings: Five Passions in World Art."

2 tablespoons butter

1 tablespoon olive oil

1 cup chopped onions

1 cup chopped celery

1 cup peeled and chopped carrots

1 cup peeled and diced potato

½ teaspoon salt

½ teaspoon white pepper

½ cup white wine

2 cups vegetable stock (see appendix A)

8 ounces Brie cheese, chopped

2 ounces smoked salmon, chopped

¾ cup heavy cream

1.  Melt butter and oil over low heat in a medium-size soup pot. Add onions, celery, carrots, potatoes, salt, and pepper. Simmer covered until vegetables are tender, about 20 minutes. Stir often. Do not let burn.

2.  Add wine and stock and stir. Uncover and bring to a boil; then reduce heat to simmer, and cook uncovered about 10 minutes.

3.  Add Brie and salmon, and stir until Brie has melted. Remove Brie rind and discard.

4.  Remove pot from heat. Put all ingredients into blender and puree until smooth about 5–7 minutes.

5.  Pour soup back into medium-size soup pot. Bring to a soft boil; turn heat to simmer and whisk in cream to blend completely. Remove from heat and serve.

Makes 4 servings.

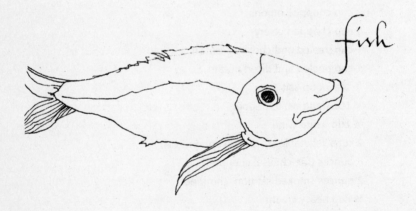

fish

# *I Love To*

Briefly, I look at you and no longer can I speak, for I know you will seduce me and gladly will I give in to your embrace. It is only a matter of time. But when I love thee, what is it that I love?

I love to gaze at your amber bubbly broth that barely coats my tongue and easily flows to the sides of my mouth while my jaws secrete yearning saliva, rushing to catch drips of your juices just before you quickly flow past without pausing to be fondled.

I love to watch the sweet corn kernels as they lead the dance with speckles of green diced scallions floating freely with full feathery parsley and bold minced onions and garlic following closely behind while the pink crawfish curl into themselves and await someone to bite their tails.

I love to inhale you, not in an ordinary way, you see, as I lower my face to the realm of the bowl to allow the perfumed aroma of the married flavors to pierce my nostrils and penetrate my pores, feeling the need for nothing more.

I love to taste your creamy spicy broth that forever satisfies my pains of desire with each bite into your tender crawfish tails, then to fresh crunchy corn, and further on to flavors of Worcestershire sauce coating the parsley and the scallions and the onions and the garlic, altogether well endowed with the necessities of lust in a bowl.

I love to swallow you as you cushion my esophagus and descend into an erotic abyss, piercing my belly like a godhead ejecting into my extremities determined to make me holler.

## Crawfish and Corn Bisque

Pinch the tail, pull the meat, and suck the head to get to the good fat. This is a pretty good description of how to eat one of the most delectable morsels on this planet: boiled crawfish. They are most often eaten at Louisiana family gatherings following a crawfish boil—cooked with potatoes in a spicy broth and thrown on the table for everyone to devour. Deciding if you gonna suck the heads or be dainty and use your fingers to get the good meat out is the test of a true devotee in the ritual of the crawfish boil. Fortunately, though, you can buy peeled crawfish meat that is neatly packed in pound bags and prepare étouffées to creamy risottos to this wonderful crawfish bisque that is a delicious introduction to crawdad heaven.

¼ cup vegetable oil

¼ cup flour

½ cup finely chopped onions

2 cloves finely chopped garlic

2 cups fresh yellow corn kernels

¾ teaspoon salt

¼ teaspoon white pepper

1 cup shrimp stock (see appendix A)

2 bay leaves

½ cup whole milk

1½ cups heavy cream

1 teaspoon Creole seasoning (see appendix B)

½ pound crawfish tails

½ teaspoon Worcestershire sauce

¼ cup green onions, chopped

¼ cup fresh parsley, chopped

1. Pour oil and then flour into a large Dutch oven over medium-low heat, and stir constantly for 8 minutes to make a blond roux (see appendix A). Do not allow to brown.

2. Add the onions and garlic. Sauté 2 minutes. Stir constantly. Add corn and sauté 1 minute. Add salt and pepper.

3. Whisk in stock and bay leaves, and bring to a boil. Add milk and cream, and bring back to a boil; then reduce heat to low and simmer for 5 minutes. Stir occasionally.

4. Sprinkle Creole seasoning over crawfish tails. Add crawfish to pot. Bring to slight boil, then lower heat and simmer 1 minute. Add Worcestershire sauce and green onions, and simmer for 8 minutes, stirring occasionally. Stir in parsley. Remove from heat and discard bay leaves. And serve.

Makes 4 servings.

# *Good Stuff*

My dear Good Stuff—

I close my eyes and I see you coming. And I know that you will be most good to me. And I know that I will cherish each moment of your presence. And I know that your departure will be greatly mourned. I say this for I dearly need you to know how dreadful it is for me after having you, how not having you affects me most drastically and most dearly. Please be aware, though, that I am not crazy. I am not crazy. I am just crazy for you. There is a distinction, you know. My mind is clear. My heart, I must admit, is not. And I offer what little I have left of my heart; all that I have not already delivered, head bowed, I offer to you, my love. Please accept this as the smallness of what is left to offer. My whole heart is yours at will.

Loving you always,
*Sweetheart*

My dear Sweetheart—

You are most gracious, my love. Yes, I am good. We know this. But I am good because of you. You chose to take the time to make me good and even make me better. What was I before you but a shrimp at heart and loose shells?

Most sincere,
*Good Stuff*

## Shrimp Bisque

"Good Stuff" was my immediate reaction from the first glance and first spoonful of this simply sensually good-looking and good-tasting soup. I thought after having it of not having it and easily transposed the thought of a lover who is so absolutely good to me, and the idea of losing or being without such a love is so drastically devastating and crazy driven. But try not to go crazy when thinking about lost love. And don't go crazy when thinking about pureeing the shrimp shells to make this bisque. It works.

½ pound medium-size shrimp

2 tablespoons butter

4 tablespoons olive oil

1 small carrot, chopped

1 small onion, chopped

1 garlic clove, sliced

1 celery stalk, chopped

1 bay leaf

2 sprigs fresh thyme

2 tablespoons tomato paste

⅛ cup brandy

4 cups shrimp stock (see appendix A) or store-bought
   low-sodium shrimp broth

¼ cup white wine

½ teaspoon salt

¼ teaspoon cayenne pepper

⅓ cup rice, uncooked

½ cup water

¾ cup heavy cream

4 tablespoons butter

½ teaspoon salt

8 cooked shrimp

1. Peel and devein shrimp. Separate shrimp and shells and set aside.

2. Over medium heat, melt butter and oil until hot in medium-size saucepan. Add shells and sauté 8 minutes, stirring occasionally. Add carrots, onions, garlic, celery, bay leaf, and thyme, and sauté 5 minutes. Add tomato paste and continue to cook about 3 minutes. Add brandy and allow to cook down 1 minute.

3. Add shrimp stock, wine, salt, and cayenne, and simmer 20 minutes uncovered.

4. Add rice, and simmer 30 minutes until rice is soft. Remove from heat.

5. Remove bay leaf and thyme sprigs and discard. Pour all ingredients from saucepan, including shells, into a blender and puree about 20 minutes. Strain, pushing pureed mixture down with rubber spatula to strain completely.

6.  In a small saucepan over medium heat, pour ½ cup water and 3 table-
    spoons of the pureed mixture and bring to a quick boil; then add peeled
    shrimp, turn heat to low, and simmer about 4 minutes. Remove 8
    shrimp and set aside for garnish.

7.  Pour remaining cooked shrimp and liquid into remaining pureed mix-
    ture and stir. Pour all ingredients into blender and puree a second time
    for about 5 minutes. Strain, pushing pureed mixture down with rubber
    spatula to strain completely.

8.  Pour pureed soup into a clean medium-size saucepan and bring to a
    gentle simmer.

9.  Whisk in cream. Whisk in butter, 1 tablespoon at a time. Stir in salt.
    Divide soup among 4 soup bowls. Add 2 shrimp to each bowl and serve.

Makes 4 servings.

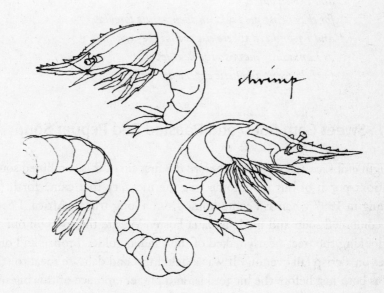

shrimp

# Naked

*Quite naked of corn kernels and pepper seeds,*
*they undressed to a seductive simplicity of smooth puree*
*that slid easily through my mouth and caused my nipples to*
  *harden*
*as they melted into each other at the center*
*I opened up*
*receiving a sweet and curious taste of mellow fresh corn*
*flowing to embrace the robust roasted red peppers*
*as they entered from the other side*
*I gathered their taste in the back of my mouth*
*and massaged my jaws with the tip of my tongue*
*to stimulate the duality of their embrace*
*and I cried out*
*for they bring me joy with their gentle foreplay*
*and I wondered where else would they take me*
*as I anxiously move to the next level*
*for I do want a holistic experience here*

## Sweet Corn Soup and Roasted Red Pepper Soup

A slight embrace and sweet kiss before the first sip of this combined soup on the front porch of our new home was the memory that came forth. That evening in 1997 when Ed came home from a long trip to Africa, I cooked this combined soup and made banana Foster. We ate the soup on our steps overlooking the trees nearly naked of their fallen golden bronze and orange leaves on a crisp fall evening. It was a delightful and delicate meal to stimulate us both just before the bigger kiss and bigger embrace of this big night.

FOR CORN SOUP:

2 tablespoons butter

½ cup chopped onions

½ tablespoon minced shallots

⅛ cup chopped carrots

⅛ cup chopped celery

½ small jalapeño pepper, seeded and chopped (wear
    rubber gloves)

2 cups fresh corn kernels (about 4 large ears of corn)

½ teaspoon chopped fresh thyme

¼ teaspoon salt

¼ teaspoon white pepper

1 cup vegetable stock (see appendix A)

½ cup heavy cream

Salt and white pepper to taste

FOR RED PEPPER SOUP:

3 medium red bell peppers, to roast

2 tablespoons butter

¼ cup chopped onions

½ tablespoon minced shallots

⅛ cup chopped carrots

⅛ cup chopped celery

½ teaspoon fresh thyme

⅛ teaspoon salt

⅛ teaspoon cayenne pepper

1 cup vegetable stock (see appendix A) or store-bought
    low-sodium vegetable broth

¼ cup heavy cream

1.  *To prepare corn soup:* Melt butter in medium saucepan over low heat. Add onions, shallots, carrots, celery, and jalapeño, and sauté about 4 minutes, stirring occasionally. Add corn kernels, thyme, salt, and pepper, and continue to sauté 5 minutes.

2.  Pour stock into pan and bring to a boil. Reduce heat and simmer 10 minutes.

3.  Puree corn soup mixture in blender 10 minutes; then strain into saucepan. Add cream and simmer 5 minutes.

4. *To prepare roasted red pepper soup:* Roast red peppers by threading them on a long skewer and holding over a gas flame on top of stove. Roast to blacken skin. If you have an electric stove, roast peppers in pan under the oven broiler to blacken skin. Using gas or electric, turn to blacken all sides. Remove from heat source and enclose in brown paper bag. After peppers have sweated for 5 to 10 minutes, remove from bag and rub off blackened skin. Do not run under water.

5. Melt butter in medium saucepan over low heat, and sauté onions, shallots, carrots, and celery, about 4 minutes. Add roasted red peppers, thyme, salt, and cayenne, and continue to sauté 5 minutes.

6. Pour stock into pan and bring to a boil. Reduce heat and simmer 10 minutes.

7. Puree in blender for 5 minutes. Pour into a separate pot. Bring to a quick boil; then lower heat, whisk in cream, and simmer 5 minutes.

Combined soup makes 4 servings. Each soup makes 2 servings.

*Note:* (Optional) Ladle ½ cup of each soup simultaneously into bowl from opposite ends. Dip a teaspoon of whipped cream in the center of the bowl.

# *Your Musk Entered the Room*

Dear Musky—

Your musk entered the room. I turned to see you gather with the others as they rushed to greet you. You covered their nakedness, and they sizzled with laughter with your arrival. I, too, stirred up the mixture in the now hot pot, and I was ignored. I wondered, had I properly ended our courtship? Did you know what I was trying to do? I didn't want to mask your natural beauty. I didn't want to lose your firm body. I didn't want to see your shapely designs and earthy shades of bronze fade. I didn't want to smother you with the groupies of onions, celery, and carrots. They always try to intoxicate you with their flavors. I wanted to taste you and only you in my mouth, with the others as a faint memory. So I held back to assure your uniqueness. Didn't you know that? I would have given more if I had thought you would be pleased and pleasing. I am a giving person. I thought you knew this. Remember, I massaged you with oils and spices, didn't I? I chose to blow you, not brush you off. Surely you remember that? I know you're wild and can't imagine a union of two. And I never asked this of you. What am I asking, then, you might ask. I am asking that when all are about you in your crowd of lovers, come for me and only me, sometimes. Please.

*Your Lady*

My Lady—

It ain't gonna happen! You knew I was wild when you met me. Look elsewhere and good luck!

*Musky*

## Wild Mushroom Soup

Unlike the preparation for making love, the preparation for cooking mushrooms calls for you simply to wipe them clean with a damp cloth or brush instead of washing them. But similar to making love, wild mushrooms are the best. However, some species are poisonous, don't you know. Therefore, it's wise to use cultivated mushrooms as opposed to the mysterious wild species that miraculously appear overnight at your doorsteps or alongside your trees after a long rain.

4 tablespoons butter

¼ cup chopped onions

1 tablespoon minced shallots

⅛ cup chopped carrots

⅛ cup chopped celery

¼ teaspoon salt

¼ teaspoon pepper

2 cups sliced mushrooms (shiitake, portobello, oyster, button)

4 cups vegetable stock (see appendix A) or store-bought low-sodium vegetable broth

1 teaspoon fresh thyme, chopped

1.  Melt butter in medium saucepan over low heat. Sauté onions, shallots, carrots, and celery about 4 minutes. Stir occasionally.

2.  Sprinkle salt and pepper over mushrooms, and toss. Add mushrooms to onion mixture, and sauté 4 minutes. Stir occasionally.

3.  Pour stock into the pan and bring to a slight boil. Reduce heat to low and simmer 10 minutes. Add thyme and simmer 2 minutes. Remove from heat. Serve.

Makes 4 servings.

mushrooms

# *You*

*You anoint me*
        *I am blessed*
*You beckon me*
        *I am yours*
*You comfort me*
        *I am fearless*
*You delight me*
        *I am happy*
*You embrace me*
        *I am cherished*
*You feed me*
        *I am satisfied*
*You glorify me*
        *I am honored*
*You hold me*
        *I am warm*
*You indulge me*
        *I am rich*
*You join me*
        *I am alive*
*You kiss me*
        *I am wet*
*You love me*
        *I am beloved*
*You mesmerize me*
        *I am spellbound*
*You nourish me*
        *I am nurtured*
*You open me*
        *I am revealed*
*You pacify me*
        *I am tranquil*

*You quicken me*
        *I am stimulated*
*You rescue me*
        *I am safe*
*You sustain me*
        *I am full*
*You tantalize me*
        *I am aroused*
*You undress me*
        *I am naked*
*You vamp me*
        *I am seduced*
*You wet me*
        *I am moist*
*You x me*
        *I am marked*
*You yearn me*
        *I am desirous*
*You Zen me*
        *I am enlightened*

*Now let me*
*live through it*
*all again*
*with you*

## Potato Leek Soup

Shower your leeks with a spray of fresh water to remove grit from the tight interlacing leaves, as you would shower between your lover's legs after lying on a sandy beach. Bathe your potatoes in a bowl of water until ready to use to prevent discoloring, and light a candle to join them in the ritual of the bath with memories of being surrounded by warm glistering water that pulsates tenderly against your joints.

¾ pound red potatoes, peeled and sliced

½ pound leeks (white part only), washed and sliced

1 quart water

4 tablespoons unsalted butter

½ tablespoon fresh thyme, chopped

¾ cup heavy cream

¼ cup milk

¾ cups liquid from potato-leek broth

1 teaspoon salt

½ teaspoon white pepper

1. Over medium-high heat in medium saucepan, place potatoes and leeks in water. Bring to a boil. Reduce heat and simmer 30 minutes.

2. Strain and set aside broth. Place potatoes and leeks in a blender and puree.

3. Melt butter in medium saucepan over medium heat. Add thyme and sauté 30 seconds. Remove from heat, and add potato-leek mixture, cream, milk, broth, salt, and pepper, and whisk contents. Return to heat, and whisk to blend, about 2 minutes. Remove from heat and serve.

Makes 4 servings.

onion, peppers

# *No Strings Attached*

Honey—

It can be simple. No strings attached. No complications of history. No long strong commitments. It can be just pleasure for the moment of a gathering of two. You and me. Can you see it?

Look—

You have misjudged me. I want strings. I want commitments. That's what life is about—history. Don't mess with me.

## Spinach Soup

Substituting canned or frozen spinach over fresh spinach is like choosing a lazy, unattentive, ugly boyfriend over a vibrant, thoughtful, handsome lover. Need I say more? And, of course, though roots in our love life are what we desire, stems must be removed in the life of spinach. Just prior to cooking, cut stems from spinach leaves. This helps eliminate the bitter taste created by the oxalic acid contained in spinach.

> 1 cup peeled and bite-size cubed potatoes
> 4 cups julienned spinach, stemmed and then blanched
> 4 tablespoons butter
> 4 tablespoons finely chopped shallots
> ¼ teaspoon salt
> ¼ teaspoon pepper
> 2 cups vegetable stock (see appendix A) or store-bought low-sodium vegetable broth
> ½ cup heavy cream

1. Over medium heat, place potatoes in medium saucepan and cover with water. Cook until tender and easily pierced with a fork without breaking them, about 8 minutes. Drain and place potatoes on paper towel.

2.  Blanch spinach in boiling water, about 1 minute. Drain spinach and place in ice water to stop cooking. Let sit about 1 minute. Remove spinach from cold water and place on paper towel. Use your hands to squeeze out water. Separate paper towel from spinach. Set spinach aside.

3.  Over medium heat, melt butter in medium saucepan. Add shallots and sauté 1 minute.

4.  Add spinach, then potatoes, and continue sautéing 4 minutes. Stir occasionally. Add salt and pepper. Add stock and bring to a slight boil; lower heat and simmer about 2 minutes. With a fork, mash at least half the potatoes. Whisk in cream and simmer 1 minute. Remove from heat. Ready to serve.

Makes 4 servings.

# *I Love All of You*

*I love all of you and will not be the selective lover*
*unabashed and stupid, this is the lover I am for you*
*for it is with all of you that I have fallen*
*and it is with all of you that I will forever desire*
*the sweet basil freckled in my bowl*
*the garlic and onions pureed into you deep*
*the white wine hallowed just above you gloriously*
*the salt mastering your savory entrance*
*the black pepper backing up the master*
*the cayenne lighting up your erogenous spark*
*the butter bringing flavors that melt nature*
*the tomatoes obviously your face of grace*
*no, I will not strain this love*
*I will not dissect your being*
*or separate that that I adorn and adorn less*
*Lord have mercy*
*for every ounce of you I want*
*in my life*
*in my body*
*all up in me*
*Lord have mercy again*
*the smooth and the rough*
*of you*
*must come in*
*to this*
*our bowl*
*our life*
*all of you*

# Tomato Basil Soup

I tasted this soup strained and unstrained and decided that the unstrained tomato basil soup captured more of the essence of what I was looking for, which was a full-flavored, bold taste. I was also pleased to see the soup ingredients individually and together, from green specks of basil to tiny chunks of red tomatoes. Like keeping the lights on, it's more delightful that way. Summer-seasoned tomatoes are best for your tomato dishes. Substitute drained canned Italian plum tomatoes during the winter months for a delicious result.

> 4 medium-firm summer tomatoes (cored, skinned, and chopped)
> 4 tablespoons unsalted butter
> 2 small onions, finely chopped
> 2 garlic cloves, minced
> ½ cup white wine
> 1½ cups chicken stock (see appendix A) or store-bought low-sodium chicken broth
> 1¼ teaspoons salt
> ¼ teaspoon black pepper
> Pinch of cayenne pepper (less than ⅛ teaspoon)
> 1 cup chopped fresh basil, in all
> ½ cup heavy cream

1. Core tomatoes and peel skin away. Discard skin. Chop tomatoes.

2. Melt butter in medium saucepan over low heat. Add onions and garlic, and sauté 2 minutes. Add tomatoes and sauté 4 minutes. Stir occasionally. Add wine and simmer 2 minutes.

3. Add stock, salt, pepper, and cayenne. Bring to a boil, then simmer 15 minutes. Add half the basil and remove saucepan from heat. Allow to sit 4 minutes. Remove tomato mixture and set aside. Set aside broth.

4. Puree the tomato mixture with 1 cup of tomato broth in blender 1 minute; add remaining basil and puree until smooth, about 3 minutes.

5. Return to saucepan and bring to a simmer. Remove from heat. Whisk in cream. Serve.

Makes 4 servings.

# *If Something Goes Wrong*

From Teary Eyes—

You tingle my taste buds. You're more than I expected. It's hard to get on your right side. Because of your simplicity, you are complicated. If something goes wrong, a cover-up only messes things up. So, there you are. I thought you'd wronged me. I thought you were turning against me. I didn't know that time was on my side. I didn't know that you weren't finished. I needed more thyme. For I thought you weren't giving me all I wanted, all I knew you had to give. Forgive me. It worked out though. Didn't it? Please don't turn against me. Look at you. Your earthy glossy broth is perfect in color as I remembered it should be. Your caramelized onion rings are intact and flavor your *juice* as it should. I promise, I won't ask you to change. I will accept you as simply as you are. I promise, I won't mess up this good thing.

Forever,
*Teary Eyes*

To Teary Eyes—

You didn't trust me. That is your flaw. This time, thyme was okay. But who knows how you will distort my true character next time? Just promise me that you will be patient. Yes, I am simple in my makeup, but I am true, too. What you see is what you get from me. But you must accept me as I truly am.

*Onion*

## French Onion Soup

As you uncover his layers, you will become more susceptible to his fumes and will discover more of who he is. He may make you cry initially, but he will indeed bring joy, eventually. Hang in there, for it is with the peeling away that you get to true love—the onion. And the essence of slow-cooked onions in a rich, intensely flavored broth is what makes a good onion soup.

To achieve this the best way, you must first caramelize lots of onions to a deep bronze color. Then you must make a strong homemade beef stock—no canned broth or beef bouillon will do. Top with a slice of French bread and fresh Gruyère and nothing will go wrong.

Preheat oven to 425 degrees.

FOR THE BEEF STOCK (MAKES 3 QUARTS):

2 tablespoons olive oil

3 pounds beef bones

1 cup tomato paste

2 stalks celery, quartered

1 large onion, quartered

1 carrot, peeled and quartered

4 garlic cloves, halved

5 quarts cold water

4 bay leaves

6 whole black peppercorns

1 teaspoon dried thyme

1 teaspoon dried basil

1 teaspoon salt

FOR THE ONION SOUP:

3 tablespoons butter

1 tablespoon olive oil

2 pounds yellow onions, thinly sliced (4 large onions)

½ teaspoon sugar (helps caramelize onions)

¼ teaspoon salt

1 tablespoon flour

2 quarts homemade beef stock (see above)
    (do not use store-bought broth)

1 cup white wine

1 thyme sprig

1½ teaspoons salt

½ teaspoon pepper

Slices of French bread, ½ inch thick

¼ pound Gruyère cheese, thinly sliced

**TO PREPARE THE BEEF STOCK:**

1   Drizzle oil over bones and roast 15 minutes.

2.  Brush tomato paste over bones and add celery, onion, carrot, and garlic. Continue to roast 25 minutes. Remove from oven.

3.  Place bones and vegetables in a large stockpot. Add water and remaining ingredients. Bring to a boil; then simmer for 3 hours. Strain. Skim oil from top and discard. Keep warm for immediate use, or freeze, tightly covered, up to one week for use later.

**TO PREPARE ONION SOUP:**

4.  Over low-to-medium heat, melt butter and oil in large saucepan. Add onions and spread out. After 10 minutes, sprinkle with sugar and salt. Stir occasionally to prevent sticking. Cook 1 hour or until onions are golden brown and caramelized. Be careful not to burn. Sprinkle with flour and stir to blend.

5.  Gradually add beef stock, wine, and thyme. Add remaining 1½ teaspoons salt and ½ teaspoon pepper. Bring to a simmer and cook an additional 25 minutes. Remove thyme sprig.

6.  Preheat broiler. Toast bread slices under broiler.

7.  Pour soup into bowls. Place bread over soup to cover. Top bread with sliced Gruyère cheese. Place bowls under broiler about 20 seconds or until cheese melts and turns slightly golden. Remove and serve hot.

Makes 4 servings.

# *A Swift Soft Sphere*

*You move like a swift soft sphere*
        *so comforting so decisive*
*touching all of me with*
        *your smooth sweet squash*
*melting in my mouth quite quietly*
        *conquering me*

        *so comforting so decisive*
*I hold on to your flavor as*
        *you fly fast deep into me*
*I feel the gentle breeze shaping my body as*
        *I open up*

        *so comforting so decisive*
*hugging my stomach with your warmth*
        *moving speedily caressing my navel*
*piercing my appetite you satisfy my desire of*
        *something full something warm something familiar*

        *so comforting so decisive*
*flowing sinking downward*
        *in that dark light of delight you're*
*loving me alone by myself as*
        *I want this to—this to—this to*
*last forever*

## Butternut Squash Soup

This soup's texture is silky smooth and so pleasant in its simplicity of pure butternut squash taste. Its texture is magna cum laude. A smooth and creamy pureed soup that flows into your mouth is ideal. So I worked at being more exact in adding the broth to the soup to create the feel of a swift soft sphere in my mouth from this squash soup.

> 4 cups vegetable stock (see appendix A) or store-bought
>   low-sodium broth
> 4 cups chopped butternut squash
> 1 cup chopped Granny Smith apple
> 1 cup peeled and chopped red potatoes
> 1 cup chopped onions
> 1 tablespoon garlic, chopped
> ¼ teaspoon powdered ginger
> 1 cup stock
> ½ cup heavy cream
> 1 teaspoon salt
> ½ teaspoon White pepper

1. Pour stock into medium Dutch oven over medium heat. Peel, seed, and chop butternut squash and apples. Put squash, apples, potatoes, onions, and garlic in pot as each is cut, and add ginger.

2. Bring to a boil, reduce to simmer, and cover. Cook about 30 minutes. Drain squash mixture and set stock aside.

3. Place squash mixture and 1 cup of the stock in blender and puree. Pour back into clean Dutch oven.

4. Whisk in cream. Add salt and pepper.

Makes 4 servings.

# *My Dear Baby*

My dear Baby—

Where were you? Is it now too late for us? Chill, I hear. Take these moments with grace. For I say to myself, I am here. You are here. No matter where we have been without each other, we are here now with each other.

My dearest Baby—

No regrets. For we have entered this life in this life. Be it thirty minutes or thirty years, we gave love and received love. And this gift will be with us forever. No regrets.

## Roasted Peppers and Pear Soup

I sliced the sweet bell pepper lengthwise and paused. There was a moment of reflection as I carefully removed the stem and then the seeds. Its hollow entrance was small. I gently pulled away the pale fibrous tissue at its top, causing a slight widening of its opening. It was firm and steady. It was ripe. I gathered the remaining seeds that had fallen deep inside. Its texture was dry for now. Its heart-shaped inner curves were erratic and erotic. I poured virgin olive oil on the tips of my fingers and followed the inner curves over and under, going in and around the skin. It is now smooth and silky and wide open. A sweet trip into a sweet pepper.

> 6 assorted small red, yellow, and orange bell peppers
> 4 tablespoons butter
> ½ cup chopped onions
> 2 tablespoons shallots, minced
> ¼ cup carrots, chopped
> ¼ cup celery, chopped
> 1 Bosc pear, chopped
> ½ teaspoon salt
> ¼ teaspoon cayenne pepper

2 cups vegetable stock (see appendix A) or store-bought
     low-sodium vegetable broth
1 cup heavy cream

1.  Roast pepper over high heat on top of gas stove or in electric stove (see p. 16). Cut in half lengthwise, and remove seeds and stems and set aside.

2.  Melt butter in a medium saucepan over low heat, and sauté the onions, shallots, carrots, and celery about 5 minutes. Stir occasionally.

3.  Add peppers, pear, salt, and cayenne, and continue to sauté about 5 minutes. Stir occasionally.

4.  Add stock to pan and bring to a boil. Reduce heat and simmer 10 minutes. Drain to separate broth from pepper-pear mixture and place each in a separate bowl. Place pepper-pear mixture and ½ cup of the broth in blender and puree. Pour pureed mixture back into saucepan and bring to slight simmer. Whisk in ½ cup of broth and cream. Simmer about 2 minutes. Remove from heat and serve with warm bread.

Makes 4 servings.

*Note:* Roast red pepper by threading it on a long skewer and holding over a gas flame on top of stove. Roast to blacken skin. Turn to blacken all sides. Remove from flame and enclose in brown paper bag. After pepper has sweated for 5 to 10 minutes, remove from bag and rub off blackened skin. Do not run under water.

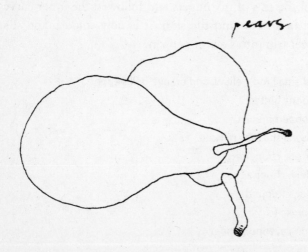

pears

# Ed Fed Me First

It doesn't take much for me to think of good food. I mean food that's not only well prepared but prepared with love and affection and care that transmits into the food, to make it, or create what I call good food—like good love. Love full of consideration and warmth and freedom and trust and friendship to reach into the purest of that which can be love or become love. That's what I mean when I say good food. It's as seductive as a good lover is.

Ed makes turtle soup for me on Mother's Day. Ed knows me well. I am the official taster whenever he cooks, so I get the first licking of his turtle soup. When I stir the soup, spices jump into my nostrils. Exotic spices of turtle nectar surround and enrapture me, causing me to spin around to catch their drift. I catch myself, pause, and scoop up a tablespoon of his turtle soup. I slowly carry the soup toward my lips. I glance at him; he looks nervous but patient. I sip his soup. I close my eyes. I stammer. Smoke emits from my breast. I hold my head so as not to lose it. I feel as though my entire body is floating with the sweetest thoughts of a man who has made me the most delicious, most sensual, and loving soup in this world. I cannot move. I do not move. I stay where I am for this moment to treasure this, his turtle soup.

He caught me, this man and his soup. My thoughts are never far from that day and Ed's turtle soup. Even at this moment, my mouth is watering at the memory. It is powerful. It is love. So when I am the taster of Ed's food, I run to the kitchen and wait patiently while he stirs the pot and gives me a spoonful, just enough to savor the taste and the aroma, until later. And later always brings forth further transformations of what Ed's turtle soup can do and has done. Ed is a master Louisiana cook from way back. All the men I know from Louisiana can cook, and cook well. But Ed fed me first.

## Ed's Turtle Soup

When Ed first offered to cook me turtle soup, I thought, "This man does not love me." And as you now may be thinking, "Why on earth did she include this 'turtle' recipe in her cookbook?" I offer it because it is extraordinarily good. Though different and maybe difficult for many to imagine, eating turtle is a culinary treasure. Try it at least once. And do add the sherry at the end. It is wondrous. You can order turtle meat by mail order (see appendix B).

FOR SEASONING MIX:

1 bay leaf

¾ teaspoon garlic powder

½ teaspoon salt

½ teaspoon cayenne pepper

¼ teaspoon white pepper

¼ teaspoon onion powder

¼ teaspoon dried thyme

¼ teaspoon dried mustard

¼ teaspoon black pepper

¼ teaspoon dried basil leaves

Pinch of ground cumin

FOR SOUP:

1 tablespoon unsalted butter

1 tablespoon margarine

1 pound fresh turtle meat

3 cups chopped fresh spinach

1 small onion, chopped

1 rib celery, chopped

1¼ cups tomato sauce

3½ tablespoons flour

½ teaspoon minced garlic

3½ cups chicken broth (see appendix A) or store-bought
  low-sodium chicken broth

¾ cup beef broth (see appendix A) or store-bought
  low-sodium beef broth

Salt and pepper

3 to 6 teaspoons dry sherry (optional)

1. *To prepare seasoning mix:* Combine all seasonings in a small bowl and set aside.

2.   *To prepare soup:* Melt butter and margarine over medium-high heat in a large Dutch oven. Add turtle meat and brown for 6 minutes; stir occasionally. Stir in seasoning mix, spinach, onion, and celery; turn heat to low and cook 15 minutes. Stir in tomato sauce and cook 10 minutes. Add flour and garlic, and cook 5 minutes. Add chicken and beef broths and bring to a boil, stirring occasionally. Turn heat to low, cover, and cook on low heat 45 minutes. Remove bay leaves and discard. Salt and pepper to taste. Stir in 1 teaspoon sherry, if using, per soup bowl.

Makes 6 servings.

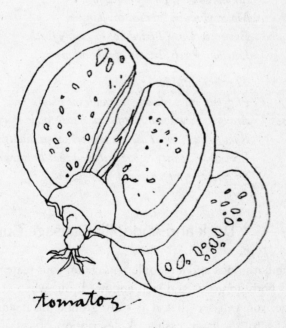

tomatos

# *Dark and Succulent*

*The Roux*
*Dark, silky, you are so perfect so aromatic*
*Hot, tasty, you are fully developed*
*Royal, fancy, you coated my lips*
*Rich, racy, you flew straight to my heart*
*Bold, sassy, you gave all that I desired*

*The Duck*
*Tender, juicy, I swallowed your juices*
*Plump, savory, I ate you too fast*
*Moist, yummy, I sensed the danger*
*Exotic, whimsy, I tried not to go any further*
*Luscious, lovely, I want it all and more*

*The Andouille Sausage*
*Pungent, spicy, what game will we play*
*Aroused, sexy, what justifies such satisfaction*
*Robust, fiery, what use are prayers when sausage enters*
*Provocative, lusty, what is it then that I must give back*
*Succulent, meaty, what is more sweet*

## Duck and Andouille Sausage Gumbo

Having both duck and andouille sausage on your plate is like having a lover who is both gorgeous and well endowed. But when you look closer at the sausage, you can see that it is only ground meat and seasonings gently pushed into a sausage casing. A description of sausage casing from Julia Child and Simone Beck's *Mastering the Art of French Cooking*:

> Professionals use a stuffing machine, poussoir, which is a large cylin-
> der with a pushing plate at one end and a nozzle at the other: the
> meat goes into the cylinder; the casing is slid up from the outside of

the nozzle; and a crank operates the plate, pushing the meat from the cylinder through the nozzle and into the casing which slowly, evenly fills up the meat, as it slides from the nozzle . . . anyone going into serious sausage making should certainly have one.

4 duck thighs and 4 legs

1 tablespoon Creole seasoning

½ cup vegetable oil

½ cup flour

1 cup chopped onions

¾ cup chopped celery

1 cup chopped green bell peppers

½ pound Andouille sausage, sliced into 1-inch pieces (see appendix B)

1 teaspoon minced garlic

2 bay leaves

8 cups chicken stock (see appendix A) or sodium-free chicken broth

1 tablespoon filé powder

¼ cup chopped green onions

2 cups white rice, cooked

1. Remove duck skin and fat and discard.

2. Season duck pieces with 1 tablespoon Creole seasoning.

3. Heat oil in Dutch oven at medium-high heat. Fry duck and brown 4 minutes per side. Place duck on paper towels and set aside. When cooled, chop into bite-size pieces. Keep oil sediments in Dutch oven. Measure oil to make sure ½ cup remains. Add additional vegetable oil to make ½ cup, if needed.

4. Reduce heat to medium and stir in ½ cup flour. Stir slowly and constantly to make a dark brown roux (see appendix A), cooking about 10 minutes. Do not burn.

5. Remove pan from heat, and add onions, celery, and peppers; stir constantly until roux stops getting darker.

6. Return pan to heat and cook until vegetables are soft, about 5 minutes. Add sausage, garlic, and bay leaves, and continue cooking 3 minutes.

7.  Add stock and bring to a boil. Reduce heat and simmer uncovered 30 minutes.

8.  Bring to a quick boil and whisk in filé powder. Reduce to simmer. Add duck and simmer 30 minutes. Remove from heat and discard bay leaves. Skim oil from top of gumbo. Stir in green onions. Serve in soup bowl. Add ½ cup rice over gumbo.

Makes 4 servings.

*Note:* I use Tony Chachere's Creole seasoning (see appendix B).

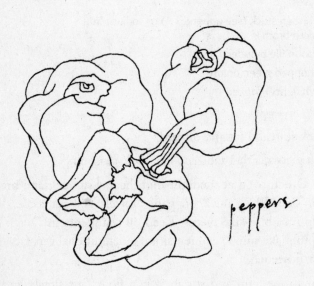

peppers

# *My Morning Glory*

My dear Morning Glory—

I have turned to your side of the bed many mornings, wishing for your return as I cushion the pillow next to me so as to turn your face toward mine. And I pull the covers up enough to cover your absence. And I move closer toward your space to be with you, for memories of you bring warmth to my heart. I brace myself with your pillow against my face to receive your gentleness and lean forward toward your flow of love in your space that even when not there, is ever so present. It gratifies me greatly that you entered my life with your large, thick sweet root that has comforted me quite often in memories only, lately. I wish dearly for the next morning each morning to taste again your natural sweetness. I am forever yearning in the A.M.

My dear Morning Grace—

Warm your bowl before you ladle me in and I will come.

## Roasted Sweet Potato Soup with Andouille Sausage

Sweet potatoes belong to the morning glory family. Defined: a twining plant having funnel-shaped flowers of various colors. Girls, imagine a twining plant having a funnel shape that we can call our own—fun, fun, fun.
Preheat oven to 450 degrees

> 1 large sweet potato
> ½ cup diced Andouille sausage (see appendix B)
> 2 tablespoons unsalted butter, in all
> 2 tablespoons chopped shallots
> ¼ teaspoon mace
> ¼ teaspoon cinnamon
> ½ teaspoon salt
> 1 ¼ cup chicken stock (see appendix A) or store-bought
>    low-sodium chicken broth

½ **teaspoon honey**
½ **cup heavy cream**
½ **cup milk**

1. Roast sweet potato until soft to the touch, about 45 minutes. When cooled, peel and discard skin, and set potato aside.

2. Fry sausage in small skillet, browning on both sides. Drain on paper towel, dice, and set aside.

3. Melt 1 tablespoon of the butter in medium saucepan at medium heat and sauté shallots about 1 minute. Add potatoes, mace, cinnamon, and salt, and stir to blend. Add 1¼ cup stock. Bring to a gentle boil; then simmer about 10 minutes. Stir occasionally.

4. Pour potato mixture into blender and puree 3 minutes. Pour back into saucepan. Add remaining butter, honey, cream, and milk. Whisk. Return to medium heat and simmer 2 minutes. Remove from heat. Serve in soup bowls. Sprinkle diced sausage in center of soup bowl.

Makes 2 servings.

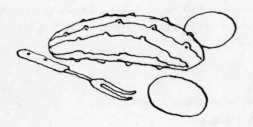

# CHAPTER TWO

## Salacious Seafood

as I sit trembling
before you
I start the end
and fold back your skin
to taste your tender flesh
and am delighted
by your texture
that dissolves in
my mouth
while your thick stuffing
coats my tongue
—YELLOWTAIL SNAPPER WITH CRABMEAT
STUFFING, "I MISS YOU"

**RECIPES:**

"I Miss You" / Yellowtail Snapper with Crabmeat Stuffing

"Sonnet to Crawfish Risotto" / Crawfish Risotto

"Reckless Love Affairs" / Shrimp Étouffée

"The Soul of Your Broth" / Fish Stew

"I Am King Salmon" / Seared Salmon with Shiitake Mushrooms, French Beans, and Tomatoes

"Beauty, What Is It?" / Braised Red Snapper with White Wine and Tomatoes

"I Dipped My Fingers in Its Sauce" / Barbecue Shrimp

"But It's My Vessel" / Salmon Soufflé

"Come Home Sweet Love" / Sautéed Striped Sea Bass

"Forgive Me" / Braised Rainbow Trout with Crawfish Potato Hash

"You Know Them Well" / Crab Cakes with Whipped Potatoes
    and Coleslaw

"Simple Love" / Garlic Shrimp

"Swim Upstream with Me" / Salmon with Mozzarella and
    Asiago Quiche

"Sweet You Are" / Shrimp and Grits

"They Came to Be Fed" / Salmon in Puff Pastry

# I Miss You

*Even now as I eat you*
*I miss you*
*and know that it can end*
*it will end*
*bite by bite*
*you disappear*
*to leave me alone*
*lonely for your moist flesh*
*and glistening skin*
*of yellow stripes*
*and that tail*
*oh that tail*
*that flips up when heated*
*and shines a brilliant*
*shade of yellow*
*yes I want you whole*
*full and always*
*head first*
*baked only twenty minutes*
*or less*
*just enough*
*to make your juices swell*
*your tail crisp and*
*your stuffing firm*

*I miss you even now*
*and know that*
*I can never regain*
*that which*
*I have eaten*
*as I sit trembling*
*before you*

*I start the end*
*and fold back your skin*
*to taste your tender flesh*
*and am delighted*
*by your texture*
*that dissolves*
*in my mouth*
*while your thick stuffing*
*coats my tongue*
*and tickles*
*my taste buds*
*with crabmeat*
*powders of garlic*
*buttered celery*
*onions*
*and bread crumbs*
*dancing from jawbone*
*to jawbone*
*over and*
*yet once over again*

*Exhausted am I*
*even now*
*for you have*
*aroused me so*
*upon your departure*
*as I have devoured*
*all of you*
*yet*
*by heart*
*I know*
*you were here*
*and pray*
*you visit*
*again*

# Yellowtail Snapper with Crabmeat Stuffing

This combo of yellowtail snapper and crabmeat would be on the "A List" of Hollywood's couples. If served alone, they would still be superb. Their look, texture, and taste are quite satisfying. I prepared the crabmeat stuffing as part of the birthday menu for my dear friend, Mtamanika. Many years have passed since that most memorable gala, but even now, when I see some of the our friends who gathered at her home that evening, they first inquire about the crabmeat stuffing, especially James and Gedney, and ask when might they get some again. Serve with Sautéed French Beans (see p. 221) and Roasted Rosemary Potatoes (p. 186).

Preheat oven to 350 degrees

1 2½-pound yellowtail snapper with head on (deboned with scales and fins removed)

FOR SEASONING AND STUFFING FISH:

¼ teaspoon salt

¼ teaspoon pepper

¾ teaspoon Creole seasoning

1 tablespoon olive oil

4 medium shrimp, peeled, deveined and sliced

¼ pound fresh lump crabmeat

1 tablespoon butter

½ tablespoon olive oil

⅛ cup chopped onion

⅛ cup chopped celery

½ teaspoon garlic, minced

⅛ cup chopped green bell pepper

1 teaspoon chopped parsley

⅛ cup bread crumbs

1 tablespoon butter

½ teaspoon Worcestershire sauce

FOR BASTING SAUCE FOR FISH:

¼ cup olive oil

1 tablespoon lemon juice

1 tablespoon Worcestershire sauce

1. Wash snapper under cold running water and pat dry with paper towel.

2. *To season fish:* Season fish inside and out with salt, pepper, and Creole seasoning. Drizzle inside and out with olive oil. Put in refrigerator until ready to stuff and cook.

3. *To prepare stuffing:* Season shrimp and crabmeat with ½ teaspoon Creole seasoning. Put in refrigerator until ready to use.

4. Put 1 tablespoon of butter and oil in large skillet over low-medium heat and sauté onions, celery, garlic, and green peppers until onions are translucent, about 1 minute, stirring constantly. Sprinkle with ¼ teaspoon Creole seasoning. Add parsley and continue cooking 1 minute. Stir in bread crumbs, sauté 1 minute. Remove from heat.

5. Melt 1 tablespoon butter in another small skillet, over low heat and add shrimp, sauté 1 minute, stirring constantly. Add crabmeat and sauté 1 minute. Remove from heat.

6. In a large mixing bowl, combine shrimp-crabmeat mixture with vegetables and stir until well blended. Add Worcestershire sauce and stir.

7. Stuff snapper with shrimp-crabmeat and tie fish with 3 strips of kitchen twine to close. Put fish in an ovenproof skillet.

8. *To prepare basting sauce:* In a small bowl, combine olive oil, lemon juice, and Worcestershire sauce. Drizzle sauce over fish and bake uncovered until fish is done, about 20 minutes. Baste fish every 5 minutes. Remove from oven. Remove twine, put fish on serving platter, and serve.

Makes 2 servings.

*Note:* I use Tony Chachere's Creole seasoning (see appendix B).

# Sonnet to Crawfish Risotto

Adapted from Shakespeare's Sonnet XL, "Take all my loves, my love, yea, take them all"

Take all I have, my love, yea, take it all
    the juice of my tails
    the aroma of my concoction
    the hue of my meat
    the curl of my body
  What more is there now than before
No truer love than thou can call true
  All my love was yours before you asked
Then because of my love, you are loved
    your look of handsome beauty
    your taste of relished savor
    your texture of tender delicacy
    your moistness of warm water
  I cannot blame you for using me
But yet I do if you don't come out right
  by willful taste of that that is not delicious
I do not forgive you of robbing me of my good dish, gentle one
    when in an instant you turn on me
    when no longer are you moist with flavors
    when dryness from overcooking seeps in
    when, salt forgotten, you are flat of flavor
  Although you steal me empty of taste
And yet love of food knows of a greater loss
  To bear a bad recipe and then hate the food
    lascivious grace upon all foods
    kill the cook, save the recipe

# Crawfish Risotto

Just looking at this dish of stimulating edibles will bring forth love. It is so tenderly beautiful as the red pink crawfish enraptures the creamy adorable risotto. Only passion of the heart resides here. Passion overflow is good. As is a little stock overflow in the risotto once cooked. Remember, risottos continue to cook even after you remove them from the heat. The rice continues to absorb the liquid to continue embellishing its creaminess. So it's best to serve risottos minutes after they are cooked.

2 tablespoons olive oil

1 tablespoon butter

1 small onion, finely chopped

1 garlic clove, crushed

1 teaspoon Creole seasoning (see appendix B)

½ pound crawfish meat

1 cup Arborio rice, uncooked

Pinch of salt (less than ⅛ teaspoon)

⅛ teaspoon pepper

½ cup white wine

3 cups shrimp stock (see appendix A), simmering, or store-bought low-sodium shrimp broth

¼ cup heavy cream

¼ cup chopped fresh parsley

½ cup grated fresh Parmesan

1. Pour olive oil and butter into wide heavy-duty saucepan over medium heat. Add onion and garlic, and sauté about 2 minutes. Season crawfish with Creole seasoning. Add to pan and sauté 4 minutes. Add rice and stir to coat about 1 minute. Add salt and pepper, and stir briefly.

2. Add wine and stir until all liquid has been absorbed, about 1 minute. Stir in 1 cup of the simmering stock and cook, stirring constantly. When absorbed, about 2 minutes, stir in another cup. Repeat this for 20 minutes until rice is al dente (firm but not soft). You may not need to use all the stock. It will depend on rice. Add cream and stir 2 minutes. Add parsley and stir 1 minute. Remove pan from heat and stir in Parmesan.

Makes 2 servings.

# Reckless Love Affairs

Shrimp étouffée creates reckless love affairs. As its definition implies. étouffée smothers you with a passion that drives you like a tidal wave that wipes
and twirls your culinary senses, leaving chaos in its path. That's why when
Ed served it to me for the first time, I jumped over the table. I was out of
control when I wrapped my body around his chest. I admit it. But after eating the shrimp étouffée, I had to seduce somebody.

The luscious, handsome mahogany roux of fiery oil and flour stirred to a
perfectly smooth texture was the malefactor. Its fluid essence had no beginning, no end, just eternal lustful pleasure. This aesthetic beauty was full of
nature's true stimulant, cocky red-hot cayenne peppers that would make the
world surrender. Its seasonal partners in crime, devoted black and white
pepper, royal green basil leaves, pungent thyme, and, of course, king salt,
perpetuated my somewhat forward behavior.

He, on the other hand, was baffled, bewildered, and confused. His bowl
was full, you see. He had not yet had the chance to taste that which was before him. But how could he, now that I had locked my legs around him?
Will he ever have the chance to savor, but more important, respond to this
spirited manipulator of lust? I do want an agreeable partner. So as not to run
him off, I apologetically gathered my senses, unglued myself from his chest,
slid down, climbed off the table, unruffled my dress, pulled my chair closer
to him, and sat down.

I turned to his plate. The prima donna shrimps were strutting their pink
butts in the deep brown roux. I looked on them as the provocateurs, while
the moist pearl rice in the center of the dark-tanned étouffée surreptitiously
winked as if to acknowledge their performance as they met again to ex-
change juices. I humbly eased his plate to him and motioned him to taste
this wondrous dish. He looked at me and saw that I was calm and with some
sense; then he looked down into the shrimp étouffée. With abrupt but constant glances at me, he reluctantly reached for his fork and pulled his plate
closer. He lowered his fork into the étouffée. I held my breath and closed my
eyes so as not to interfere. I sensed his watchful glances. I lowered my head
and peeked at his plate. His fork was still sitting in the étouffée. I thought—

Get involved! Looking at him with an inviting but innocent smile, I licked my lips and threw him a kiss. He caught it. Slowly stirring the snow-white rice into the rich dark roux and plump shrimp, he gathered up a heaping forkful. Without losing a drop, he eased the titillating dish into his mouth.

I was ecstatic. I rushed to catch up with him and devoured a couple of spoonfuls. Then, it happened. The roux began to coat us like the coming of love. We quivered from the étoufées' pulsating passion now deep within us. But it has to rise up, you see. For if it does not rise to escape, it will ignite our souls. It has only moments to live within us. And it must do its job, to create crazy mad love and bold sex in those who devour this shrimp étouffée. So, I grabbed him. With a big, wet, long, twisting kiss. I exploded in his mouth. In miniseconds, he picked me up with his left arm and cleared the table with his right. There, in my kitchen, the white laced tablecloth was creating new designs in motion from side to side, as we raced to catch the eroticism of the moment.

## Shrimp Étouffée

I really did take Ed by his collar and pulled him to me across my small two-seater kitchen table and extended my lips to his to give him a big, fat, wet kiss of gratitude. It was the first time I had eaten this traditional Creole dish, and it was so good I had to seduce the cook. This sensual dish is best served over rice and with a simple salad.

> 4 teaspoons Creole seasoning, in all
> 2 pounds medium shrimp, peeled and deveined
> ½ cup vegetable oil
> ½ cup flour
> ¼ cup chopped onion
> 1 garlic clove, minced
> ¼ cup chopped green bell pepper
> ¼ cup chopped celery
> 2 bay leaves
> 4 tablespoons butter
> ½ cup chopped green onion
> ¼ cup chopped fresh parsley
> 2 cups shrimp stock (see appendix A)

1 tablespoon chopped fresh thyme
1 teaspoon salt
3 cups cooked rice

1. Sprinkle 2 teaspoons of the Creole seasoning over shrimp and mix well. Set aside.

2. Heat oil over medium heat in cast-iron skillet until slightly smoking, about 3 minutes. Use wooden spoon to stir in flour. Stir constantly, about 3 minutes, until roux (see appendix A) is dark brown.

3. Remove skillet from heat. Stir in onions, garlic, green pepper, celery, and bay leaves. Stir 2 minutes off the heat. Set aside.

4. In another medium-size skillet, melt butter over medium heat. Add shrimp, green onion, and parsley, and sauté 2 minutes. Add stock, thyme and salt, simmer 1 minute.

5. Place skillet with roux and vegetables over medium heat. Pour shrimp and stock mixture into roux and vegetables and stir. Simmer 2 minutes. Remove from heat and discard bay leaves. Serve over rice.

Makes 4–6 servings.

*Note:* I use Tony Chachere's Creole seasoning (see appendix B).

onion, peppers

# *The Soul of Your Broth*

*The soul of your broth comes to me*
*with a juice that justifies its being*
*with a spice that spits its glory*
*with a fluid that flows easily into me*
*with a taste that testifies to its goodness*
*with a warmth that welcomes all of eternity*

*The soul of your broth speaks to me*
*of yearnings yet fulfilled*
*of slow stewing gathering steam*
*of aroused emotions just under the lid*
*of aromas raising me up to lay me down*
*of flavors causing me to offer my life*

*The soul of your broth comes to me*
*as an orgasm*
*intense yet warm*
*wild yet tame*
*loving me mightily*
*as I stir through its myriad*
*as I float into its daze*
*as I simmer in its glory*
*as I tenderize its reality*
*as I blend into its spirituality*
*and drown in its love*

## Fish Stew

Soul: The immaterial essence; principal or actuating cause of an individual life; the spiritual principle embodied in human beings; a person's total self; the quality that arouses emotion and sentiment; a moving spirit; a strong positive feeling, as of intense sensitivity and emotional fervor—as defined by Webster.

Stew: Cooking slowly and gently, always at a simmering point, with the food barely covered with liquid to blend flavors deliciously and make tender all that is tough—as defined by Valinda. Serve this stew with warm bread and love.

¼ cup olive oil

1 large thinly sliced onion

3 garlic cloves, crushed

1 12-ounce can Italian plum tomatoes, cut into bite-size pieces, with juice

2 bay leaves

1 cup white wine

½ teaspoon saffron threads, and stir in wine

4 small potatoes, peeled and cut bite-size

4 cups fish stock (see appendix A) or store-bought low-sodium fish broth

Dash of Tabasco hot sauce

1½ teaspoons salt

½ teaspoon pepper

FOR SEAFOOD SEASONING:

1 teaspoon Creole seasoning

½ teaspoon salt

¼ teaspoon pepper

½ pound red snapper fillet, cut bite-size

½ pound halibut fillet, cut bite-size

½ pound perch fillet, cut bite-size

12 large shrimp, peeled and deveined

½ cup chopped fresh parsley

¼ cup heavy cream

1. Heat olive oil in large saucepan over medium heat. Sauté onions and garlic in oil until soft, about 2 minutes. Add tomatoes and bay leaves. Bring to a slight boil; then simmer about 10 minutes. Stir occasionally.

2. Add wine, saffron, and potatoes. Bring to boil; then simmer about 3 minutes. Add stock. Add dash of hot sauce. Add 1½ teaspoons salt and ½ teaspoon pepper. Bring to boil, then simmer about 10 minutes.

3. Sprinkle Creole seasoning, salt, and pepper over seafood.

4.  Add snapper, halibut, and perch to pot. Bring to boil; then simmer about 3 minutes. Add shrimp and simmer 4 minutes. Add parsley and stir. Add cream and simmer 1 minute. Remove from heat, discard bay leaves, and serve in soup bowls.

Makes 6 servings.

*Note:* I use Tony Chachere's Creole seasoning (see appendix B).

# *I Am King Salmon*

*They lay beneath me ready to cushion my hot plate.*
*French beans, Shiitake mushrooms, and tomatoes rush to*
*     comfort me.*
*For I am King Salmon, the best fuck they ever had.*
*I fight against odds to get what I want.*
*My meat is outstanding with or without salt.*
*Butt naked or dressed, I am divine.*
*My flavors exceed the most well-seasoned fish.*
*Vegetables trounce at my door to get next to me.*
*Just being in my sphere makes them creatures of desire.*
*Buttering themselves up in fiery sautéed pans, they wait in my*
*     bed all scattered about.*
*And I, of course, always on top, deliver sweet juices that flow*
*     throughout.*
*They like it, yes they do, and crave to please me with color and*
*     texture.*
*But with them or not, I will be eaten up oh so soon.*
*For my fat firm flesh outshines them all seared, smoked, or eaten*
*     raw.*

## Seared Salmon with Shiitake Mushrooms, French Beans, and Tomatoes

Whether you choose to steam, roast, or sear salmon, you'll find it deliciously richer than most any other fish. You should be ensured that, as long as you do not overcook this fish, you will experience a succulent epicurean delight. I also found the combination of shiitake mushrooms, French beans, and tomatoes with this fish is most pleasant to the taste and intensely attractive.

Preheat oven to 350 degrees.

FOR THE SAUCE:
1 12-ounce can Italian plum tomatoes, chopped, with juice
2 garlic cloves, halved
2 sprigs fresh basil
½ cup olive oil
¼ cup white wine
¼ teaspoon salt
¼ teaspoon pepper

FOR THE VEGETABLES:
4 tablespoons butter
½ pound shiitake mushrooms, stem removed and sliced
½ pound French beans, blanched, stems cut (see p. 57)
1 cup chopped Italian plum tomatoes
Salt and pepper

FOR THE SALMON:
4 8-ounce skinless salmon fillets
1 teaspoon salt
1 teaspoon pepper
2 tablespoons clarified butter (see note at end of recipe)

1. In a medium saucepan over medium heat, add tomatoes with juice, garlic, basil, and oil, and bring to a quick boil then lower heat to simmer 15 minutes. Add wine. Season with salt and pepper, and simmer 5 minutes. Remove from heat and strain, pressing tomatoes down. Keep warm.

2. Melt 4 tablespoons butter in a large skillet over medium-high heat. Add mushrooms and pinch of salt and pepper; sauté 3 minutes. Stir occasionally.

3. Stir in the French beans and pinch of salt and pepper and sauté 1 minute.

4. Add tomatoes and pinch of salt and pepper and sauté 1 minute.

5. Remove from heat, transfer to platter, and keep warm.

6. Season salmon with salt and pepper.

7. Heat butter in large ovenproof skillet over high heat. Sear salmon topside until golden, about 3 minutes. Turn salmon over and place skillet in oven.

8. Cook salmon until done, 3–4 minutes. Remove from oven.

9. Transfer salmon to center of platter with mushrooms, tomatoes, and French beans. Reheat and whisk sauce. Pour ½ cup of sauce over salmon. Serve with warm bread.

Makes 4 servings.

*Notes:* 1. *To clarify butter:* Clarified butter has the water and milk solids removed. Clarified butter is heated unsalted butter. It forms three layers. The top layer is foam, and it should be skimmed off with spoon. The milk solids drop to bottom. The middle layer is clarified butter. Allow butter to sit for a few minutes; then either strain through cheesecloth-lined strainer or fine sieve or gently pour off butter from the milk solids, leaving clarified butter (butterfat).

2. *To blanch French Beans:* Immerse the beans briefly in boiling water, then into cold water to stop the cooking process.

# *Beauty, What Is It?*

*Beauty, what is it?*
*Is it your symmetry of exactness*
*    with nature's design*
*    in scaled calligraphy?*
*Is it your perfumed aroma*
*    distinctly yours*
*    and yet unknowing?*
*Is it the split just under your belly*
*    that's not too tight*
*    and not too wide?*
*Is it your eyes of clear fantasy*
*    watching me*
*    watching you?*
*Is it your moist taste*
*    causing infinite pleasures*
*    from the depth of your flesh?*
*Is it your moderate weight*
*    as I hold you*
*    knowing you are a perfect fit?*
*Is it your firm lean body*
*    that's prominently plump*
*    just at your chest?*
*Is it your rich glow*
*    radiating your desire*
*    for me?*
*Is it your now-smooth skin*
*    as I oil you down in that direction*
*    as I should?*
*Is it your delicacy*
*    that melts on my tongue*
*    on impact?*

*Is it the seeing*
*and knowing you*
*that lifts my heart?*
*Is it your savory sauce*
*that makes me cry*
*each time I sip?*
*Or is it the wine*
*and my hunger*
*that's causing me to trip?*

## Braised Red Snapper with White Wine and Tomatoes

I consider red snapper and sea bass to be the most beautiful fish in the sea. Their naturally scaled symmetry and firm and curved plump bodies are examples of nature's perfection. I initially planned to fillet this fish, but after removing it from the refrigerator and uncovering it, I just looked at its body and could not image slicing it into fillets. I had to honor this beauty and cook it whole. Serve with Saffron Parmesan Risotto (see p. 201).

Preheat oven to 425 degrees.

2-2-pound red snappers with heads, cleaned and scaled
½ teaspoon salt
½ teaspoon pepper
½ teaspoon Creole seasoning
2 tablespoons olive oil, in all
2 tablespoons butter
2 tablespoons diced shallots
1 small onion, diced
2 garlic cloves, diced
1-16-ounce can Italian plum tomatoes with juices, chopped
4 sprigs fresh thyme
Pinch of salt and pepper
½ cup white wine
½ cup fish stock
2 tablespoons chopped fresh parsley
Pinch of salt and pepper

1. Season fish inside and out with salt, pepper, and Creole seasoning. Drizzle inside and out with 1 tablespoon of the olive oil.

2. Put remaining olive oil and the butter in medium ovenproof skillet over medium heat. Add shallots, onions, and garlic, and sauté about 3 minutes. Stir occasionally. Add tomatoes, thyme, and pinch of salt and pepper, and simmer 2 minutes. Add wine and stock and simmer about 1½ minutes. Place fish in center and baste. Sprinkle parsley and pinch of salt and pepper over fish. Place in oven and bake until done, about 20 minutes. Remove from oven.

Makes 4 servings.

*Notes:* 1. I use Tony Chachere's Creole seasoning (see appendix B).

2. Serve with Saffron Parmesan Risotto (see p. 201).

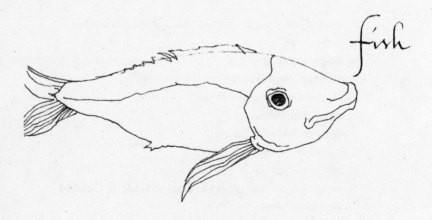

# I Dipped My Fingers in Its Sauce

*I dipped my fingers in its sauce . . . I couldn't stop sucking*
*I held my head deep down into it . . . the spirits intoxicated me*
*I bit into it toward the center . . . the juices ooze there*
*I removed my socks . . . it was now too hot*
*I took a deep breath . . . I wanted to embrace it as it entered*
*I surrender*

*I dipped my fingers in its sauce . . . I couldn't stop sucking*
*I savored its glorious richness . . . the enchantment was*
   *captivating*
*I pulled out its tail between my lips . . . it lingered there*
*I rubbed my thighs . . . a protective measure*
*I closed my eyes . . . I wanted to see it as a memory*
*I surrender*

*I dipped my fingers in its sauce . . . I couldn't stop sucking*
*I gazed at the empty pink tails . . . the vanishing spicy cream*
   *stared at me*
*I swirled one last sop of the sparkling amber liquid . . . it danced*
   *with me*
*I massaged my breast . . . the tender spell was over*
*I wept . . . it was so good*
*I surrender*

## Barbecue Shrimp

I remember lowering my face down into the bowl of this gloriously golden sauce and then inhaling the aroma and then holding my fork to capture a shrimp to scoop up some of the sauce. I then realized that by using a fork, I was not able to capture the full sensuality of receiving this dish. I thought it was most important that the shrimp and sauce be eaten and touched at the same time. So dipping my finger into the sauce with the shrimp and not stopping until all was devoured, was exactly how this poem began literally and figuratively. And with each dip and each line written, I ate and I wrote and I surrendered.

    1½ pound large shrimp, shells on, deveined
    1½ tablespoons Creole seasoning, in all
    1 teaspoon cracked black pepper
    3 tablespoons olive oil
    ⅓ cup chopped onions
    1 tablespoon garlic, minced
    2 bay leaves
    1 small lemon, sliced
    2 tablespoons Worcestershire sauce
    1 teaspoon Tabasco sauce
    ½ cup beer
    ½ cup heavy cream
    8 tablespoons butter, cut into 8 pieces
    Pinch salt

1. Devein shrimp, cutting through shells. Sprinkle shrimp with 1 tablespoon Creole seasoning and pepper. Set aside.
2. Pour oil into large cast iron skillet over medium heat. When oil smokes slightly, add onions and garlic, and sauté 1 minute, stirring constantly.
3. Add shrimp and stir.
4. Add remaining Creole seasoning, bay leaves, lemon, Worcestershire sauce, and Tabasco sauce, and stir. Add beer and stir.
5. Lower heat and simmer about 1 minute. Remove lemon slices. Stir in cream. Whisk in butter, 1 tablespoon at a time, within 2 minutes. Stir in pinch of salt.
6. Remove from heat. Remove bay leaves.

Makes 4 servings.

*Notes:* 1. I use Tony Chachere's Creole seasoning (see appendix B).

2. Serve in soup bowls with warm French bread.

# But It's My Vessel

*How much space do you need*
*I've buttered the inside for you to slide forward*
*I've folded you gently*
*and rolled you over*
*I want you hot and rising*
*but do you need to take up that much space*
*Sorry*
*I do*
*yes I do want it all*
*all of you hot and rising*
*but is not my vessel deep enough*
*should we always plan to add a collar*
*for your glorious rise*
*Sorry*
*not that I'm complaining*
*not that I don't appreciate your*
*hot and rising self*
*I do*
*but I do want to know*
*I want to try it next time*
*with certainty*
*using my vessel as it is*
*or maybe*
*Lord forbid*
*less of you*
*Sorry*
*is it me*
*I know that this has been*
*going on for years*
*using collars of parchment or foil*
*to facilitate your hot and rising self*

*to maybe two or three or four inches more*
*Sorry*
*no complaints*
*it's all good*
*indeed*
*be it overflowing*
*or neatly nestled*
*in my vessel*
*for your expansion*
*gives me joy of knowing*
*that I have caused*
*you to be hot and rising*
*and that your farewell*
*comes only after you*
*leave my vessel*

## Salmon Soufflé

How to beat egg whites: Beating is tricky. And it is the drama of beating that is seductive—egg whites, that is. A copper bowl is best for producing stable beaten egg whites, stainless steel is next best, and glass is third. Whichever you use, the bowl should be clean and dry to obtain the fullest volume. With mixer, beat the whites until they are smooth, have a velvety sheen, and are firm enough to allow their peaks to stand up.

How to fold egg whites: Like tender moments of lovemaking, you must be gentle and delicate to retain volume of egg whites, that is. Use a rubber spatula and spoon to scoop up the whites and place them on top of the soufflé mix. Gently fold into the mix by placing your spatula into the bottom of the bowl and bringing it toward you from the edge of the bowl. Lift up and carry over onto the top of the soufflé mix, and repeat until the whites are completely blended into the soufflé. This should take 1 minute. Overfolding will cause the soufflé to deflate. You got that?

Preheat oven to 400 degrees, then turn down to 375 degrees.

4 ounces salmon fillet, skin removed

⅛ teaspoon salt

⅛ teaspoon pepper

1½ tablespoons clarified butter, in all (see p. 57)

2 1-cup ramekins

3 tablespoons grated Parmesan, in all

1½ tablespoons butter

1 tablespoon finely chopped shallots

1½ tablespoons flour

½ cup milk, hot

2 egg yolks

1 teaspoon Creole seasoning

⅛ teaspoon salt

ice for ice bath

4 egg whites

1. Season salmon with salt and pepper. Into ovenproof skillet, pour 1 tablespoon clarified butter over medium-high heat. Sauté salmon about 2 minutes. Turn salmon over and place in oven. Cook about 2 minutes. Remove from skillet. Place in food processor and chop finely.

2. Place baking sheet in preheating oven.

3. Use remaining ½ tablespoon clarified butter to rub ramekins; dust with 1 tablespoon Parmesan and set aside.

4. Over medium-low heat, melt 1½ tablespoons butter in medium saucepan and add shallots. Sauté about 30 seconds. Add flour and stir over low heat about 2 minutes to make a blond roux (see appendix A). Stir constantly. Remove from heat and slowly add hot milk, stirring constantly. Return to heat and beat in egg yolks one at a time, stirring constantly. Cook and stir about 2 minutes, until mixture is thickened. Remove from heat and mix in salmon. Add Creole seasoning, 2 tablespoons Parmesan, and salt, and mix. Place salmon mixture in a medium metal bowl, and set bowl in ice bath to cool completely.

5. Whisk egg whites in separate medium metal bowl until they form soft peaks. With spatula, fold one third of whites into salmon mixture and

continue to fold lightly in until all the whites are well blended. Fold soufflé mixture into ramekins.

6. Place ramekins on baking sheet in oven and bake until done, 12 to 15 minutes, or until skewer inserted comes out slightly moist. Serve immediately.

Makes 2 servings.

*Note:* I use Tony Chachere's Creole seasoning (see appendix B).

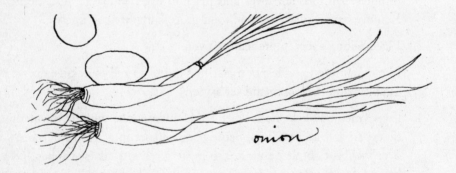

# *Come Home Sweet Love*

*Come home sweet love*
*breed here with me*
*for I am the fresh water you seek*
*I am the seabed of your desire*
*your anadromous ascent*
*must lead to me*

*Come home sweet love*
*breed here with me*
*your absence fares not well*
*for I am lonely and worthless*
*without you*
*come please come*
*or I will die*

*Come home sweet love*
*breed here with me*
*let me see your swelling flesh*
*as I lay on my back*
*and see you coming*
*in my dreams*
*I await you patiently*

*Come home sweet love*
*breed here with me*
*your rare appearance*
*sheds tears of longings*
*for your skin next to mine*
*tight*
*breathing into each other*
*giving of nothing*
*not even air*

*Come home sweet love*
*breed here with me*
*I am exhausted*
*at the thought*
*of your prolonged absence*
*and know no purpose*
*beyond serving*
*and being served*
*you*

*Come home sweet love*
*breed here with me*
*I am exhausted*
*at the thought*
*of you without me*
*of me without you*
*and breathe not*
*one ounce of life*
*for there is no purpose*
*without you*
*come home*

## Sautéed Striped Sea Bass

"Come Home Sweet Love" came from defining striped bass as anadromous in that it ascends from a saltwater habitat to spawn in fresh water. Fighting against odds to be in the company of love is what we live for. And the thought of coming home to create, to love, and to be loved is what "Come Home Sweet Love" speaks to. Serve this loving dish with Roasted Portobello Mushrooms (see p. 215) and Roasted Garlic Whipped Potatoes (see p. 227).

Preheat oven to 400 degrees

   ¼ teaspoon salt
   ¼ teaspoon white pepper
   2 8-ounce bass fillets with skin on
   4 tablespoons clarified butter

1. Salt and pepper fillets on both sides.

2. Heat butter about 1 minute over medium heat in medium cast-iron skillet. Put fillets in pan skin side up and cook 2 minutes.

3. Turn fillets skin side down, and cook until skin begins to brown, about 5 minutes.

4. Place skillet with bass in oven and roast until bass is done, 6 to 7 minutes, depending on thickness.

5. Remove from oven. Place fillets, skin down, on serving platter, and pour butter sauce from skillet over fillets.

Makes 2 servings.

# *Forgive Me*

*Forgive me*
*as I flip back your skin*
*too quickly*
*that easily yields*
*in my direction*
*for I seek your wet meat*
*that's tender and juicy*
*even though*
*your skin*
*that*
*I seasoned first*
*is what brought me*
*to this place*
*of massaging you*
*gently*
*in my hand*
*pulling out the best*
*in you*
*I offered rhythmic*
*strokes*
*with oil*
*to calm the initial touch*
*then what must be*
*food's air*
*salt*
*upon which I sprinkled*
*on you*
*and caused your flavor*
*to swell*
*to then create*
*a more pungent taste*

*I offered exotic bits of*
*black pepper*
*and your meat*
*got a little*
*heat*
*of cayenne*
*that cried for*
*attention*
*until*
*that is*
*crawfish potato*
*hash*
*took over*
*and*
*sorry*
*I had to leave*
*quickly*
*'cause*
*she got me*
*all wowed up*
*gee golly*
*she's so pretty*

## Braised Rainbow Trout with Crawfish Potato Hash

Because of the crawfish potato hash's multiple flavors of deliciously sautéed crawfish, crisp yet moist potatoes, and red bell peppers, the hash steals the show. It is so attractive and so good that you must select a handsome trout to complement this twosome. Serve with a salad or Sautéed Spinach (see p. 213).

Preheat oven to 400 degrees.

    1 2-pound rainbow trout, gutted, deboned, and fins removed
    ½ teaspoon salt
    ½ teaspoon pepper
    1 teaspoon olive oil

½ cup fish stock (see appendix A) or store-bought low-sodium
    fish broth

¼ cup white wine

3 tablespoons olive oil, in all

3 tablespoons butter, in all

1 small onion, chopped

1 tablespoon chopped shallots

2 cups potatoes, cut in small cubes

1 small red bell pepper, diced

1 tablespoon chopped fresh thyme

2 teaspoons Creole seasoning

¼ cup grated Asiago cheese

¼ pound crawfish tails

⅓ cup chopped fresh parsley

1. Rub skin of trout and inside cavity with salt and pepper. Drizzle oil inside and on both sides of trout.

2. Pour fish stock and wine in ovenproof skillet. Place fish in skillet and put in oven, and bake 20 minutes or until skin of fish easily pulls away from meat. Baste occasionally.

3. Meanwhile, over medium heat in medium skillet, put 1 tablespoon oil and 2 tablespoons butter. Add onion and shallots, and cook 2 minutes. Add potatoes and stir to coat with oil and vegetables. Add red pepper and stir. Add thyme and 1 teaspoon of the Creole seasoning and stir. Cook to brown potatoes slightly, 15 to 20 minutes. Remove from heat and add Asiago cheese. Stir until potatoes are well coated with cheese.

4. Melt remaining oil and butter in small saucepan over medium heat.

5. Sprinkle remaining teaspoon of Creole seasoning over crawfish; stir into skillet and sauté about 4 minutes, stirring often. Add to potato mixture. Add parsley and stir well.

6. On serving platter, gently place fish in center and put crawfish potato hash around fish.

Makes 2 servings.

*Note:* I use Tony Chachere's Creole seasoning (see appendix B).

# *You Know Them Well*

*You know them well*
> *both delicate, round and plump*
> *slightly tan*
> *soft and meaty inside*
> *seared to a crisp crust outside*
> *you stare and dare*
> *forsake all around them*
> *as they lie in shadows of white creamy potatoes*

*You taste, you nibble*
> *you hold your head between them*
> *their aroma keeps you there*
> *their firm tips around the edge*
> *where they are most golden*
> *ache for your lips*
> *as both are squeezed by seasoned bread crumbs,*
> *and embraced by onions, celery, and green peppers*

*You eat them*
> *gently*
> *it is a soft bite that collapses upon the first bite*
> *the bite needs no teeth just curved lips*
> *that protrude to catch all the drippings*
> *and a tongue to suck the delicate meat*
> *to extract their mouthwatering morsels*
> *they are but a palmful, so*
> *eat slowly*
> *caress*
> *eat slowly*
> *caress*
> *eat slowly*
> *caress*
> *swallow*

# Crab Cakes with Whipped Potatoes and Coleslaw

Whenever I eat crab cakes, I must have at least two. This has become a ritual for me, as it must be for most everybody in the whole wide world. Even restaurants have come to this realization and always serve up two with an order. What would happen if we just got one? Would we, with serious indignation, get up and leave a restaurant immediately, our culinary sense insulted? Would we end a lifelong relationship with someone who invites us to his or her home and has the nerve to serve a plate with only one crab cake? Absolutely.

FOR THE COLESLAW:

1 small cabbage, shredded

2 medium carrots, shredded

½ cup dill pickle relish

½ small onion, chopped

1 cup mayonnaise

1 teaspoon salt

½ teaspoon pepper

FOR THE WHIPPED POTATOES:

4 pounds white potatoes

1 cup heavy cream

2 teaspoons salt

1 teaspoon pepper

1½ sticks butter

FOR THE CRAB CAKES (MAKES ABOUT 8):

2 tablespoons vegetable oil

½ cup chopped green onions

½ jalapeño pepper, seeded and diced (wear rubber gloves)

2 teaspoons Creole seasoning (see appendix B), in all

2 eggs

¼ cup bread crumbs

1 pound lump crabmeat

¼ teaspoon salt

⅛ teaspoon pepper

6 tablespoons vegetable oil, in all

1. *To prepare the coleslaw:* Mix all ingredients in large mixing bowl. Keep covered in refrigerator until ready to serve.

2. *To prepare the potatoes:* Peel and cut potatoes and place in medium pot. Cover potatoes with water and bring to boil. Simmer until potatoes are soft and slightly breaking apart. Drain potatoes in colander.

3. Place drained potatoes in large mixing bowl. Add cream, salt, and pepper, and whip with an electric mixer. Mix until potatoes are smooth. Add butter and stir well. Season with additional salt and pepper to taste. Keep warm.

4. *To prepare crab cakes:* Heat 1 tablespoon oil in large skillet over medium heat. Add onions, jalapeño, and sauté 30 seconds. Remove from heat. Stir in 1 teaspoon Creole seasoning. Remove from heat and put in large mixing bowl.

5. Stir eggs, bread crumbs, and remaining 1 teaspoon Creole seasoning into vegetables. Add crabmeat, salt, and pepper and mix well.

6. Measure ¼ cup of the crabmeat mixture and form small ball using your hands. Pat down slightly. Makes about 8 crabmeat balls.

7. Heat 3 tablespoons of the oil in medium skillet over high heat. Fry half of the crab cakes until brown, about 2 minutes on each side. Drain crab cakes on paper towels. Repeat with remaining crab cakes and oil. Serve hot.

Makes 4 servings.

crabs

# Simple Love

*Simple love, please give me some.*
*Uncomplicated, naked love*
*is what I want.*
*That which I can taste first*
*then taste again*
*and know it well.*

*Simple love, please give me some.*
*No labyrinth of seasonings*
*no layers of herbs.*
*Possessive tomatoes, insecure carrots*
*demanding onions*
*need not come a' courting.*
*Just olive oil and lemon juice*
*to marinate*
*nothing more.*

*Simple love, please give me some.*
*Unentangled, intently gentle*
*is what I want.*
*A dish that is purely itself*
*secure in its understanding of what it is—*
*brief offerings of joy*
*seeking nothing in return.*

*Simple love, please give me some.*
*Not smothered, not sauced*
*only clarified butter*
*over a full flame*
*transforming gray shrimp into*
*radiant pink victuals with sprinkles of*
*garlic masters*
*needing nothing else*
*to engage my taste buds.*

*Simple love, please give me some.*
*Unadulterated, innocent love*
*is what I want.*
*Soft embraces*
*sweet kisses*
*sensual appetites*
*sexual souls*
*please give me some.*

## Garlic Shrimp

Simple love. Is not that what we all want? Uncomplicated, true love. And how better to achieve such than with a quick preparation and deliciously delivered sauté of garlic and shrimp in butter to share with your lover? You can serve this simple, sensuous dish with rice and sautéed spinach.

½ pound medium-to-large shrimp, shelled and deveined
½ teaspoon salt
¼ teaspoon pepper
4 tablespoons olive oil
1 tablespoon lemon juice
8 tablespoons clarified butter (see p. 57)
6 large garlic cloves, thinly sliced
2 cups cooked rice seasoned with salt

1. Season shrimp with salt and pepper. Pour olive oil and lemon juice over shrimp, and marinate shrimp 30 minutes in refrigerator.
2. Heat clarified butter in large skillet over medium heat. Sauté garlic about 1 minute. Add shrimp and its marinade, and sauté until shrimp are done, about 2 to 3 minutes. Stir occasionally to cook shrimp on all sides. Remove from heat.

Serve shrimp with its sauce over rice.

Makes 2 servings.

# *Swim Upstream with Me*

*Swim upstream with me*
*for in this life*
*as we live it*
*there are high waves all about*
*and oceans to cross*

*Swim upstream with me*
*there is but*
*fresh water*
*awaiting us if we dive forward*
*to spawn*

*Swim upstream with me*
*let me wash*
*your silvery blue back*
*and your middle*
*indeed your best part*

*Swim upstream with me*
*as we search*
*for our calmness*
*our wet ground of serenity*
*to find our sexual mist*

## Salmon with Mozzarella and Asiago Quiche

The idea of swimming upstream and fighting against the current to return to the spawning ground is a most loving and tender image. Young salmon remain in fresh water for about two years and then begin to migrate toward the sea where they reach maturity. The duration of their stay in the sea is variable, as it depends on when they become sexually mature, don't you know. Wouldn't we all love to live by the sea upon our sexual maturity? Serve with a salad of mixed greens with grilled figs or with a bowl of watermelon.

Preheat oven to 425 degrees.

> 1 8-ounce salmon fillet, boned and skinned
> 1/8 teaspoon salt
> 1/8 teaspoon pepper
> 1 tablespoon butter, in all
> 1 9-inch deep-dish piecrust, store bought
> 2 tablespoons chopped onions
> 1 tablespoon chopped fresh thyme
> 3/4 cup light cream
> 3 eggs
> 1/2 teaspoon salt
> 1/4 teaspoon pepper
> 1/4 teaspoon nutmeg
> 1 cup shredded mozzarella
> 1 cup shredded Asiago cheese

1. Season salmon with salt and pepper. Over medium heat, melt 1/2 table-spoon butter in small cast-iron skillet. Place salmon in hot butter and cook about 2 minutes. Turn salmon over, place skillet in oven, and continue to cook salmon for 3 minutes. Remove from oven and place salmon on platter. When slightly cooled, break salmon into small bite-size pieces.

2. With fork, prick the piecrust all over sides and bottom. Bake 3 minutes. Prick to deflate and bake until crust is slightly brown, another 1 to 2 minutes. Remove from oven.

3. Melt remaining butter in separate skillet over medium heat. Add onions and thyme and sauté about 2 minutes. Remove from heat. Mix salmon into onion mixture. Set aside.

4. Mix 3/4 cup cream with 3 eggs. Whisk to blend. Add salt, pepper, and nutmeg, and whisk.

5. Sprinkle 1/4 of the mozzarella and Asiago cheeses to cover bottom of pie crust. Whisk 1/4 of the cheeses into egg mixture. Pour salmon mixture

into piecrust. Pour egg mixture over salmon. Sprinkle remaining cheeses to cover egg and salmon mixture.

6. Bake in 425-degree oven for 10 minutes, then reduce heat to 375 degrees and bake 15 minutes. Turn oven back to 425 degrees for 5 minutes. Remove from oven, and place on rack to cool, about 10 minutes. Slice and serve.

Makes 4 servings.

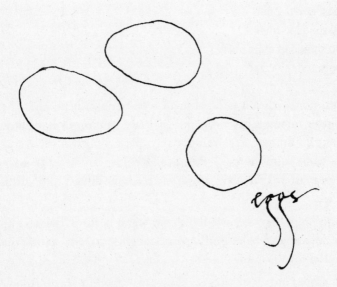

eggs

# Sweet You Are

*Sweet you are*
*    with your red, yellow, and green peppers.*
*You bite my tongue*
*    with your jalapeño heat.*
*You suck my juices*
*    leaving only yours to savor.*

*I unzip my pants and*
*    you swell me up.*
*Your big shrimp are hot*
*    with Creole flavors.*
*I lick the split part that's plump and prime*
*    with the tip of my tongue curved to press between the lips.*

*Sweet you are*
*    with your creamy white grits.*
*You lie over silky golden butter*
*    with freshly chopped green thyme and parsley.*
*You float in a walnut brown roux*
*    with diced onions and garlic stroking the sauce.*

*I rear back and unfold my legs 'cause*
*    your hominy grains penetrate me*
*with sable full-bodied soy and Worcestershire sauce*
*    embracing all that they touch with delicious manly flavors.*
*Oh, yes, it is so sweet to be with you and so bitter to be without.*

## Shrimp and Grits

Grits are cheap thrills, costing nearly nothing but causing warm sensations upon their being eaten. During the process of transforming corn into traditional hominy grits, I'm told, the kernels of the corn shell pop off and the kernel swells to twice its size. Wow! The key to good creamy grits is the ratio of water to grits (4 to 1)—stirring to prevent lumps and adding lots of butter. Serve this dish with fresh tomato slices and hot buttery bread.

FOR SHRIMP SAUCE:

4 tablespoons oil, in all

6 tablespoons butter, in all

1 large onion, diced

½ medium red, yellow, and green bell peppers, diced

1 jalapeño pepper, seeded and thinly sliced (wear rubber gloves)

2 garlic cloves, minced

2 pounds large shrimp, shelled and deveined

½ teaspoon salt

1 tablespoon Creole seasoning (see appendix B)

½ cup flour, to coat shrimp

3 tablespoons flour

3 cups shrimp stock (see appendix A), or store-bought low-sodium shrimp broth

4 tablespoons Worcestershire sauce

2 tablespoons soy sauce

1 tablespoon chopped fresh thyme

2 tablespoons chopped fresh parsley

FOR THE GRITS:

6 cups water

1½ cups grits

1 teaspoon salt

4 tablespoons butter

1. *To cook shrimp sauce:* Over medium-high heat, melt 2 tablespoons oil and 2 tablespoons butter in medium Dutch oven. Add onions, bell peppers, jalapeño, and garlic, and sauté about 3 minutes. Remove vegetables from Dutch oven and drain in colander. Set aside.

2. Season shrimp with salt and Creole seasoning, then dredge shrimp in flour. Over medium-high heat, add remaining 2 tablespoons oil and 2 tablespoons of the butter to pan, and sauté shrimp 2 minutes. Toss to

cook both sides of shrimp. Remove shrimp from Dutch oven, place in bowl, and set aside.

3.  Place Dutch oven back over medium-high heat, and add remaining 2 tablespoons butter. Stir in vegetable mixture. Sprinkle with 3 tablespoons flour, and sauté over medium heat about 2 minutes.

4.  Add stock, Worcestershire sauce, and soy sauce. Bring to boil, turn heat to low, and simmer 8 minutes. Add shrimp, thyme, and parsley. Simmer 3 minutes. Remove from heat.

5.  *To cook grits:* In large pot, bring 6 cups water to boil. Stir in 1½ cups grits and 1 teaspoon salt, and stir vigorously 30 seconds to prevent lumps. Turn heat to low. Cover and cook, stirring occasionally. Cook about 15 minutes or until grits are creamy. Remove from heat. Add 4 tablespoons butter and stir. Divide grits among six dinner plates. Pour 1 cup of shrimp and vegetable sauce over grits. Serve hot.

Makes 6 servings.

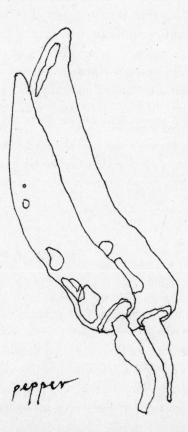

pepper

# *They Came to Be Fed*

At seven in the evening . . . dressed in apron only . . . I received them . . . one by one they came to be fed. Salmon in puff pastry was my choice . . . full . . . firm . . . sweet and big. Big enough to serve three lovers who had come to eat in silence . . . as long as they could.

They watched me as I marched them into a narrow room and sat them at a long table with white linen and red candles. But I was not to be served on the silver platter tonight. The seducer is yet to come, for she is still in the oven releasing the last explosions of puff layers encasing her, while crawfish mousse deep inside bubbles from her heat . . . she is almost done.

Three, four, five minutes more and she will swell up to her optimum size . . . but time is running out. The polite ritual of waiting for the sake of savory and sweet pleasure is wearing thin. The suitors begin to tap spoons against saucers, creating African rhythms summoning us to appear. I hear . . . but cannot come . . . not yet . . . but I will answer my lovers and fully penetrate their culinary abyss . . . this night, too.

Five minutes up. She's swollen and golden. Hot buttery juices flow from her bottom crevice . . . she's ready . . . so am I. We heed the call and march into the narrow room past the shadows of twilight beaming through the bay windows . . . I place her on the table . . . they smile . . . chaotic tenderness of excitement permeates the air as I reach out for their plates to begin the feast.

## Salmon in Puff Pastry

Puff pastry is one of the most impressive foods you can present to your lover. In cooking school, I was the master puff pastry dough maker in my class. At least, I thought so. I believe I was so successful because of my gentle folding of butter into the dough and my thoughtful and precise rolling of the dough, gently folding it again, and repeating this process about ten times in between refrigerating. For me, folding pastry dough created a sensual serenity similar to a calm orgasm that often brought slow tears to my eyes. I may have missed my calling—that of a baker. I have found that the folding of dough is the second most sensual act you can perform on your kitchen counter. Serve with Grilled Vegetables (see p. 198).

Adapted from Wolfgang Puck's *Modern French Cooking*.

2 8-ounce salmon fillets, skinned and boned
¼ teaspoon salt
¼ teaspoon pepper
1 tablespoon chopped fresh tarragon
1 tablespoon chopped fresh parsley

FOR CRAWFISH MOUSSE:

⅛ pound crawfish tails (about 12 crawfish tails)
⅛ teaspoon Creole seasoning
1 tablespoon butter
1 egg beaten
pinch salt and pepper
¼ cup heavy cream
puff pastry sheets, thawed (see note at end of recipe)
1 egg, lightly beaten
1 tablespoon water

1. Cut pocket into each salmon fillet. Do not cut all the way through salmon. Sprinkle salmon with salt and pepper, tarragon, and parsley. Cover with plastic wrap and refrigerate until ready to stuff.

2. *To make crawfish mousse:* Sprinkle crawfish with Creole seasoning. Put crawfish and butter in food processor to chop 5 seconds. Add ½ of beaten egg and mix 3 seconds. Remove crawfish mixture from food processor. Sprinkle a pinch each of salt and pepper, and stir. Put in medium bowl. Cover. Put in refrigerator to chill. Whip cream to stiff peaks and fold half of cream into crawfish mixture.

3. Remove salmon and crawfish mousse from refrigerator. Spoon crawfish mousse into salmon pocket. Do not overstuff; turn salmon fillet with open fillet pocket at top. Refrigerate at least 20 minutes.

4. Allow pastry sheets to thaw so that you can easily roll dough without cracking seams. Roll dough on floured marble surface. With 1 sheet,

place 1 salmon fillet on pastry dough to about an inch from its edge. Fold dough over salmon. Trim pastry following outline of salmon. Seal edges using a baker's brush dipped lightly in water. Press edges together. Repeat with second salmon fillet. Place on parchment-covered baking sheet and refrigerate for at least 20 minutes. Preheat oven to 375 degrees.

5.  Lightly beat 1 egg and 1 tablespoon of water for egg wash. Remove pastry-covered salmon on baking sheet from refrigerator. Brush the egg wash generously on pastry dough.

6.  Bake until salmon is done, about 16 to 20 minutes, or until pastry is golden brown and when skewer inserted into middle of salmon for 1 minute comes out hot. Do not overcook.

Makes 2 servings.

*Notes:* 1. I use Tony Chachere's Creole seasoning (see appendix B).

2. Frozen puff pastry sheets can be purchased from a gourmet shop and at some grocery stores.

## CHAPTER THREE

# Mannish Meats

*Shall I compare thee to a stuffed leg of lamb?*
*Thou art more abundant and more tender.*
—Leg of Lamb Stuffed with Spinach and Mint,
  "Sonnet to a Stuffed Leg of Lamb"

**RECIPES:**

"Succulent Tails" / Braised Oxtails in Red Wine Sauce

"Sonnet to a Stuffed Leg of Lamb" / Leg of Lamb Stuffed with
    Spinach and Mint

"As Good As Sex: A Testimonial" / Chili

"Comforting Love" / Stuffed Peppers and Collard Greens

"Metamorphosis" / Braised Roast Chuck with Caramelized Onion
    Po' Boy

"He Said She Said" / Braised Lamb Shanks

"Meatballs" / Spicy Meatballs with Angel-Hair Pasta

"Curry Me There" / Curried Lamb

"He's a Ladies' Man" / Roast Leg of Lamb with Vegetables

"Though Not My First Choice" / Beef Stew Provence

"Quickies Are Good" / Stir-Fry Beef Strips with Roasted Peppers

"Tie Me Up, You Say" / Osso Buco

"To Shape Thy Lover's Love Parts" / Beef Wellington for Two

"May I Lick Your Plate" / Sirloin Steak with Shallot Brandy Sauce

"Grill Me Baby, Grill Me" / Grilled T-Bone Steak

# Succulent Tails

I wrap my hand around your long slenderness and stare at you in solitude. In your raw state, you are but a bony, thick piece of meat. And as I consider your perception and your bare image, your appearance eclipses your savory taste, causing you not to be considered a culinary muse.

But if I may hold you tenderly, soak you deeply, heat you slowly, I might then see your immense beauty. For as in any romance that lasts, indulgence, attentiveness, and forgiveness know no bounds. So we share a bottle of wine and relax, for I do know that you require time to reach your fullness as a succulent tail. Here, red Burgundy suits you best. Absorb its tenderizing qualities—a full day at least. It relaxes your muscles, causing you to dispel that tough image and begin to become the sweet, gentle tails that you are.

Then shall we slow dance in the kitchen. A low sultry simmer is what we need to cause you to swell into a fat juicy luscious meat. Time matters not, you see, because the ultimate deliverance of your taste is timeless. But the hours—they do pass by endlessly. Two . . . three . . . four hours, and on and on, until you reach out slightly away from your secure joints to then be ready to be sucked from your bones ever so delicately.

I, with deliberate care, scoop you up and ladle you down inside a deep white plate surrounded by the dark Burgundy sauce of your juices, and surely, if there is anything left, it is but a bone.

## Braised Oxtails in Red Wine Sauce

Oxtails were a staple food, along with collard greens, fried chicken, and catfish, when I was growing up in Atlanta. They were affordable and abundant, like most foods found on our working-class table, and were not considered a special meal in our home or our community. It was only as an adult that I learned we were eating what is now considered a delicacy. Several years ago, I interviewed Chef Michel Bourdin of London's Connaught Hotel. He had been serving oxtails in his restaurant for over 25 years. "There is a tendency," Chef Bourdin said, "to go back to the original cooking—home cooking. And

I think oxtails are a typical dish that is found in the homes and now restaurants. It is what we call bourgeois cooking." Adapted from a recipe in *Gourmet* in 1987, "Braised Oxtails and Spring Vegetables" by Chef Michel Bourdin.

> 3 pounds meaty oxtails
> ½ bottle red Burgundy
> 1 carrot, sliced
> 1 medium onion, chopped
> 1 garlic clove, chopped
> 5 peppercorns
> 2 herb bundles tied together, *each* with 2 parsley stems, 1 bay leaf, 2 thyme stems
> 1 tablespoon salt
> 2 teaspoons pepper
> 4 tablespoons vegetable oil
> 3 tablespoons vegetable oil
> ¼ cup vegetable oil
> ¼ cup flour
> 1 28-ounce can Italian plum tomatoes, with juice
> 3 cups beef stock (see appendix A), or store-bought low-sodium beef broth
> 1 teaspoon salt
> 1 teaspoon pepper

1. Marinate oxtails overnight in wine with carrots, onions, garlic, peppercorns, and 1 herb bundle.
2. Strain oxtails and vegetables into bowl, and set aside the wine marinade. Pat oxtails dry. Salt and pepper both sides and put on plate. Place vegetables on paper towel and discard tied herbs.
3. Heat 4 tablespoons oil in large skillet and brown oxtails about 10 minutes on both sides; place in large Dutch oven.
4. Heat 3 tablespoons oil in skillet and sauté vegetables until soft, about 5 minutes; place in Dutch oven with oxtails.
5. Over medium-high heat, pour ¼ cup oil into skillet used to brown oxtails. When oil is smoking slightly, whisk flour into skillet and stir to make dark roux (see appendix A). Cook and stir 5 to 7 minutes. Pour

roux into the Dutch oven. Add tomatoes, stock, and wine marinade, and bring to boil; lower heat to slow simmer. Add second bundle of herbs. Season with salt and pepper. Cover partially, and simmer until meat is tender, 3 to 4 hours. Remove from heat.

6.   Place oxtails on platter and strain sauce. Pour sauce over oxtails.

Makes 4 servings.

*Note:* Serve over Whipped Potatoes (see p. 74).

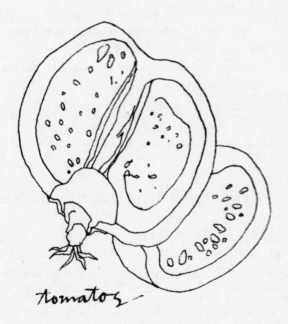

tomatos -

# Sonnet to a Stuffed Leg of Lamb

Adapted from Shakespeare's Sonnet XVIII, "Shall I compare thee to a summer's day?"

> *Shall I compare thee to a stuffed leg of lamb?*
>> *Thou art more abundant and more tender.*
> *Young cooks do toughen the darling's leg*
>> *And lamb's rendezvous hath all too swift a passage.*
> *Sometimes too quick the leg is caressed with oil,*
>> *and often too long is its meat in heat.*
> *Though every good morsel is eaten to the bone,*
>> *by chance when seasoning is applied generously.*
> *But thy immense leg of lamb has no end,*
>> *nor lose supremacy of that gentle genital thou ownest;*
> *nor is the heat ever too hot in a sultry skillet for thee,*
>> *when in life's passionate pleasures thou endures.*
> *So long as women long for men,*
>> *so long as women long for men.*

## Leg of Lamb Stuffed with Spinach and Mint

When I prepared the stuffed leg of lamb and sat down to write about it, I did not hear its sensual voice. I thought that we would just have to share this delicious dish with company for dinner and be satisfied. But the following day as I was driving to the market, I heard Garrison Keillor on National Public Radio's *The Writer's Almanac* reciting Shakespeare's Sonnet XVIII; "Shall I compare thee to a summer's day." It was as though he spoke only to me, for I was still hoping to be seduced by that leg of lamb. On hearing Keillor recite the first two lines, "Shall I compare thee to a summer's day? Thou art more lovely and more temperate," I pulled out pen and paper and wrote, "Shall I compare thee to a stuffed leg of lamb? Thou art more abundant and more tender." I finished my leg of lamb sonnet driving down the highway to the market that Saturday morning. "Be well, do good work, and keep in touch," as Keillor would say. Serve with Risotto with Wild Mushrooms (see p. 180). Adapted from Emeril Lagasse's *Emeril's New Orleans Cooking*.

Preheat oven to 375 degrees.

> 4 tablespoons olive oil
> 7 ounces diced lamb meat, from inside leg of lamb
> 1 teaspoon Creole seasoning
> Pinch of salt
> ⅓ cup onions, chopped
> 1 small shallot, chopped
> 2 garlic cloves, minced
> 1 tablespoon chopped fresh parsley
> 2 cups chopped fresh spinach
> ⅓ cup chopped fresh mint
> 3 ounces fresh Parmesan, shaved
> 1 5-pound leg of lamb, boned and butterflied
> 2 tablespoons Creole seasoning
> ⅛ teaspoon salt
> 3 tablespoons olive oil
> ½ cup beef stock (see appendix A) or store-bought low-sodium broth

1. Heat 4 tablespoons olive oil in large cast-iron skillet over medium-high heat.

2. Season diced lamb with Creole seasoning and salt. Sauté in skillet about 2 minutes. Add onions, shallot, garlic, and parsley, and sauté 2 minutes. Remove from heat. Stir in spinach, mint, and Parmesan. Set stuffing aside to cool.

3. Place lamb on a work surface with inside of butterflied side up. Spread cooled stuffing evenly over lamb. Fold lamb over to close and cover stuffing. Tie tightly with kitchen twine. Rub outside of lamb with 2 tablespoons Creole seasoning and salt.

4. Heat 3 tablespoons olive oil in cast-iron skillet over medium-high heat. Place lamb in skillet, and cook on both sides, about 3 minutes per side. Place skillet in oven, and roast 40 to 50 minutes. Baste occasionally.

5.   Remove lamb from pan and place on platter. Spoon off fat. Place pan on top of stove at high heat; add stock to deglaze pan, scraping and stirring browned bits with wooden spoon. Lower heat and simmer until stock is slightly thickened, about 5 minutes. Strain, set aside, and keep warm. Remove twine from lamb and slice to serve.

Makes 8 servings.

*Notes:* 1. I use Tony Chachere's Creole seasoning (see appendix B).

2. To serve, slice lamb and pour lamb juice over lamb.

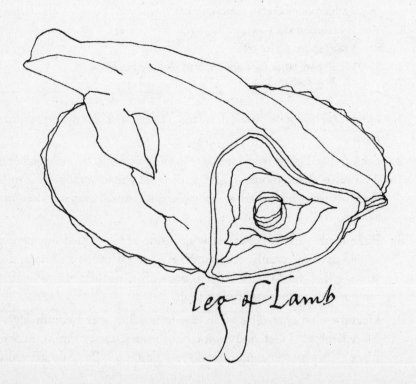

Leg of Lamb

# As Good As Sex: A Testimonial

*As good as sex, I say*
*Yes*
*it is*
*and I've had good sex*
*so as I eat this chili*
*my body and mind responds*
*to the sexual thrill*
*of my memories*
*of extraordinarily*
*rambunctious deliciously*
*exuberating sex*
*And the best treat of it all*
*was that it was not expected*
*not from a bowl of chili*
*as in lovers who perform*
*breathtaking sex*
*Please forgive me when I say*
*you can't tell a book by its cover*
*So be open to the phenomenon*
*of the possibility of*
*getting dazzling wondrous sex*
*from that that might not look*
*too great on the outside*
*or that that your imagination*
*has not yet "reached"*
*Never had I imagined*
*this common chili propelling*
*my sexual cells into*
*a climactically sensual*
*state of being*
*This was the case*
*for this chili with me*

*It was not a part of this book*
*It was only a pot of chili*
*planned to comfort me and Ed*
*on this first ice storm*
*of January 2005*
*I got up early*
*as I normally do*
*I wrote some*
*read some*
*and this time*
*cooked on this early morning*
*I began to gather my ingredients*
*ground beef, garlic, tomatoes,*
*thyme, cumin, oregano, chili peppers,*
*coriander, salt, pepper*
*And near panic when I discovered that*
*I had only two small onions*
*I looked out the window*
*Ice everywhere*
*No way could I get more onions*
*So I opened the refrigerator*
*began the hunt for whatever*
*else I could substitute for the*
*two onions*
*I saw peppers*
*assorted pepper caps and bottoms*
*of red, yellow, and orange*
*leftovers from last week's*
*shrimp and grits*
*I diced them up nicely*
*then my two small onions*
*and garlic*
*I had no beef stock or beef bouillons*
*and didn't feel like making any*
*So I used water and*
*vegetable bouillons*
*to add more flavor*
*Then you chili lovers*

*you know the drill*
*I tossed everything else in*
*to sauté before simmering*
*No big deal*
*It's just chili*
*OK, I said and walked away*
*Let it cook about one hour*
*then added the kidney beans, canned OK*
*Nothing special*
*But after an hour of simmering*
*I stirred in the beans and*
*witnessed something*
*kind of extraordinary*
*a beauty unimaginable*
*that struck me upon first glance*
*a swirling liquid of red hues*
*dancing in circles*
*with the deep royal red*
*portion of the steaming liquid*
*floating just above*
*Surely the engagement of*
*the pungent chili powders and oil of the meat*
*outstanding in its appearance*
*I was mesmerized by its enchantment*
*like coming upon a potential lover*
*not too impressive at first glance*
*but later discovering compassion*
*thoughtfulness and sincerity*
*And oh, by the way*
*abundance*
*in the right places*
*Needless to say*
*I was impressed*
*But, I asked, does it taste good?*
*That is the question*
*What the hell am I going*
*to do with compassion*
*and even this enormous*

*pot of chili*
*if it doesn't taste good*
*forgive me, please*
*I must excuse myself*
*and go get me mo*
*for it is*
*God good*

# Chili

This chili has become one of my grandchildren's favorite dishes. They eat it with a dollop of sour cream and a sprinkling of grated cheddar cheese. With each spoonful of chili, they turn to me and thank me with "We're so glad you're our grandma." Serve this warm spicy dish with corn muffins.

3 tablespoons olive oil

2 medium onions, chopped

3 garlic cloves, chopped fine

½ of medium diced red, yellow, and green bell peppers

2 tablespoons chili powder

4½ teaspoons cumin

3 teaspoons coriander

2 teaspoons dry thyme

2 teaspoons dry oregano

2 teaspoons crushed red pepper

2 teaspoons salt

2 teaspoons pepper

2 pounds ground chuck

1 6-ounce can tomato paste

1 28-ounce can roasted tomatoes with juice

1½ teaspoons sugar

7 cups water

2 cups vegetable stock (see appendix A) (can use vegetable bouillon cubes or store-bought low-sodium vegetable broth)

2 tablespoons masa harina flour (see note at end of recipe)

2 8-ounce cans of dark red kidney beans, drained

1.  Heat oil in large pot over medium-high heat. Add onions and sauté about 2 minutes. Add garlic and bell peppers and sauté 3 minutes.

2.  Sprinkle chili powder, cumin, coriander, thyme, oregano, crushed red pepper, salt, and pepper over ground chuck, and mix well to distribute the seasonings.

3.  Add meat to pot, and stir into onion and pepper mixture. Cook and stir until meat is brown, about 5 minutes. Add tomato paste, blend into meat, and stir about 1 minute. Add roasted tomatoes and sugar. Mix well and stir about 3 minutes.

4.  Mix water, stock, and masa harina flour, and stir into pot. Bring to a boil, then simmer about 1 hour. Add beans and simmer 45 minutes. Serve hot.

Makes 8–10 servings.

*Note:* You can find masa harina flour in large grocery stores and Mexican American markets in the flour and cornmeal sections.

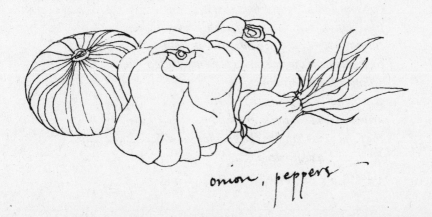

onion, peppers

# *Comforting Love*

While we move fast all about us,
    there is a comforting love.
Not passion driven,
    but a mellow knowing.
Filled with wide smiles and warm embraces
    of aged tears of remembrance
    and love shared.

While we move fast all about us,
    looking back speeding past,
    there is a life just before us
    ready to touch, ready to taste.
Now shall we slow the life
    to absorb that that is before us,
    to experience that that we experience,
    to love that that we love,
    to appreciate the comforts of life right now—
waking up and getting up on Saturday mornings,
eating stuffed peppers on their second day,
a kiss in the park,
roast garlic mashed potatoes floating in a sea of butter,
bedroom darkness just before sleep,
fried catfish, coleslaw, and grits on Friday nights,
turning over for a kiss, a hug, and anything else,
fresh lemonade over ice on a hot Sunday afternoon,
falling asleep in his arms,
waking up in his arms,
drinking good hot coffee in the a.m.,
the palm of his hand on the middle of your back as you sleep,
lunch with a dear friend,
Häagen-Dazs ice cream on sale,

*collard greens with corn bread crumbs in its pot liquor,*
*seeing daybreak arrive,*
*seeing daybreak arrive again*

## Stuffed Peppers and Collard Greens

There is much to be said about "soul food," now often referred to as "comfort food," generally defined as traditional African American food of the South, like collard greens, oxtails, grits, black-eyed peas, sweet potatoes, and fried chicken. Soul food is a wool blanket on a cold winter's night; it is loving arms and legs wrapped snugly around each other in bed following an over-time love session. It is what we seek after we've had the most glamorous fou fou of gourmet foods. Even though it refers most often to Black Southern cuisine in the United States, it is any authentic ethnic food from any group of people. It is the food you come home to. Serve this dish with whipped po-tatoes (see p. 74).

FOR THE STUFFED PEPPERS:

4 each medium bell peppers, red, yellow, green, and orange, seeded and tops sliced off

4 teaspoons olive oil for each pepper

1 teaspoon salt to season 4 peppers

1 teaspoon pepper to season 4 peppers

2 tablespoons olive oil, to sauté vegetables

1 large onion, chopped

3 large chopped garlic cloves

chopped bell pepper tops

1½ pounds ground chuck

3 teaspoon dried oregano

3 teaspoon dried thyme

4 teaspoons Worcestershire sauce

1 6-ounce can tomato paste

1 teaspoon salt

1 teaspoon pepper

½ cup seasoned bread crumbs

½ cup beef stock (see appendix A) or store-bought low-sodium
   beef broth

½ cup grated Parmesan cheese

1 cup boiling water to come up midpoint of peppers

FOR THE COLLARD GREENS:

5 cups water

4 large smoked turkey wings

1 large onion, peeled and quartered

1 bunch collard greens, leaves quartered, stems removed and
   discarded.

1 jalapeño pepper, seeded and diced (wear rubber gloves)

2 teaspoons salt

2 beef bouillon cubes

¼ teaspoon cayenne pepper

2 tablespoons apple cider vinegar

Salt

1. *To prepare the stuffed peppers:* Cut tops of bell peppers about ½ inch from stems and remove seeds. Set aside. Rub oil inside and outside peppers; sprinkle salt and pepper inside. Set aside.

2. Heat 2 tablespoons oil in a large skillet over low-medium heat. Add onion, garlic, and chopped bell pepper tops, and sauté about 3 minutes. Preheat oven to 350 degrees. Add meat, oregano, and thyme, and sauté about 3 minutes. Add Worcestershire sauce, tomato paste, and salt and pepper, and sauté about 3 minutes. Add bread crumbs, and sauté about 2 minutes. Stir in stock and half the cheese, and simmer about 1 minute.

3. Spoon meat mixture into the bell peppers, filling them completely. Place peppers in a baking dish and fill the dish with boiling water that comes up to mid-point of peppers. Bake until peppers are tender and stuffing is hot, about 45 minutes. Sprinkle with remaining cheese, and cook until cheese is melted, about 2 minutes.

4. *To prepare the collard greens:* In stockpot, bring water with turkey and onion to boil, then simmer for 30 minutes.

5. Wash greens in cold water. Place greens in pot. Add jalapeño, salt, beef bouillon, cayenne, and vinegar; stir and cover. Bring to a boil; then turn down to simmer. Stir occasionally. Cover to cook 30 minutes. Uncover

and continue to cook 30 minutes or until greens are tender but not too soft. Season with salt to taste.

Makes 4 servings.

*Note:* For collard greens to be ready at same time as peppers, I would put peppers in oven 15 minutes after the first collard green simmer starts in step #5. If you do that, do not preheat oven until step #2 after sautéing onion, garlic, and pepper tops. Place peppers in baking dish, and add boiling water when ready to put in oven after the 15-minute preheat is up.

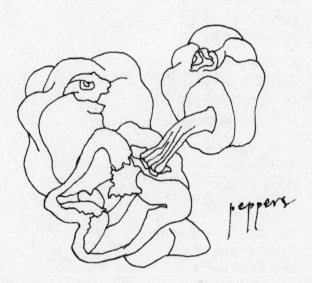

peppers

# *Metamorphosis*

*A liquid eroticism in my pot*
*simmering, bubbling, slowly*
*metamorphosing your cock*

*not that your present state*
*is not a perfect bait*
*it's the gift of your transition*
*that's heavenly mate*

*thick, tough, and tantalizing*
*you are an admirable sight*
*good enough as you are*
*good enough so far*

*but you're now in my pot*
*surrounded by my heat*
*and the lid is tight*
*to release a tender meat*

*this is the journey*
*this is the quest*
*there is no escape*
*for this is your fate*

*once your amorous incursions*
*lay you upon me*
*the sauce thickens*
*the metamorphosis quickens*

## Braised Chuck Roast with Caramelized Onion Po' Boy

It is reported that the first po' boy was made during the Depression in a New Orleans bar near the Mississippi River. Most of the bar's customers were longshoremen. The owner wanted to create a sandwich big enough to satisfy the longshoremen and cheap enough for the "poor boys" who lived near the depressed riverfront. The rest is history. I had my first po' boy at our dear friend Lionel McIntyre's home in New Orleans. He unwrapped white butcher paper on his small kitchen table and revealed several po' boys overflowing with fried shrimp and fried catfish with shreds of lettuce, tomato slices, and pickles dangling out with a thick rémoulade sauce oozing from the French loaf. I wondered, what a big, messy looking sandwich and besides, who's gonna eat all that? After my first delicious bite, it took only seconds to devour my po' boy. I then turned to Ed to sample his catfish po' boy. I was hooked.

Preheat oven to 325 degrees.

> FOR THE CHUCK ROAST:
> 2½ to 3 pounds boneless beef chuck roast
> 2 teaspoons salt
> 2 teaspoons pepper
> 3 tablespoons olive oil, in all
> 3 onions, peeled and thinly sliced across
> 1 large garlic clove, sliced thin
> 1 medium carrot, sliced into 3-inch pieces
> 1 tablespoon tomato paste
> 1 cup red wine
> 1½ cups beef stock (see appendix A) or store-bought low-sodium broth
> 1 teaspoon chopped fresh thyme
> 2 tablespoons chopped fresh parsley

1. *To prepare the chuck roast:* Season the meat with salt and pepper, and pour 1 tablespoon olive oil over it. Pierce meat with fork and massage oil into meat.

2. Pour remaining oil into large heavy-duty, ovenproof pot. Heat oil until smoking slightly. Place meat in pot, and brown roast on both sides, about 5 minutes each side. Remove meat to plate and lower heat to medium low.

3. *To caramelize onions:* In same pot, add sliced onions, and let cook slowly, tossing to brown on all sides. Cook about 50 minutes or until onions are caramel colored or golden brown.

4.  Add garlic, carrots, and tomato paste, and sauté to blend, about 1
    minute. Add wine and stock and bring to boil. Place meat back in pot;
    cover tightly. Place pot in oven. Braise 1 hour, then turn meat over and
    continue cooking until meat is tender, about 1 hour. Stir in thyme and
    parsley. Cook uncovered 10 minutes.

Makes 6–8 servings.

*Note:* Place slices of beef, sauce, and onion over hot-buttered French bread.
Serve with Potato Salad (see p. 239).

garlic

# *He Said She Said*

*Do you wish to watch me undress, she said*
*Yes I wish to watch you undress, he said*

*Do you wish to loosen my loin, he said*
*Yes I wish to loosen your loin, she said*

*Do you wish to caress my thigh, she said*
*Yes I wish to caress your thigh, he said*

*Do you wish to see me simmer, he said*
*Yes I wish to see you simmer, she said*

*Do you wish to see my beauty, she said*
*Yes I wish to see your beauty, he said*

*Do you wish to see my magic, he said*
*Yes I wish to see your magic, she said*

*Do you wish to turn me over, she said*
*Yes I wish to turn you over, he said*

*Do you wish to see my meat moisten, he said*
*Yes I wish to see your meat moisten, she said*

*Do you wish to make me tender, she said*
*Yes I wish to make you tender, he said*

*Do you wish for me to satisfy you, he said*
*Yes I wish for you to satisfy me, she said*

*Do you wish for me to satisfy you, she said*
*Yes I wish for you to satisfy me, he said*

*Then do as you are told*
*Stew me gently*
    *Season me generously*
    *Watch me carefully*

*Baste me frequently*
*Cover me completely*
*Uncover me*
*When I say so*
*And your wish is my command*

## Braised Lamb Shanks

I begged the young man for the lamb shanks. He told me he only had two lambs and a lady had ordered the shanks for today. He said I should come back tomorrow morning when the market gets more lamb. I said, But I want them today. The lady may not come today, I said. He smiled and walked away. I looked behind the glass counter to see if he had overlooked a lamb. I walked up and down the glass counter eyeing leg of lamb, lamb stew, rack of lamb, lamb breast, lamb tongue, and lamb chuck. I went back to my position, in the middle of the counter. I stared at the sign, "American Lamb Shanks," but there were no shanks. From the end of the counter, he smiled. We laughed. He yelled, She may be here anytime. I leaned against the counter watching shoppers pass by, disappointed but not defeated. I turned to search for the young man yet again. He walked toward me. He reached for the lamb shanks. Two only! he said. Yes, yes, two will do, I said. I thanked him, smiled, and walked quickly away.

Preheat oven to 300 degrees.

2 medium lamb shanks
½ teaspoon salt
½ teaspoon pepper
4 tablespoons olive oil, in all
½ cup chopped onions
¼ cup chopped carrots
2 large garlic cloves, minced
1 cup chopped Italian plum tomatoes with juice
1 cup red wine
2 cups beef stock (see appendix A) or store-bought low-sodium beef broth
½ teaspoon dry basil

½ teaspoon dry oregano
1 bay leaf

1.  Season lamb with salt and pepper. Massage with 2 tablespoons of the olive oil.

2.  Pour remaining oil into a Dutch oven over medium-high heat. When oil is hot and begins to smoke slightly, sear lamb shanks on both sides until brown, about 3 minutes each. Remove from pot.

3.  Remove pot from heat and let cool slightly about 2 minutes. Turn heat to medium and return pot to heat. Add onions, carrots, and garlic. Sauté about 2 minutes. Add tomatoes, wine, and stock. Bring to boil; lower heat and simmer about 1 minute. Add basil, oregano, and bay leaf, and simmer 1 minute.

4.  Return lamb shanks to pot and stir. Cover and cook 30 minutes, baste and turn over. Repeat every 30 minutes. Cook lamb shanks until they are tender and done, about 1 hour and 45 minutes. Discard bay leaf.

Makes 2 servings.

*Note:* Serve over Saffron Parmesan Risotto (see p. 201).

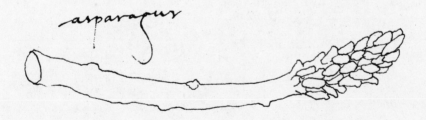

# *Meatballs*

*Meatballs*
*Meatballs Meatballs Meatballs*

      *Meat*
           *Balls*

      *Meat*

           *Balls*

*Meat*
*Balls*

*Meat*
      *Balls*

           *Meatballs*

*Balls*

      *Balls*

           *Balls*

              *Meatballs*

           *Meat*

      *Meat*

*Meat*

*MeatballsMeatballsMeatballsMeatballsMeatballsMeatballs*

*MEATBALLSMEATBALLSMEATBALLSMEATBALLS*

*MeeeeeeeeeeeeeatBaaaaaaaaaaaaaaaaaaaalls*

*M . . . e . . . a . . . t . . . b . . . a . . . l . . . l . . . s*

# Spicy Meatballs with Angel-Hair Pasta

Baking the meatballs instead of the usual cooking method of frying creates an evenly cooked meatball that is also less greasy. Do not overcook them, for they will become tough. Also, remember, they will cook further when simmered in the sauce. Take care to make the meatballs the same size. This will further ensure cooking consistency for all the balls. Indeed, we want to treat the balls equally.

FOR THE SAUCE:

1 tablespoon butter

1 shallot, peeled and chopped

1 12-ounce can Italian plum tomatoes, chopped, with juice

1 teaspoon oregano

1 teaspoon basil

½ teaspoon salt

½ teaspoon pepper

¼ cup chopped parsley

Dash of Tabasco sauce

15-ounce can tomato sauce

FOR THE MEATBALLS:

Preheat oven to 350 degrees

2 tablespoons vegetable oil

½ cup chopped onion

2 garlic cloves, minced

1 pound ground beef

¼ cup bread crumbs

¼ cup pine nuts, chopped slightly

¼ cup grated fresh Parmesan

2 eggs

2 tablespoons chopped fresh parsley

3 tablespoons chopped fresh basil, in all

½ teaspoon salt

¼ teaspoon pepper

¼ teaspoon Creole seasoning

**FOR THE PASTA:**
1 teaspoon salt, in all
4 tablespoons olive oil, in all
1 1-pound bag angel-hair pasta
2 tablespoons grated Parmesan

1. *To prepare the sauce:* Melt butter in a medium saucepan over medium heat. Add shallots and sauté 1 minute. Pulse tomatoes and juice in a food processor to chop. Add tomatoes and juice to saucepan. Add oregano, basil, salt, and pepper, and simmer about 5 minutes. Add parsley and hot sauce, and simmer about 2 minutes. Add 15 ounce can of tomato sauce and stir. Remove from heat.

2. *To prepare the meatballs:* Heat oil in skillet over medium-high heat. Add onions and garlic, and sauté about 1½ minutes. Remove from skillet and let cool slightly. Add onions and garlic to ground beef in mixing bowl, and add bread crumbs, pine nuts, Parmesan, eggs, parsley, basil, salt, pepper, and Creole seasoning. Mix well.

3. Use a ⅓-cup measure to scoop out ground beef mixture. Make rounds with palms of your hands. Place on a half-sheet baking pan, and bake for 10 to 12 minutes. Turn meatballs over and cook another 10 to 12 minutes. Remove from oven. Place meatballs in sauce and cover pan and simmer about 5 minutes.

4. *To prepare the pasta:* In large pot of boiling water, add ½ teaspoon salt and 2 tablespoons of the olive oil. Add pasta and stir; cook until al dente (firm but not soft), according to package directions. Drain.

5. Drizzle remaining olive oil over pasta, and season with remaining salt to taste. Stir in Parmesan.

Makes 4–6 servings.

*Notes:* 1. I use Tony Chachere's Creole seasoning (see appendix B).

2. Serve meatballs over pasta.

# Curry Me There

*Curry me there*
  *amidst thy glorious flavors*
  *perfume me with turmeric as you lay the first thought*
  *embrace me with clover to open my flower bud*
  *lick me with ginger to tickle my clitoris*
  *anoint me with fragrant fennel to widen the funnel*
  *massage me with sweet and bitter fenugreek for love's yin*
    *yang*
  *kiss me hard and long with warm spicy cardamom*
  *possess me with your pungent maleness of coriander*
  *enter me with cumin's nutty seeds*
*Curry me there, again*

## Curried Lamb

Slowly caramelizing onions to make a curry dish is the trick to preparing a good curry. I have used store-bought curry powder to prepare this dish, and I have made a curry powder mixture with all the different seasonings to make curry. I have found the difference not to be substantial. Buying curry powder mix is also a lot less expensive. So I would recommend purchasing a good curry powder instead of buying the individual seasonings. Saffron Parmesan Risotto (see p. 201) complements this dish quite nicely.

  ¼ cup curry powder
  2 pounds lamb stew meat with bone in, cut into 2-inch pieces
  2 tablespoons olive oil, in all
  1 large russet potato, cut into 2-inch pieces
  ¼ cup clarified butter (see p. 57)
  2 medium onions, sliced thinly
  ½ cup Italian plum tomatoes, quartered
  1½ cups coconut milk
  3–4 cups cooked rice (optional)

1. Sprinkle curry powder (hold out ½ teaspoon for potatoes) over lamb. Massage into meat. Pour 1 tablespoon of the olive oil over lamb and massage. Let sit 30 minutes, covered in refrigerator.

2. Boil potatoes until just soft and easily pierced with fork, about 7 minutes. Drain. Sprinkle ½ teaspoon of the curry powder over potatoes and stir. Set aside.

3. Heat butter in a medium saucepan over low heat. When hot, add onions and sauté about 25 minutes. Stir occasionally. Remove onions from pan and set aside.

4. Add remaining tablespoon of oil to same saucepan and increase heat to medium high. Add lamb and cook 3 minutes on one side. Turn lamb over. Pour onions on top and cook 2 minutes. Add potatoes, tomatoes, and coconut milk, and simmer until lamb is tender, about 25 minutes. Remove from heat, and serve.

Makes 4 servings.

*Note:* Serve over rice or without rice.

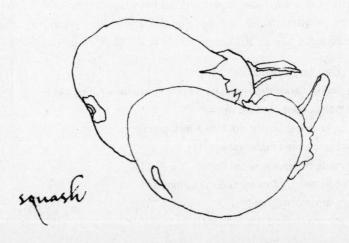

squash

# He's a Ladies' Man

He's a ladies' man
can't you see
        cuddling in the middle of them
        expanding his leg to them
            to be touched
            by his saintly prowl
        they're well served
He's a ladies' man
don't you know
        attending to them all
        he anoints them all
            with juicy kisses
            front center sideways
        they're well served
He's a ladies' man
we are told
        ensuring a cozy gathering with them
        in a tight-fitted roaster with them
            when the heat commence
            all joyously lament
        they're well served
He's a ladies' man
sure he is
        his nature is gentle yet strong with them all
        abundant to their call with them all
            blessed are they truly
            to be at his side 'cause
        they say, he's a ladies' man
Yeah, um hum
        We're Carla Carrots and we speak for the crew
        we sweeten him freely
        but don't take credit easily

*'cause he's so generous when teasily*
*we hug his leg gaily*
       *'cause we love him mightily*
*we're Reddie his potatoes*
*sucking up his pathos*
*we know we will overdose*
*from his well-endowed legos*
*wrapping all our potatoes*
       *'cause we find him grandiose*
*Excuse me Madame*
*we're French beans*
*his true lovers on weekends*
*our length complements his yang yen*
*in unison we mise-en-scène*
       *'cause we love his Big Ben*

## Roast Leg of Lamb with Vegetables

Shopping for a leg of lamb is such a treat. I study the legs through the butcher's windows. Some are bigger than others. Some are more muscular than others. And some are indeed more tender than others. I always feel that the most tender, most well-shaped leg is just waiting for me to hold, to massage, and to lay down in my kitchen, in my oven. Serve with Risotto with Red Wine and Parmesan (see p. 217).

 1 2-pound leg of lamb
 4 rosemary sprigs
 2 garlic cloves, sliced
 2 teaspoons salt, in all
 2 teaspoons pepper, in all
 ½ cup plus 1 tablespoon olive oil
 3 small onions, peeled and quartered
 6 small red potatoes, washed and dried
 1 cup beef stock (see appendix A) or store bought low-sodium
    beef broth
 1 cup white wine
 ½ pound baby carrots with stems (see note at end of recipe)

½ pound French beans
salt and pepper

1.  Make 1-inch slits on both sides of lamb, leaving 3 to 4 inches apart. Insert 2-inch pieces of rosemary and garlic slices into each slit. Sprinkle 1 teaspoon of the salt and 1 teaspoon of the pepper over lamb. Pour ½ cup of the olive oil over lamb, and massage into lamb. Place all in plastic bag and seal. Refrigerate at least 2 hours.

2.  Preheat oven to 350 degrees. Remove lamb from plastic bag. Place medium roasting pan over medium-high heat. Put remaining tablespoon of olive oil in pan. When hot, brown lamb on both sides, about 5 minutes each.

3.  Place onions and potatoes around lamb in pan. Cover and place in oven, and cook 20 minutes. Add stock, wine, and carrots. Turn lamb over, and stir onions and potatoes. Cook 30 minutes. Spoon juices over vegetables. Baste lamb and turn it over. Add beans. Cook until lamb is tender, an additional 20 to 30 minutes. Season with salt and pepper to taste.

Makes 4 servings.

*Note:* Baby carrots in the bag will be fine, not as pretty, if you cannot locate them with stems.

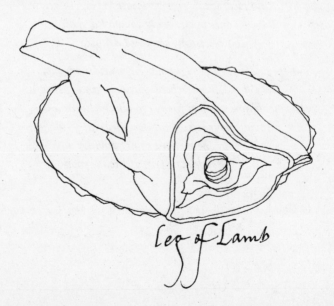

Leg of Lamb

# *Though Not My First Choice*

*Though not my first choice how rude*
   *'cause stew never burnt me with desire*
*yet I have been deliciously wooed*
    *as you entered me like a flaming fire*
     *tenderly enjoining my lips*
     *with a savory meat well equipped*

*Were your name filet mignon or Wellington*
   *surely impressed would be I*
*I would greet your moist tenderloin*
   *quite openly and unashamed for I*
    *seek taste and quality I do*
    *though taste I do get from you*

*Saturated with a jus of Southern comfort*
   *and a hint of wine that makes you mellow*
*with mouth-size morsels coming easy without effort*
   *and pleasant flavors permeate me herein below*
    *once upon eating you do I despair*
    *I've lost my way oh I declare*

*For I want what I thought best for my culinary mojo*
   *a T-bone, a porterhouse, or some kind of sirloin*
*that would proudly satisfy my ego plus my so-and-so*
   *though your stew meat does pleasantly rally my she-loin*
    *for shame am I to not publicly adore you*
    *forgive me again as I rendezvous*

# Beef Stew Provence

Beef stew is a poor man's dish. From the scrapings of the carving of the more expensive cuts, we get what is leftover beef for stew. Yes, filet mignon is my first choice if my beef is lined up waiting for me to select. But with beef stew, I don't have to get dressed up. I can pull out a cold beer with a hot plate of beef stew over rice and feel quite comfortable and be deliciously satisfied from the comfort of this most comforting food.

> 1 pound beef-stew meat, cubed to bite size
> ½ teaspoon salt
> ½ teaspoon pepper
> 3 tablespoons flour
> 4 tablespoons olive oil, in all
> 1 medium onion, chopped
> 2 garlic cloves, sliced
> ½ cup red wine
> 1 cup Italian plum tomatoes with juice
> 2 cups of beef stock (see appendix A) or store-bought
>     low-sodium canned beef broth
> 1 carrot, cut into 2-inch slices

1.  Season meat with salt and pepper. Coat with flour.

2.  Heat 1½ teaspoons oil in medium Dutch oven over medium-high heat. Brown one batch of the meat, about 4 minutes on each side. Repeat with 1½ teaspoons oil and the remaining meat.

3.  Remove meat from pan and set aside.

4.  Pour remaining 1 teaspoon oil in pan. When oil is hot, put onions and garlic in pan, and sauté 3 minutes. Deglaze pan with wine, scraping and stirring brown bits with wooden spoon, and simmer 1 minute. Add tomatoes and stock and bring to boil; then lower heat to simmer and add meat and carrot. Simmer 30 minutes. Stir occasionally. Cook until meat is tender, about 30 minutes more. Remove from heat.

Makes 4 servings.

# Quickies Are Good

*Quickies are good*
*when you can get some*
*immediate gratification*
*ain't bad*
*though*
*I love the drama of a*
*well-planned seduction*
*that introduces*
*suspense, intrigue, and delight*
*it's time well spent*
*when all is spiced just right*
*in the art of making love*
*but in between*
*let's just have quickies*

## Stir-Fry Beef Strips with Roasted Peppers

This is a wonderfully quick, delicious, and attractive beef dish to prepare. With the sautéed beef strips and red, yellow, and green peppers to serve with a creamy Parmesan risotto (see p. 217), you have before you a lovely dish to offer. You also have deliciously different textures of seasoned meaty beef, roasted and sautéed peppers, and a creamy risotto that complement each other to make this quickie good.

½ pound steak strips, cut into ½-inch strips
½ teaspoon salt
½ teaspoon pepper
2 tablespoons Worcestershire sauce
2 tablespoons soy sauce
1 small red pepper, roasted, seeded, halved, and sliced lengthwise

1 small green pepper, roasted, seeded, halved, and sliced
   lengthwise

1 small yellow pepper, roasted, seeded, halved, and sliced
   lengthwise

Flour to coat meat

4 tablespoons olive oil, in all

1 medium onion, halved and sliced lengthwise

1 small jalapeño pepper, seeded, halved, and diced
   (wear rubber gloves)

2 garlic cloves, finely chopped

¼ cup chopped fresh parsley

1. Sprinkle steak with salt and pepper. Marinate steak in Worcestershire and soy sauce 30 minutes. Discard marinade. Wipe dry with paper towel.

2. Roast red, green and yellow peppers over high heat on top of gas stove or in electric oven (see p. 16). Cut in half lengthwise and remove seeds and stems. Thinly slice lengthwise.

3. Coat steak with flour. Heat skillet with 2 tablespoons oil over medium-high heat until slightly smoking. Add steak and cook, shaking skillet to cook all sides. Cook 5 minutes. Remove steak from skillet. Add remaining 2 tablespoons of oil. When hot add onion, peppers, jalapeño, and garlic. Cook 1 minute. Add steak. Stir occasionally, and cook additional 7 minutes more for medium well. Remove from heat. Add parsley and stir.

Makes 2 servings.

# *Tie Me Up, You Say*

*Tie me up*
   *you say*
*You like it that way*
   *you say*
*it's more intense*
   *you say*
*and what do I get out of it*
   *I say*
*A tender but firm meat*
   *you say*
*And juices up the wazoo*
   *you say*
*a flavor that ignites lust*
   *you say*
*You've been here before*
   *I say*
*Always and forever*
   *you say*
*Squeezing tight all parts*
   *you say*
*Makes it bigger and better*
   *you say*
*I'll say*

## Osso Buco

Giuliano Bugialli tells us in *The Fine Art of Italian Cooking* that osso buco means "hole in the bone" and refers to veal shank, cut into horizontal slices, with the piece of bone in the middle open and revealing a section of marrow. The slices are tied up prior to cooking to hold the meat around the bone.

The general practice in Italy, he says, is to serve pasta and rice as a separate course. Ed and I eat osso buco on top of a pile of whipped potatoes.

4 meaty veal shanks (1½ inch thick, crosscut)
2 teaspoons salt
1 teaspoon pepper
1 cup flour
4 tablespoons butter
¼ cup olive oil
2 large garlic cloves, whole
2 medium onions, finely chopped
1 medium carrot, finely chopped
1 celery stalk, finely chopped
4 garlic cloves, minced
1 28-ounce can Italian plum tomatoes
1 cup white wine
1 herb bundle tied together of 5 sprigs fresh thyme, 5 sprigs
    fresh parsley, and 2 bay leaves
3 cups chicken or veal stock (see appendix A) or store-bought
    low-sodium broth
Salt
½ cup finely chopped fresh parsley
Grated zest of 1 lemon

1. Wash and pat dry veal shanks. Tie each shank around middle with kitchen twine. Salt and pepper. Dust with flour.

2. Over medium heat in Dutch oven, place 2 tablespoons of the butter and ⅛ cup of the oil, let butter melt. Add garlic cloves and veal. Cook to brown, about 6 minutes on each side. Remove shanks and place on platter. Remove garlic.

3. Add remaining butter and oil to Dutch oven. Let butter melt. Add onions, carrots, celery, garlic, and sauté 5 minutes, stirring occasionally.

4. Break tomatoes into pieces by hand over onion and carrot mixture, and simmer 10 minutes. Add wine and herb bundle. Simmer 3 minutes.

5. Place veal shanks back into Dutch oven in one layer. Add stock just to cover shanks. Salt to taste. Put in oven and bake covered 1½

hours. Remove lid and bake uncovered 30 minutes or until shanks are tender.

6. Mix parsley and lemon zest and sprinkle over shanks. Remove herb bundle. Skim excess fat.

Makes 4 servings.

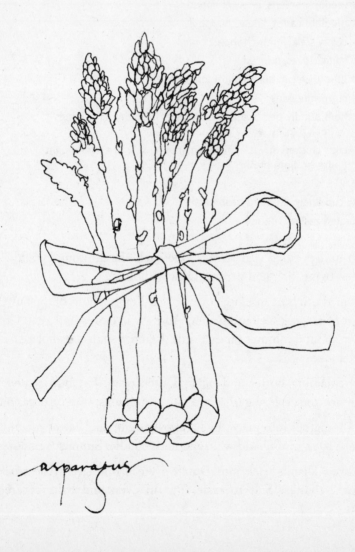

# To Shape Thy Lover's Love Parts

What a life of joy
    when in the middle
    of my solitude
    all surprises I thinkest
    have unfolded.
    Then cometh thee
    dear Wellington
    offering such a lusty treat
    a gift of erotic sovereignty
    to shape thy lover's love parts
    precisely as I wish.

I laughed out loud
    with this discovery
    for never did I seek
    such commanding joy
    for my lover's parts are
    more than abundant
    to bring forth alien sounds
    of pleasure.

But what a treasure indeed
    to become the creator of love's
    shape, size, and stature
    to form, fondle, and fold
    for consistency,
    plumpness, and length
    God what else is there
    to hold
    dear heart
    when you get
    to shape thy lover's love parts.

# Beef Wellington for Two

This was really a great idea to prepare Beef Wellington for two with the use of a shoulder loin instead of an entire fillet of beef. It's just enough for two to share this elegant dish, unlike a full fillet that is enough for twenty. And like most good ideas, it came about by accident. I could not afford the fillet, but I saw the shoulder loin next to it, costing a fraction of the fillet. So, I said to myself, what the heck, it's a loin and it's just the right size. Bingo! Serve with Sautéed French Beans (see p. 221).

1 shoulder loin (about 8 inches long)
salt
Pepper to cover both sides generously
2 tablespoons olive oil, in all
12-ounce bunch spinach, stems removed
1 bowl ice water
2 tablespoons pine nuts
1 shallot, chopped
2 tablespoons honey
Salt and pepper
1 sheet frozen puff pastry dough, thawed
   (see note at end of recipe)
1 egg, lightly beaten

1. Season loin with salt and pepper. Pat with 1 tablespoon of the olive oil. Heat remaining oil in skillet over medium-high heat. When hot, add loin and sear on all sides, about 4 minutes total. Remove from skillet and place on plate to cool.

2. Blanch spinach in boiling salted water for 20 seconds. Drain spinach and place in ice water. Drain spinach again and squeeze with paper towel to remove as much liquid as possible.

3. Grind pine nuts in food processor. Add spinach and shallots, and pulse until smooth. Place in bowl, add honey, and mix well. Salt and pepper to taste.

4. Allow pastry sheet to thaw so that you can easily roll dough without cracking seams. Roll pastry dough on a lightly floured surface. Roll into a rectangle just big enough to cover loin completely. Spread spinach

mixture over the pastry. Leave edges clear. Mix egg with 1 tablespoon of water to make egg wash. Brush edge of dough with egg wash. Lay loin on pastry and wrap in pastry. Press seams firmly. Place pastry-covered loin, seam down, on a parchment-paper-covered baking sheet. Lightly beat egg for egg wash. Brush the egg wash generously on pastry dough. Decorate with leaves made from leftover pastry, egg wash leaves, and press on top of pastry. Refrigerate to cool at least 30 minutes. After being in refrigerator for 15 minutes, preheat oven to 400 degrees. Remove from refrigerator, and bake until pastry is golden brown, 20 to 25 minutes.

Makes 2 serving.

*Note:* Frozen puff pastry sheets can be purchased from a gourmet shop and at some grocery stores.

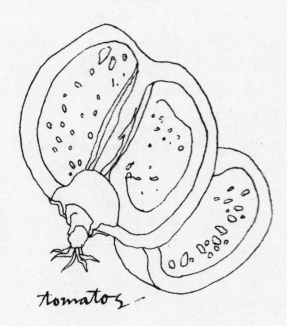

tomatos

# *May I Lick Your Plate*

*May I lick your plate*
*while it's hot please quick*
*hold it up and stick it*
*gently to my lip*
         *It's in my brain*
*I'll lick fast all around*
*I'll get the sauce*
*as it flows down*
*hold the plate up here*
*as I slurp*
         *It's in my brain*
*turn it to the left*
*I'll turn my tongue*
*left*
*turn it to the right*
*I'll turn my tongue*
*right*
*I'll lick up*
*I'll lick down*
*I'll lick it 'round and 'round*
         *It's in my brain*
*It's in my mouth*
*It's in my eyes*
*It's on my ears*
*now your plate is clean*
*oh my*

# Sirloin Steak with Shallot Brandy Sauce

This is a very simple and pleasant dish. The shallot brandy sauce makes it royal. Shallots, which are in the onion family, are underused. I use shallots instead of onions when I desire a milder onioney flavor. Even though they might be considered a cross between the onion and garlic, shallots are unique. Unlike the onion's bold flavor, shallots' flavors are subtle. Serve this dish with Roasted Garlic Whipped Potatoes (see p. 227).

> 1 pound sirloin steak cut in strips
> ½ teaspoon salt
> 1 teaspoon pepper
> 2 tablespoons olive oil, in all
> 4 tablespoons butter, in all
> 3 large shallots, sliced
> 1 cup beef stock (see appendix A) or store-bought
>     low-sodium beef broth
> 2 tablespoons Worcestershire sauce
> 1 tablespoon brandy
> 2 teaspoons lemon juice
> 1 tablespoon chopped fresh parsley

1. Season steak with salt and pepper.

2. Heat 1 tablespoon of the olive oil and 2 tablespoons of the butter in medium skillet over high heat. When hot, sear steak to brown, 2 minutes on each side. Remove steak and place on platter.

3. Lower heat; put remaining butter and oil into skillet and add shallots to caramelize (turn onions golden brown). Sauté about 3 minutes. Stir in stock, Worcestershire sauce, and brandy. Bring to slight boil, then turn down to simmer about 2 minutes. Add steaks and simmer 2 minutes. Remove from heat. Add lemon juice and parsley to steaks.

Makes 4 servings.

# Grill Me Baby, Grill Me

Adapted from Sam Cooke's song "Soothe Me."

*Grill me baby*
    *grill me*
*grill me with your grill marks*
*'cause I know your flaming fire*
    *is soothing to me*

*I used to go in ovens*
    *with lots of sauce on the side*
*since I been grilled by you though*
*I don't go in ovens no mo'*

*Grill me baby*
    *grill me*
*grill me with your watchful loving*
*'cause tossing me at*
    *that right time*
    *is soothing to me*

*Oh, how I used to sauté about*
    *oh how I used to fry*
*since I laid on your hot rods*
    *all I want to be*
    *is grilled at home*
    *by you*

## Grilled T-bone Steak

The placement of the T-bone steak on the grill is essential to preventing the tenderloin portion (the smaller more tender meat of the bone) of the steak from overcooking. Allow the tenderloin to cook over lower flames, while the strip portion cooks over the hottest. T-bone steaks are so large that one 1½-inch steak can serve two. But when you cut to share, make sure that the cut is equal and attractive and, most importantly, that you share the tenderloin. Serve with a salad and Roasted Rosemary Potatoes (see p. 186).

> 2 T-bone steaks, 1½ inches thick
> ½ teaspoon salt
> 1 teaspoon pepper

1. Season both sides of steaks with salt and pepper. Over hot charcoal flames, grill steaks uncovered until browned, about 3 minutes on each side. Slide steaks to lower flame on the grill and grill about 7 to 8 minutes for medium rare. Remove from grill and serve.

Makes 4 servings.

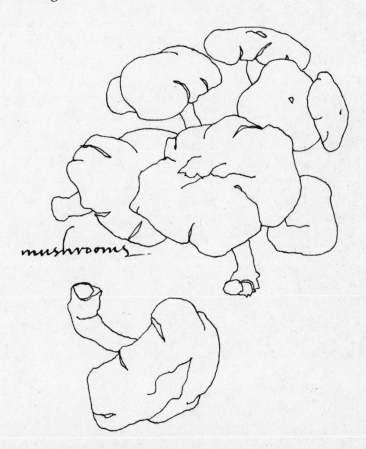

mushrooms

# CHAPTER FOUR

## Flirtatious Fowl

*I saw you in the farmers' market. You stood out
from the rest... I wanted to see under them to see
if you were as full there as you were up front.*

—SEARED DUCK BREASTS WITH FIG SAUCE,
"BREASTS IN AN OPEN MARKET"

**RECIPES:**

"Your Labia Minora" / Duck à l'Orange

"Breasts in an Open Market" / Seared Duck Breasts with
Fig Sauce

"You Surprised Me Today" / Chicken Chasseur

"Hold Her Gently" / Roasted Quail with Pecans and Grapes

"Oh to Be a Shiitake" / Chicken Shiitake Mushroom Risotto

"I Fear Your Seducktion" / Roasted Duck

"Just Eat Me" / Quail in Wine Sauce

"How Long Have I Known You" / Southern Fried Chicken

"He Caused Me to Dream" / Cornish Hens

"Enjoy the Ride" / Quail with Cherries

"I Turn Up the Heat" / Roasted Rosemary Chicken

"How Deep" / Chicken and Andouille Sausage with Parmesan
Penne Pasta

"I'm So Happy" / Roasted Chicken Breast Stuffed with Spinach
and Goat Cheese

"A Chick's Coming Out" / Curried Chicken

"A Love Supreme" / Barbecued Chicken

# Your Labia Minora

There is a sweetness inside
we both know
and we want that sweetness
to come up from below
to penetrate your skin
to surface in an easy flow
this is what we admire
this is what we desire
but
to get to your sweet meat
we must go through
your fat
that cushions and
protects the treasure
the meaty pleasure
of your duck meat
that is massage
that is quince
that is pinch
but
you seem not to
welcome my pricks
or allow my honey
to fragrance
love's commence
my sweet duck
allow me to enter
that sacred space
allow me to sweeten

*that which will be eaten*
*we can get through this*
*that fat*
*we can unfold your aurora*
*we can open up your pandora*
*your labia minora*

## Duck à l'Orange

Ducks are known for their dark succulent meat. They are also known for their lack of meat and fatty content. Do not be discouraged, though. There will always be obstacles to receiving the best in life. Be it a duck or a dude, hunker down, if you believe there is something good in anything. Get through the fat.

**TO STEAM DUCK:**

1 4½-pound duck
bamboo steamer and large skillet to steam duck
large pot of boiling water
1 teaspoon salt
1 teaspoon pepper

**TO MAKE ORANGE GLAZE:**

1 cup orange juice from 2 large oranges
¼ cup of orange liqueur
3 tablespoons honey

Special equipment: Medium-large bamboo steamer; kitchen twine.

1. Cut excess fat at neck and bottom of duck. Discard fat. With kitchen twine, tie duck legs together and wings together.

2. Lay duck, breast up, on a bamboo steamer. Put bamboo steamer in large skillet. With skillet over high heat, pour boiling water into bottom of skillet until water is just below duck but not allowing water to touch duck. Cover steamer and cook 40 minutes. Add additional boiling water as water boils down.

3. Preheat oven to 425 degrees.

4.  Remove duck from steamer and season with salt and pepper on both sides. Lay duck, breast side down, on a cooking rack that sits in a slightly oiled roasting pan. Roast 20 minutes. Turn duck breast side up and continue to roast 30 to 40 minutes or until duck is done.

5.  About 30 minutes before duck is done, cook glaze. Pour orange juice, liqueur, and honey in a small pot over medium-high heat. Cook to reduce to ¼ cup, about 20 to 30 minutes, and glaze is syrupy.

6.  *To glaze duck:* Remove duck from oven when done. Brush all of glaze over duck, top and bottom. Put duck back on rack in roasting pan, breast side up, and put back in oven to roast 5 to 7 minutes more. Remove duck from oven and put on serving platter. Serve immediately.

Makes 2–4 servings.

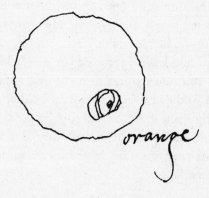

orange

## *Breasts in an Open Market*

I saw you in the farmers' market. You stood out from the rest with your broad plump breasts. I wanted to see under them to see if you were as full there as you were up front. I asked to touch you. Holding you was a sensation for me. I had never held breasts like this. Standing before them, looking straight at breasts like this was not the usual way I saw them. My position was usually above breasts, looking down upon them, over my stove. But this was different. It was a more enlightened stance, one in which I could enjoy all your dimensions, your size, your thickness, your softness. You were full in my hands but hung over slightly off my hands from your fullness. As I squeezed you gently, you oozed firmly through the cracks of my fingers and almost slipped out of my hand. I turned around to see if anyone was looking. I felt ashamed at my awkwardness. I quickly grabbed you again with both hands so as not to release your tender meat. And as I held both of you, I knew that you were the ones to come home with me this day. After taking one more look at your perfect plumpness and squeezing you one last time, not really wanting to leave that moment though, I knew I had to move on to the next thing. So I motioned the young dark-haired man with massive black eyebrows, "Yes, these are the ones," and I gingerly gave you to him, holding you near my heart. He was obviously inexperienced, for he handled you briskly and held you with only one hand. Half of you drooping from his grasp, he almost dropped you without a flicker of emotion. I rushed him to complete his task and give me my breasts. He didn't understand why I was so hasty and he really didn't care, but he quickly delivered you to me in hopes that I would leave. I received you and held you tightly against my chest and kissed you quickly and turned toward the entrance to dash away. We escaped! And as I rushed to my car holding you alongside me, I thought that this bright, clear, sunny, and cool Saturday morning would be a lovely day to have breasts so full, fresh, and tasty. But half the joy had been holding you and caressing you at my leisure for my pleasure while the world passed me by at the market.

# Seared Duck Breasts with Fig Sauce

I have found so much pleasure in going to the DeKalb Farmers' Market here to shop for fresh foods. It is huge, the size of a football field, enclosed with aluminum siding. Its employees, patrons, and foods are a mix from around the world. Ask fellow customers how they prepare particular foods and you get a welcoming response and elaborate description, and often a little story, too. You do not have to do much to fresh foods to get good taste. Like a good man or woman, the essence of goodness will rise to the occasion.

2 6-ounce duck breasts

TO SEAR DUCK BREASTS:
1 teaspoon salt
1 teaspoon pepper
1 teaspoon clarified butter
1 teaspoons cinnamon

FOR THE FIG SAUCE:
6 whole figs, cut in half
¼ cup honey
2 tablespoons water

1. *To steam duck breasts:* In a double boiler, steam duck, with skin down, over boiling water at high heat, about 10 minutes. Remove from heat and put duck on cutting board.

2. *To sear duck breasts:* Score duck skin with sharp knife. Do not cut into meat. Season with salt and pepper on both sides. Sprinkle cinnamon over skin and press down.

3. Heat butter in medium cast-iron skillet. When butter is hot, sear duck with skin side down, about 2 minutes. Turn duck over and cook 2 minutes. Remove duck from pan. Cut each into 4 slices.

4. *To prepare fig sauce:* Place figs, honey, and water into a saucepan at low heat. Cook until figs are tender, about 15 minutes. Pour half of fig mixture into blender and puree. Pour puree mixture back in with remaining cooked figs. To serve, pour sauce over duck.

Makes 2 servings.

# *You Surprised Me Today*

*You surprised me*
*today*
*and how delicious it is*
*that you do so*
*for your reputation*
*calls for common things*
*common experiences*
*common taste*
*except*
*when you're*
*fried to the bone*
*but today*
*even though you had to*
*get a little tipsy*
*you portray another side*
*that today*
*was quite manly*

*I thought I knew you*
*and*
*your limitations*
*fried with a Southern accent*
*smothered that country way*
*roasted for Sunday company*
*but this day*
*you came to me*
*dressed differently*
*sophisticated*
*in a knowing but*
*not showing-off way*
*with this*
*you approach me*

*I turn your way*
*and know that you're*
*unlike the others*
*yet familiar*
*of which we seek often*
*yes*
*there is a paradox*
*we seek the comfort of knowing*
*and erotic risk of the unknown*
*we seek taste of memories*
*and succulence from dreams to dream*
*and as I stare at you*
*I'm guessing*
*can you deliver*

*You play the part*
*of hunter*
*and me the hunted*
*as your luscious golden skin*
*seared quickly*
*pulls back*
*slightly*
*to reveal your meat*
*round and moist*
*today*
*in your sizzled sauce*
*bubbling explosions of flavor*
*in my room*
*creating excitement of lust*
*yes lust for immediate pleasure*
*I do expect this of you*
*this day*
*and let me tell you how*
*indulge me*
*allow me to savor your juices*
*first*
*hold your ego*
*as I contemplate*

*me as the hunter*
*and capture the musk*
*of your mushrooms*
*biting into them*
*gently*
*until they are all in*
*my mouth*
*however*
*it is you*
*the mainly tipsy one*
*who is expected to*
*turn me on*
*and you do*
*do understand*
*we come differently too*
*we come full and explosive too*
*and serving or being served*
*that that is of our familiar*
*or that that is only in our dreams*
*is welcomed at our table*
*when true passion says*
*come here*
*we go there*
*did I surprise you*
*today?*

## Chicken Chasseur

This dish has a distinctive, strong flavor as I learned when I cooked it with our 2004 Thanksgiving dinner. It is a take-charge, look-at-me kind of dish. As I ate it along with our turkducken and cornbread rice dressing and seafood dressing and collard greens and sweet potatoes and potato salad and macaroni and cheese and red beans and rice and braised goat and barbecue ribs and Ed's gumbo—yeah, all of that—the chicken chasseur was kicking for recognition. Its flavor refused to blend in. It tried to steal the spotlight, but Ed's gumbo won by a landslide. To keep the peace, allow this chicken chasseur to head the table and serve it with rice and a simple salad only.

2 thighs with skin on

2 drumsticks with skin on

1 teaspoon salt

1 teaspoon pepper

2 tablespoons olive oil

2 tablespoons clarified butter

2 tablespoons butter

2 shallots, chopped

1 large garlic clove, minced

1 cup sliced button mushrooms

1 tablespoon flour

2 teaspoons tomato paste

½ cup white wine

1 tablespoon brandy

1 cup chicken stock (see appendix A) or store-bought
   low-sodium chicken broth

2 teaspoons chopped fresh thyme

1 tablespoon chopped fresh parsley

¼ cup heavy cream

2 cups rice, cooked

1. Season chicken parts with salt and pepper, and massage into chicken.

2. Heat oil and clarified butter in cast-iron pan. When oil and butter are hot, add chicken. Fry until golden brown about 8 minutes one side, turn to fry 5 minutes more. Remove from pan and pour out oil.

3. With pan off heat, melt 2 tablespoons butter in pan. Add shallots and garlic, and stir about 1 minute. Put pan back over heat and add mushrooms, and sauté about 3 minutes. Sprinkle flour over mushrooms, and stir about 1 minute. Stir in tomato paste and cook 1 minute. Add wine, brandy, and stock, and bring to a slight boil, then reduce heat to simmer. Return chicken parts to pan and add thyme. Cover and simmer for 30 minutes. Add parsley and cream, and simmer 2 minutes; then remove from heat.

Makes 2 servings.

*Note:* Serve over rice.

# *Hold Her Gently*

*As you hold her gently with her breast upright,*
  *massage her insides to season her well.*
*One finger will do with salt and pepper*
  *'cause her tender meat needs not much.*
*One teaspoon and a pinch, no more,*
  *will season the juices that flow from inside out.*
*Then rub her skin down to relax her muscles*
  *and brush the dark honey balsamic glaze over her body.*
*Start at the rear with strokes down her back, as*
  *long, even rhythmic strokes are best for spontaneous flavor.*
*Pull her legs slightly back to coat her thighs,*
  *then turn her over, be generous with your sauce.*
*Brush across her breast with a stream of balsamic*
  *and lower, painting her frame completely mahogany.*
*Lay her softly atop the pecans*
  *gathering the sizzling red grapes to join in.*
*Roast them together not long at 425*
  *just 'til they marry their memories of savory and sweet lust.*
*Fifteen then five minutes will do, for*
  *a hot oven makes quick eternal love.*

## Roasted Quail with Pecans and Grapes

Quails are tender beings. Imagine your most precious loving moment. And believe me, you can get that same sensation when eating a properly cooked quail. They are delicate and delicious. They are absolutely wonderful to gaze upon when they lie on their backs, legs bent back and open for your stare and delight at what's to come. Serve with Creamy Whipped Potatoes (see p. 74) and Sautéed French Beans (see p. 221).

Preheat oven to 425 degrees.

FOR SEASONING:

½ teaspoon salt

½ teaspoon pepper

½ teaspoon garlic powder

½ teaspoon onion powder

FOR QUAIL:

4 5-ounce quails

2 tablespoons olive oil

5 tablespoons clarified butter

2 tablespoons honey

20 pecan halves

30 red grapes

½ cup water

1. *To prepare seasoning for quail:* Mix salt, pepper, garlic powder, and onion powder.

2. *To prepare quails:* Season quails by rubbing seasoning mixture over quails and inside quail cavity.

3. Drizzle oil over quails and massage onto quails. Set aside.

4. *To cook quails:* Heat 3 tablespoons butter until it begins to sizzle in medium skillet over medium heat. Brown quails 2 minutes on each side, 1 minute on breast side and 1 minute on back.

5. Heat remaining butter in another medium ovenproof skillet over medium heat. Add honey.

6. Spread pecans in skillet and stir to coat with butter and honey.

7. Lay quails, breast up, on top of pecans.

8. Put in oven and cook 15 minutes. Baste quails generously. Turn quail over. Cook 5 more minutes or until quails are done. Add ½ cup of water and grapes, and continue to cook 3 minutes. Remove from oven and serve.

Makes 2 servings.

*Note:* You can buy or order quails at a grocery store.

# Oh to Be a Shiitake

*Oh to be a shiitake*
*wild and fancifully free*
*pretty, alluring, seductive*
*caps curled over on me*
*forever young and fine*
*forever chic and preferred*
*forever available just ask me*
*surprise yourself with thee*
*Many turn away*
*for fear of my fame*
*of my stylish name*
*and exotic claim*
*but I desire desire*
*I who smell of love want love*
*I though youthful want you full*
*of exotic flavors admired*
*Bigger here is not better*
*smaller here is prized*
*excitement of your palate*
*earthy edibles enjoined enjoyed*
*I absorb passion*
*leave not me to soak*
*too much passion weakens me*
*but weaken me I can shii-take it*

## Chicken Shiitake Mushroom Risotto

Shiitake mushrooms are the sexy mushrooms. They are cute and shapely, and unlike the large portobello mushrooms, shiitakes are small and dainty. Spring and autumn are the seasons for shiitake mushrooms. Purchase those whose caps are still curled under, and always select those that are dry and have not turned a dark brown. Serve this delightful dish with sautéed spinach (see p. 213).

> 1 chicken breast, deboned and cubed
> 1 teaspoon Creole seasoning
> 3 tablespoons olive oil
> 1 small onion, finely chopped
> 2 garlic cloves, crushed
> ¼ pound shiitake mushrooms, sliced and stems removed
> 1 cup Arborio rice, uncooked
> ¼ teaspoon salt
> ¼ teaspoon pepper
> ¼ cup green onions, sliced thinly
> 1 tablespoon chopped fresh thyme,
> ½ cup white wine
> 3 cups chicken stock (see appendix A), or store-bought low-sodium broth
> ¼ cup heavy cream
> ½ cup grated fresh Parmesan

1. Put diced chicken in bowl and season with Creole seasoning. Set aside.

2. Pour olive oil into a wide, heavy-duty saucepan over medium heat. Add onion and garlic, and sauté about 2 minutes. Add mushrooms and sauté 3 minutes. Stir occasionally. Add chicken and sauté 4 minutes. Stir constantly. Add rice, and stir to coat, about 1 minute. Add salt and pepper to taste, and stir briefly. Add green onions and thyme, and sauté 1 minute.

3. Add wine, and stir until liquid has been absorbed, about 1 minute. Stir in ½ cup of slow-simmering stock, and cook, stirring constantly. When absorbed, stir in another ½ cup. Continue this for 20 minutes until all stock has been added and rice is al dente (firm but not soft). You may not need to use all the stock. It will depend on the rice. Add cream and stir 1 minute. Remove pan from heat, and stir in Parmesan. Serve immediately.

Makes 2 servings.

# I Fear Your Seducktion

*I've tasted you before*
*I remember your succulent flavors*
*your tender dark meat*
*your crisp mahogany skin*
*I remember seeing the juices flow*
*easily*
*as I sliced you down the middle*
*you were always welcome*
*at my table*
*but now*
*time has passed*
*things have changed*
*and*
*I fear your seducktion*

*I am reluctant to commit*
*I may not live up to your standards*
*you may see me stripped*
*of ideas*
*of how best to serve you*
*to season*
*prep*
*and heat you*
*for if I cannot serve*
*I refuse to receive*
*so*

*I find reasons to avoid you*
*I read*
*I pay bills*
*I clean house*
*I don't go near the kitchen*
*and*

*heaven forbid*
*me to open the refrigerator*
*for if I see you*
*legs wide open*
*tempting me*
*with your bad self*
*I might succumb*
*unprepared*
*do understand*
*I want to*
*and*
*again*
*I want to*
*taste your wildness*
*tamed with sweet kisses*
*of cherries or plums or figs*
*if oranges don't trump*
*their indulgence*

*For there are so many choices*
*to perfection*
*so many decisions*
*not yet made*
*should I brown you first*
*in clarified butter*
*or olive's oil*
*should I steam you*
*then roast*
*should I stuff you*
*or*
*should I not*
*can't you see*
*I want to*
*bite into you*
*again and*
*experience the dual delight*
*of your tender moist meat*
*and crispy savory skin*

'cause
the mere knowing of
your culinary
succulence
feeds my addiction
fully
that's why
I fear your seducktion

'Cause I want you
the way I had you
and don't know the secrets
of your exquisite delivery
are you just bad
in that good way
or
does my foreplay
of soy sauce
cause your meat to be
more tender
or
is it the high heat
we generate
that causes your
skin to harden
as we both desire
this I know not
and fear
your next appearance
may be your last
causing me only to
live in the dream
of your seducktion

# Roasted Duck

Some of us have had the delight of eating duck and want dearly to master duck cookery. For their succulent meat and crispy skin are worth making a fool of oneself that first time. When preparing to roast a duck, prick it to help the fat flow downward and out of the body. Cook to tender, not tough. The most important thing to remember is to put it in a hot oven on a good rack so its skin turns crisp and its juice fat falls freely.

Preheat oven to 450 degrees.

> 1 4½–5-pound duck
> 2 tablespoons soy sauce
> Salt and pepper
> 1 tablespoon fresh ginger, peeled and sliced
> 2 tablespoons clarified butter (see p. 57)
> 1½ cups water

1. Tie duck legs together and tie wings together with kitchen twine. With fork, prick the duck generously. Sprinkle with soy sauce and salt and pepper. Place ginger slices inside cavity of duck.
2. Melt butter in cast-iron skillet over medium-high heat, and brown duck on both sides, about 3 minutes to each side.
3. Place duck breast side down on baking wire rack inside shallow roasting pan. Pour water into pan. Roast 40 minutes. Then turn duck breast side up, and continue roasting another 35 minutes or until golden brown and crispy. Stock will evaporate—do not replenish it.

Makes 2 servings.

# *Just Eat Me*

A little country, yes, but country ain't bad if you seek the comfort of cozy in-dulgence. My juices are just as good as, if not better than, those slick chicks with honey and grapes. That ain't my forte. And, anyway, my legs are wide open for you, not tied tight with kitchen twine. You got to know when you got something good. You got to know this. Those who stack themselves atop grilled asparagus and piles of flash-fried spinach and roasted cubed rosemary potatoes with chives sprouting further upward as if to launch off into space, all have to find their way home. When company pulls up to the table and lowers their forks to decipher what the hell's going on, I rest my case, for they have to work to the true essence of what it is that they're about to de-vour. I, on the other hand, need not a veil to pull back. I'm here simply lying on my back waiting for you. You need not tilt your head to understand what I'm all about. And there's no need to analyze my *jus*. What I offer is a sim-ple pleasure in style and taste, one that you come back to suck up with good bread. I don't cost much or ask much of you. You fool, just eat me.

## Quail in Wine Sauce

Quails are succulent, plump, tiny game birds whose meat is rich in flavor and bone-sucking good. I always suck the meat from the bone. That may not meet with Miss Manners' approval, but it can certainly inject a sly erotic twist into the meal. Serve with Creamy Southern Grits (see p. 194).

Preheat oven to 350 degrees.

    4 5-ounce quails (see note at end of recipe)
    1 teaspoon salt
    1 teaspoon pepper
    1 teaspoon onion powder
    1 teaspoon garlic powder
    1 teaspoon Creole seasoning

3 tablespoons olive oil

4 shrimp, peeled and deveined

4 garlic cloves, peeled

4 pearl onions, peeled

1 stalk celery, halved, and each slice cut in quarters

1 cup chicken stock (see appendix A) or store-bought low-sodium chicken broth

2 tablespoons vegetable oil

2 tablespoons flour

½ cup water

½ cup white wine

1. Rub quails inside and out with salt, pepper, onion powder, garlic powder, and Creole seasoning. Pour olive oil over quails and massage inside and out. Place a shrimp, garlic clove, a pearl onion and 2 slices of celery in each quail cavity. Place quails in Dutch oven. Sprinkle remaining seasoning over quails. Add stock. Cover and bake 25 minutes, basting twice.

2. Make dark roux (see p. 306). Pour oil into small saucepan over medium heat. When hot, stir in flour with a wide wooden spoon. Stir constantly until roux is dark brown, about 5 minutes. Stir in water and continue cooking about 8 minutes. Pour roux into Dutch oven with quails and stir in wine. Continue cooking quails until tender, about 30 minutes. Baste twice.

Makes 2 servings.

*Notes:* 1. You can buy or order quails at a grocery store.

2. I use Tony Chachere's Creole seasoning (see appendix B).

# *How Long Have I Known You*

*How long have I known you*
*all my life*
*and what have we shared*
*our souls*
*you have never forsaken me*
*you always bring flavor*
*you never surprise me*
*with distasteful desires*
*I have tried to always*
*make you better*
*not to change you, that is,*
*but to just take you where*
*you're supposed to be*
*where?*
*to that crispy point*
*to that tender moment*
*to that well-seasoned path*
*I know that's what you want*
*I know that's what I want*
*after all these years*
*I think it is the way*
*it is our way*
*isn't it*
*have I spoken too soon*
*have I not taken your concerns*
*to heart*
*am I taking you for granted*
*I think not*
*for it is in that silent way*

*I interpret your meaning*
*when you stop singing*
*as you sizzle*
*I understand*
*that I must remove you*
*from the heat*
*and I do*
*when the oil no longer*
*drips out*
*I understand*
*that I can now bite*
*into your meat*
*and I do*
*when I have eaten you*
*to the bone*
*I know to put the bone down*
*and I do*
*I hear your silence*
*do you hear mine*
*when I turn away*
*and wait patiently*
*for your doneness*
*it seems ever so long*
*that wait*
*for you to come*
*in that golden way*
*as a tender piece of meat*
*hot, dripping, and*
*no longer soft*
*and my choice*
*to turn you over*
*once*
*only*
*do you understand that*
*can you hear me*

*front and back*
*once*
*only*
*tossing is not my style*
*I want substantial*
*serious*
*sessions*
*per side*
*while others may toss about*
*seeking taste in different ways*
*I'm finger lickin'*
*stickin' with ya*

## Southern Fried Chicken

If you want the best chicken in the world, don't cook this recipe: go to Mrs. Willie Mae's restaurant in New Orleans. I tried to get the recipe. I cooked pound cakes for her and begged her to tell me what she does to her chicken. She just laughed. "Baby, I'm glad you like it," she said. Her restaurant is on the corner of St. Anna and N. Toni Streets. My recipe is hopefully as close to Mrs. Willie Mae's as possible. I do believe the buttermilk makes the crust golden and tenderizes the meat. Maybe Mrs. Willie Mae will see my note and give me some pointers. Fried chicken goes well with Collard Greens (see p. 228).

½ cup buttermilk
2 chicken thighs and 2 chicken legs
½ teaspoon salt
½ teaspoon pepper
½ teaspoon cayenne pepper
1 cup flour
1 cup vegetable oil
2 tablespoon butter

1. Pour buttermilk into plastic bag. Put chicken in bag and let sit in refrigerator at least 20 minutes.

2. Remove chicken from buttermilk and shake off excess. Season chicken with salt, pepper, and cayenne. Place flour in another plastic bag and drop chicken parts into bag. Shake to cover chicken parts with flour.

3. Remove chicken from flour and shake off excess. In a cast-iron skillet, heat oil and butter over medium-high heat. When oil is hot but butter is not burning, place chicken in skillet, turn heat to medium, and fry until done and golden brown, 5 to 8 minutes on each side. Place chicken on paper towels to drain.

Makes 2 servings.

breast of chicken

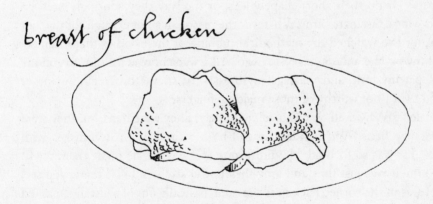

## *He Caused Me to Dream*

He caused me to dream as I watched him pour pure olive oil onto the palm of his hands and briefly rub them while oil dropped down between his fingers onto the plump breasts of the well-seasoned hens. He had already thoroughly massaged the hens with thyme, rosemary, garlic, and onion powder and sprinkled salt and pepper between their legs. He does something extra with his hands to cause them to be tender and juicy and savory. He holds them like he holds a woman, as much as he can, while tenderly squeezing them and patting them until their firm tightness becomes immensely relaxed. I watched him and wondered how long can this go on, this patting, this rubbing, this massaging of these hens. Have they not yet received enough of his holy hands? You see, I, too, have been held in the palm of his hands.

Why does he spend so much time stroking the hens? Is it their big firm breasts? Or do their short shapely legs, or the way they adoringly hold up their wings, fascinate him? Whatever the reason, it's not enough for me, not now, for I've watched the methodical rubbing of their bodies that mesmerized my psyche and damaged my ego. All I want now is for him to rub my legs, pat my butt, and massage my breasts, be they a bit small, but never mind. Am I not worthy of those majestic fingers?

Jealous? Why, well, yes. Ridiculous? Okay. They were hens, but they were free-range hens. And besides, he will be too tired when he finishes with them. He was so focused. He didn't look at me while he made them ready. For him, it was just they and only they in the kitchen. I was there, you see, but I was in the corner, back near the door, basically out of sight if you asked him. He saw me only when he needed someone to wipe his brow from the intense preparation of his darlings. But I could do more.

Oh my, how the pain of passion denied reveals one's nakedness. Turn to me, please. Give me your impetuous caresses for I, too, need to exhale. You see, the fire has scorched me. That embrace that wets me like the morning dew has adorned me. My fierce desire yells, "Molest my soul. Scorch my body. Devour me. Turn away, now, from those birds. Come lie with me. Let us fly."

This I need to convey to him as he lingers with the preparation of those lowlife biddies. Tell him of your emptiness. Yes, speak to him of your yearning for his glorious embrace. Pray him to sprinkle his seasonings upon you—cop a plea. And this, I did.

He turned to me and said, "Give me the mittens. Pass the pans. Open the oven." And this, I did.

## Cornish Hens

Early in my relationship with Ed, he prepared this dish, and it was then that I saw the relationship between the food and the love of the cook. I saw the tender strokes he gave the hens and believed that somehow that must make them more tender and delicious. In my heart, I thought that those loving strokes had to penetrate into the meat of the hens, making their best flavors rise. I know I give my best when I receive tender loving strokes. Don't you? Serve with Roasted Garlic Whipped Potatoes (see p. 227).

Preheat oven to 350 degrees.

> 2 Rock Cornish hens
> 1 teaspoon salt
> 1 teaspoon pepper
> 2 tablespoons dry thyme
> 2 teaspoons poultry seasoning
> 2 teaspoons onion powder
> 4 garlic cloves, sliced in half
> ¼ cup olive oil
> 2 cups chicken stock (see appendix A) or store-bought
>    low-sodium chicken broth

1. Rinse hens inside and out under cold running water. Pat dry with paper towel.
2. Mix salt, pepper, thyme, poultry seasoning, and onion powder, and rub over bodies and cavities of hens. Place garlic slices inside cavities.
3. Massage hens with olive oil. Place hens on wire rack in shallow roasting pan, breast-side up.

4.  Pour chicken stock into roasting pan and place hens in oven. Roast at 350 degrees until hens are done, about 45 minutes. Baste 5 times while cooking. Remove from oven.

5.  Place hens in center of serving platter, and drizzle sauce over hens.

Makes 2–4 servings.

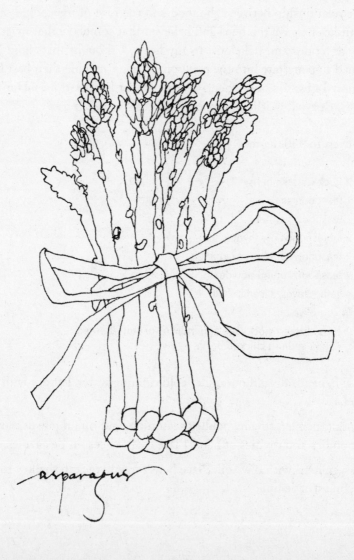

asparagus

# *Enjoy the Ride*

He sees the cherry
red, plump, and sweet
just at the gate of your meat
waiting for him to eat

He didn't want to see it first
there is so much for him to immerse
but this just excites his universe
now he can't think straight it's a curse

Love encountered has to mellow
It's not always just to pump up his fellow
he knows this, Lord we hope so
if he desires to be our gentle Joe blow

But what do you expect of him
when you pull up your dress to him
and you spread out your legs at him
you wench

He's not a fool he's just a man
he sees the cherry
he eats the cherry
sex without love is not beneficiary—Ha! Ha!

We must help him, Quailiah,
sit up and cross your legs
cover your breast with more sauce
nestle your butt deep into the potatoes

Now see, the excitement has calmed
but we know you're still the bomb
and we know the story's outcome
but the beginning and middle is full of charm

*So if we let love be the luminary*
*as it lights up his manly domiciliary*
*and if we let patience be the leader*
*as it guides him to become the cherry eater*

*We will see love rise gently*
*and share in love's discoveries intently*
*with time on our side yet not on our mind*
*as we glide in the erotic sensually*

*Yes, he needs not this melancholy*
*he would say*
*time is wasted*
*he would say*

*But we know best*
*don't we*
*we define pleasure*
*don't we*

*So much other can be discovered*
*we say*
*so much other can be enjoyed*
*we say*

*Oh, fuck, just throw the damn cherry*
*in his face*
*lie back*
*and enjoy the ride*

## Quail with Cherries

Quails are plump, succulent, and full of flavor. American quails are known to be quite sociable, and they can be extremely erotic, always holding their perky legs up high. Popping a cherry in them is a natural. Eating this tender meat with a sweet cherry is a delight. Have your lover join you in the preparation of this dish. It can be a suggestive prelude to your evening of seduction. Serve with red wine and Parmesan risotto (see p. 217).

    4 5-ounce quails

    ½ teaspoon salt

    ½ teaspoon pepper

    2 tablespoons olive oil

    1 6-ounce jar of maraschino cherries, in all

    4 shallots, peeled

    8 fresh thyme sprigs

    2 tablespoons clarified butter

    ½ cup white wine

    ¾ cup chicken stock

**TO PREPARE QUAILS:**

1.  Season quails with salt and pepper. Massage quails with olive oil. Insert 2 cherries in cavity and follow with a shallot and 2 thyme sprigs folded in half.

**TO COOK QUAILS:**

2.  Heat butter in medium skillet, over medium heat. When hot, brown quails. Cook 2 minutes each side. Cook 1 minute on breast and 1 minute on back.

3.  Turn quails breast side up and pour wine in skillet and cook 1 minute. Add stock and bring to a slight boil, then simmer 8 minutes. Pour remaining cherries and juice in skillet. Bring to a slight boil, then simmer 1 minute. Remove from heat and serve.

Makes 2 servings.

*Note:* You can buy or order quails from your grocery store.

# I Turn Up the Heat

*I hold your breast and*
*I strip the leaves from the rosemary sprigs and*
*I rub gently the rosemary leaves on each breast and*
*I lay bay leaves there twice and*
*I press lightly slices of garlic on your skin and*
*I open your legs and*
*I cushion cubes of celery and carrots in you and*
*I raise your legs again and*
*I perfume you with rosemary and*
*I blow onions there too and*
*I pour warm butter over your body and*
*I massage first your breast and your arms and*
*I pull your legs to wrap them with the butter and*
*I roll you over to rub your neck and back and*
*I pinch you with salt and pepper and*
*I make a bed of carrot halves and celery stalks and*
*I engage quartered potatoes and onions to join and*
*I moisten the bed with warm water and*
*I lay you on the bed and*
*I turn up the heat.*

## Roasted Rosemary Chicken

Free-range chickens are the elite of the poultry world. Placed in a sexual context, they would be in a fashionable brothel. They would be "in the house" being massaged and plumped up for your likin'. They would be fed special vegetarian diets and have the freedom to roam about, checking out other chicks, or just lying about grooming themselves and enhancing their chickeny flavor. They would be the youngest and most tender of chickens whose feathers would be snow white and beaks fire engine red. Oh yes, they would be expensive. Much more than the chicks on the street. Serve this delight with Vegetable Paella (see p. 182).

Preheat oven to 400 degrees.

    1 chicken (about 3 pounds)
    1 teaspoon salt
    1 teaspoon pepper
    1 teaspoon poultry seasoning
    2 sprigs fresh rosemary, chopped
    1½ tablespoons olive oil
    2 garlic cloves, peeled
    1 onion, peeled and halved
    1 celery stalk, cut in half
    1½ cups water

1.  Salt and pepper chicken inside and out. Sprinkle poultry seasonings over chicken and inside cavity. Put ¼ of the rosemary under the skin of the chicken breasts. Sprinkle remaining rosemary over chicken and inside cavity. Massage chicken with olive oil inside and out. Put garlic cloves, onion, and celery in cavity of chicken.

2.  Put chicken with breast side up on a roasting rack sitting inside a roasting pan. Pour water in pan. Put pan in oven and cook 40 minutes. Reduce heat to 350 degrees and continue to cook 30 minutes or until chicken is done. Remove from oven. Place chicken on a platter and serve.

Makes 4 servings.

# *How Deep*

*How deep will you go,*
        *far, farther is not far enough*
*but try, please try*
        *for I live, I die*
*with an ancient yearning for your taste*
        *of Parmesan cream sauce*
*over your sausage*
        *especially.*
*How deep will you go,*
        *for I am in an abyss*
*with my love of your*
        *penne al dente pasta,*
*well penetrated with virgin olive oil*
        *lying in my wet bowl,*
*sinking deep into the center*
        *of my heart.*

*How deep will you go,*
        *waiting, waiting, I have waited*
*too long in a loveless spiral*
        *descending endlessly*
*until I cooked you,*
        *until I ate you*
*and the chicken breasts of*
        *tender bites and spicy juices.*
*How deep will you go,*
        *as I spread out my soul*
*to you with immense tranquility,*
        *offering only that which*

*you have given me*
        *deliciously well-seasoned*
*flavors that seep deep into my pores*
        *burning my yearning as I am swollen*
*by you.*

## Chicken and Andouille Sausage
## with Parmesan Penne Pasta

Parmesan cheese will make anything taste good. Italy's Parmigiano-Reggiano is the king of Parmesan cheeses: Parmigiano-Reggiano is aged for more than two years, and the extended aging gives it its deliciously rich, sharp, complex flavor and extreme granular texture. Pre-grated Parmesan does not compare to the taste of freshly grated, so it is highly recommended that you purchase fresh Parmesan and grate it just before cooking.

Adapted from Emeril Lagasse's *Emeril's New New Orleans Cooking*.

large pot of boiling water
½ teaspoon salt
¼ cup olive oil, in all
2 tablespoons olive oil
1 cup Andouille sausage, cut into 1-inch slices
¼ cup green onions, chopped
¼ cup celery, chopped
1 chicken breast, boned, skinned, bite-size pieces
1 ½ teaspoons Creole seasoning (see appendix B), in all
1 cup heavy cream
½ teaspoon Worcestershire sauce
½ cup grated fresh Parmesan cheese, in all
4 tablespoons butter
salt
½ pound penne pasta

1.  *To prepare pasta:* Bring a large pot of water to a boil. Add ½ teaspoon salt and 2 tablespoons oil and lower heat to simmer until ready to cook pasta.

2.  *To prepare chicken and Andouille sausage:* Heat oil in large skillet over medium heat until oil smokes slightly. Add Andouille sausage and cook on both sides, about 2 minutes. Stir in green onions and celery and sauté 1 minute.

3.  Season chicken with 1 teaspoon Creole seasoning. Add chicken and sauté for about 1 minute, stirring constantly. Add remaining ½ teaspoon Creole seasoning. Sauté 2 minutes.

4.  Turn heat to low, add cream, and simmer 1 minute. Stir in Worcestershire sauce and ¼ cup Parmesan, and simmer 30 seconds. Whisk in butter, 1 tablespoon at a time, within 3 minutes. Remove from heat. Season with a pinch of salt.

5.  *To continue preparation of pasta:* Turn heat to high to bring simmering water to a boil. Add pasta and stir. Cook until pasta is al dente (firm but not soft), about 10 minutes. Stir occasionally. Drain. Season with a pinch of salt and drizzle remaining oil and ⅛ cup of Parmesan over pasta and stir.

6.  Mix pasta into chicken and sausage sauce, and toss until pasta is thoroughly coated. Sprinkle remaining Parmesan over pasta. Season with salt to taste. Serve immediately.

Makes 2 servings.

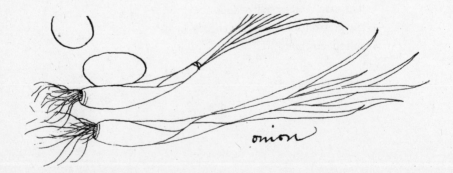

onion

# I'm So Happy

*As I welcomed this moment*
*to taste your stuffing*
*that is now warm and full of flavor*
*well seasoned you are*
*and soft to my tongue*
*you blossom in my mouth*
*your full-bodied stuff*
*your multitextures*
*melting deliciously into me*
*like dancers at midnight*
*locked lovingly in an embrace*
*I hold your stuff*
*and your breast*
*and press the thicker you*
*to open just there*
*to insert your stuff*
*most all of it*
*softly onto the breast*
*pulling away reluctantly*
*for overstuffing*
*is a no-no*
*and creates questions*
*of intent*
*ego driven mostly*
*care not to have*
*too much stuff*
*just give that which can fit*
*comfortably in the breast*
*now plump and round*

*from most all your stuff*
*tie gracious you with lace*
*so pretty so ready*
*to sizzle*
*so crisp so golden so complete*
*your stuff has made of me*
*Lord I'm so happy*
*upon me you lay*

## Roasted Chicken Breast Stuffed with Spinach and Goat Cheese

"A chicken in his pot every Sunday," France's King Henry IV said of his hopes for each peasant in his kingdom. President Herbert Hoover paraphrased it much later. To "a chicken in every pot." But for me, just give me plump breast and I will be eternally grateful. Serve with a slice of Potato Cake (see p. 207).

Preheat oven to 375 degrees.

1 tablespoon butter
1½ teaspoon chopped shallots
¾ cup chopped fresh spinach, stems removed
Salt and pepper
¼ cup crumbled goat cheese
2 medium-large boneless chicken breasts
Salt and pepper
2 tablespoons clarified butter (see p. 57)
1 tablespoon olive oil

1.  Melt 1 tablespoon butter in a skillet over medium-high heat. Sauté shallots about 1 minute. Add spinach and pinch of salt and pepper. Sauté about 1½ minutes. Remove from heat and stir in goat cheese. Set aside to cool.

2.  Cut a 4-inch-long pocket at center of breast. Season outside and inside breast with pinch of salt and pepper. Stuff breast with cooled spinach and cheese mixture. Close pocket, fold over, and tie with kitchen twine.

3.  Heat clarified butter and oil over medium-high heat in ovenproof skillet. Place breast top-side down in skillet, and fry about 2 minutes, until golden brown. Turn and fry about 1 minute. Do not overcook. Breast will cook further in oven. Turn breast topside up in the skillet and put skillet in hot oven. Cook about 2 minutes or until breasts are done. Remove from oven. Remove twine and serve.

Makes 2 servings.

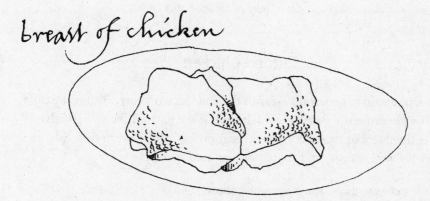

breast of chicken

# A Chick's Coming Out

*As a wanting cook takes delight*
*    in his chick's coming of spice*
*With an amber color pleasant to the sight*
*    and made royal with Basmati rice*
*Whether fried, sautéed, stewed all this night*
*    his chicks are in curried paradise*
*For all his curry spices are selective appetites*
*    that are often quite overpriced*
*And in curry's abundance may cause heat to ignite*
*    yet when scooped and stirred about will entice*
*And when his chicks are sampled, they do invite*
*    A wanting to be with them twice*
*        Or as long as they linger in the pot*
*        Or as long as the cook offers a lot*

## Curried Chicken

Do not be afraid to generously season the chicken with curry. You really can't go wrong because the curry is the deliverer of the flavor. Like salt, which enhances the flavor of foods, curry is the significant ingredient in this dish, improves the savory taste, and should not be used sparingly.

2 chicken thighs and 2 legs with bone in, chop into 2-inch pieces
¼ cup curry powder
2 tablespoons olive oil, in all
1 large russet potato, chopped into 2-inch pieces
¼ cup clarified butter (see p. 57)
2 medium onions, thinly sliced
½ cup Italian plum tomatoes, quartered, drained
1 13-ounce can coconut milk

½ teaspoon salt
¼ teaspoon pepper
4 cups cooked rice

1. Sprinkle chicken with curry powder (hold out 1 teaspoon for potatoes). Massage into chicken. Pour 1 tablespoon olive oil over chicken and massage. Let sit 30 minutes, covered in refrigerator.

2. Boil potato pieces until easily pierced with fork, about 7 minutes. Drain and put in bowl. Sprinkle 1 teaspoon curry powder over potatoes, and stir. Set aside.

3. Heat butter in a medium saucepan over low heat. When hot, add onions and sauté about 25 minutes. Stir occasionally. Remove onions from pan and set aside.

4. Add remaining tablespoon of oil to saucepan, and increase heat to medium high. Add chicken and cook 3 minutes on one side. Turn chicken over. Pour onions on top and cook 2 minutes. Add potatoes, tomatoes, coconut milk and salt and pepper, and simmer until chicken is tender, about 15 minutes. Remove from heat and serve over rice.

Makes 4 servings.

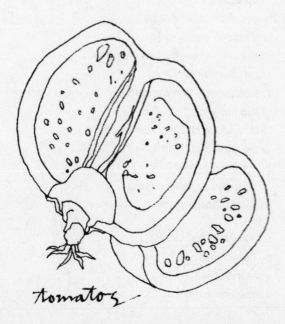

tomatos

# *A Love Supreme*

*barbecue chicken*
*on the bedroom wall*
*a love supreme*

## Barbecued Chicken

Love in the extreme in a common way.

Preheat oven to 350 degrees.

TO PREPARE BARBECUE SAUCE (MAKES 1½ CUPS):
3 tablespoons butter
1 small onion, chopped
1 garlic clove, peeled and minced
1 cup catsup
⅛ cup apple cider vinegar
½ teaspoon liquid smoke
1 tablespoon Worchestershire sauce
1 teaspoon lemon juice
½ tablespoon Dijon mustard
⅛ cup brown sugar
½ tablespoon chili powder
½ teaspoon salt
½ teaspoon pepper
¼ teaspoon cayenne pepper
Dash of Tabasco sauce

TO PREPARE THE CHICKEN:
8 chicken thighs, skin removed
1 teaspoon salt
1 teaspoon pepper

1.  Melt butter in medium saucepan over medium heat. Sauté onions and garlic 3 minutes. Add remaining ingredients and simmer 20 minutes. Puree in blender and set aside.

2.  Salt and pepper chicken. Put in roasting pan and cover. Bake 30 minutes, then turn chicken over and continue to bake 15 minutes. Remove pan from oven and pour out liquid.

3.  Pour barbecue sauce over chicken in the pan and continue to bake, uncovered, about 10 to 15 minutes. Remove from oven and put chicken and sauce on platter to serve.

Makes 4 servings.

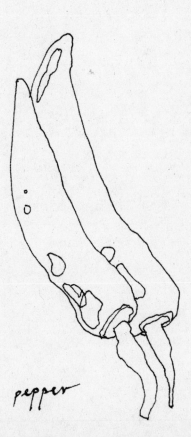

pepper

**CHAPTER FIVE**

# Vixen Veggies and Sexy Sides

*Ooh orgy. Let's dive in*
*move over mushrooms and eggplants*
*leave room for me*
*let me in between*
*onions and garlic*
*where it all begins*

—Vegetable Paella, "Ooh Orgy"

**RECIPES:**

"The Shadow of My Love" / Risotto with Wild Mushrooms

"Ooh Orgy" / Vegetable Paella

"What's Sexy About Red Beans" / Red Beans and Rice

"Dear Rosemary" / Roasted Rosemary Potatoes

"Possessed" / Fried Eggplant Frittata

"Let Everything Taste Good" / Crepes with Spinach and Ricotta

"Many a Glorious Morning" / Creamy Southern Grits

"Enter My Nakedness / Grilled Vegetables Sprinkled with Balsamic
    Vinegar and Parmesan Shavings

"A Heavenly Love Is Thee" / Saffron Parmesan Risotto

"The Recipe" / Vegetable Torte

"Layers of Love" / Potato Cake

"In My Skin" / Stuffed Roasted Eggplant

"The Art of Being Loved" / Sautéed Spinach

"Magnum Opus Pour Ma Pus" / Roasted Portobello Mushrooms

"Each Time" / Risotto with Red Wine and Parmesan

"I Fed Him" / Whipped Sweet Potatoes

"Lovely" / Sautéed French Beans
"If I Am Naked" / Eggplant Parmesan
"A Cloud of Dreams" / Roasted Garlic Whipped Potatoes
"'Cause We Have Loved That Well" / Collard Greens
"A Plate Full of Love" / Cornbread Rice Dressing
"Wherefore Do You Lie upon Me" / Southern Coleslaw
"In My Bowl" / Parmesan Penne Pasta
"Nice" / Salade Niçoise
"My Momma Told Me About You" / Potato Salad

# The Shadow of My Love

*How lucky to meet the shadow of my love*
*        with shades of you beside, behind, beneath*
*                pillowing my path*
*        with seasonings desired*
*        with heat needed to endure*
*        with time equally shared*
*                to become the thing we were*
*                to the thing we are*
*                to a simple pleasure enjoined*
*                        for life*
*Our common good in flavor*
*        our common good enriched*
*                'til satisfied palates do us entrust*
*        with each onion diced*
*        with each mushroom sautéed*
*        with each Parmesan grated*
*                you become mine*
*                I become yours*
*                together love for love*
*                        for life*
*And this I allow to meet the shadow of my love*
*        and this I allow for our common good*
*                and this I admit I have no control for*
*        you season my juice*
*        you soak my grains*
*        you spice my ri-so-tto*
*                I allow this do I*
*                and join thee with joy I do*
*                        for life*

# Risotto with Wild Mushrooms

In the kitchen, as in the bedroom, it is most important to *mise en place*—have everything ready just before you turn the heat on. In the bedroom, we line up the candles, lay out the negligee, and select the music. In the kitchen, we line up the foods, measure the spices, and pull out the utensils. This is essential when cooking risotto because the trick to this Italian dish is to stir constantly while adding ingredients. As you cook the rice to absorb the flavors of the various garnishes that follow, make sure it simmers in stock to al dente (firm but not soft) so that you can deliver a delectably creamy yet firm risotto. Much like what we desire in the bedroom. Arborio rice for risotto is usually available. Vialone Nano or Camaroli rice is also good for a risotto.

  1 tablespoon olive oil

  2 tablespoons butter

  ¼ cup chopped onion

  2 garlic cloves, minced

  1½ cups sliced fresh mushrooms (shiitakes, chanterelles,
     and buttons)

  1 cup Arborio rice, uncooked

  ½ teaspoon salt

  ½ teaspoon pepper

  2¼ cups vegetable stock (see appendix A) or store-bought
     low-sodium vegetable broth

  ¼ cup heavy cream

  ¼ cup plus 2 tablespoons grated fresh Parmesan

1.  Heat oil and 1 tablespoon of the butter to melt in large skillet over medium heat. Add onions and garlic, and sauté 1 minute. Add mushrooms and sauté 3 minutes. Add remaining 1 tablespoon butter to melt. Add rice and stir to coat for 1 minute. Add salt and pepper.

2.  Add half of the stock. Stir and lower heat to simmer. Cook approximately 5 minutes. Add remaining stock and cook 7 minutes or until rice is al dente. Stir in cream and simmer 3 minutes. Remove from heat, and fold in Parmesan. Serve immediately.

Makes 2 servings.

# *Ooh Orgy*

*Ooh orgy let's dive in*
*move over mushrooms and eggplant*
*leave room for me*
*let me in between*
*onions and garlic*
*where it all begins*
*in olive's oil and her*
*sizzling paella*
*I'm not shy*
*we know saffron is*
*she's pure as snow*
*but red as cayenne*
*most expensive of us all*
*if she were in a brothel*
*she would be top doll*
*and the triple bell peppers*
*of red, yellow, and green*
*they can orgy themselves*
*but who'll ring their bells*
*and what of the zucchini*
*God what of the zucchini*
*I mistook my place*
*let me near the zucchini*
*we can drink of the brandy*
*and swim in the broth*
*oh we forgot the rice*
*forget the rice*
*let's drink*
*no, no, rice come on in*
*without rice*
*we're nothing but veggies*
*squeeze in the plump tomatoes*

*they'll bring in some color*
*and hopefully do*
*a lap dance or two*
*oh my, here come the*
*frozen green peas*
*boring boring boring*
*push them to the other side*
*they're too cold and I'm a hottie*
*French beans are coming*
*and so are hearts of artichoke*
*I'm so glad I made this party*
*I got hearts and French kisses*
*it can't get no better.*

## Vegetable Paella

It is with paella that an orgy is welcome. The more, the merrier as the numerous ingredients join each other to simmer and bake to a most delicious and attractive consummation. The pan called a paella also names the dish. Its basic ingredients are rice, saffron, and olive oil. Traditional accompaniments are French beans, peas, artichoke hearts, red peppers, chicken, shrimp, and mussels, to name a few.

Preheat oven to 350 degrees.

10 tablespoons clarified butter, in all (see p. 57)
7 tablespoons olive oil, in all
5/8 teaspoon salt
5/8 teaspoon pepper
½ medium red bell pepper, seeds and ribs removed, cut into strips
½ medium green pepper, seeds and ribs removed, cut into strips
1 small zucchini, sliced into ½-inch pieces
8 medium button mushrooms, sliced in thirds
1 Chinese eggplant, sliced into ½-inch pieces
40 French beans, blanched (see p. 57)
1 cup chopped onions
2 garlic cloves, minced

½ stalk celery, chopped

1 cup bite-size pieces of marinated artichoke hearts

2 cups defrosted frozen green peas, drained

1 cup Italian plum tomatoes, sliced and cut in half

2 cups white long-grain rice, uncooked

½ cup brandy

4 cups hot vegetable stock (see appendix A) or store-bought, low-sodium broth

2 teaspoons saffron threads (infused in stock for 15 minutes) (see note end of recipe)

Salt and pepper

Special equipment: Medium-large paella pan or large ovenproof skillet

1. In a paella pan over medium heat, pour 1½ tablespoons of the clarified butter and 1 tablespoon oil into pan. Sprinkle ⅛ teaspoon salt and ⅛ teaspoon pepper over red and green peppers. Sauté peppers 2 minutes. Remove from pan, and place peppers in small bowl.

2. Repeat step 1 with zucchini, and place in bowl with peppers.

3. Repeat step 1 with mushrooms.

4. Repeat step 1 with eggplant.

5. Repeat step 1 with blanched French beans, but sauté 1 minute.

6. Pour 2 tablespoons olive oil and the remaining 2½ tablespoons butter in pan. When oil is hot, sauté onion, garlic, and celery for 2 minutes. Add artichokes, peas, and tomatoes, and stir. Add peppers, zucchini, mushrooms, eggplant, and French beans, and stir. Add rice and brandy, and stir well. Simmer 1 minute. Add stock and saffron, and stir. Bring to boil, then simmer 2 minutes. Season with salt to taste. Cover and place in oven, and bake until rice is al dente (firm but not soft), 15 to 20 minutes. Remove from oven and uncover. Serve hot.

Makes 10 servings.

*Note:* Infusing saffron is to let the saffron steep in stock like tea to bring out the flavor. Do not strain stock.

# *What's Sexy About Red Beans*

*What's sexy about red beans*
*they give more than they take*
*you put them on*
*you leave them alone*
*no high maintenance*
*no gourmet preps*
*just let them soak*
*or not*
*add no-fuss ingredients*
*onions, garlic, celery,*
*bay leaves*
*let them come out*
*after an hour or two*
*to cream your palate*
*no showstoppers here*
*it's not their desire*
*but they give good heads*
*a better mind*
*to understand the nature*
*of what's sexy.*

## Red Beans and Rice

Red beans and rice is a traditional Monday meal in New Orleans. Mondays were washdays. You could put on a pot of red beans and let them simmer for hours without tending to them, and they still cooked up deliciously. They are usually cooked with ham or smoked sausage. It is now becoming a gourmet dish in trendy restaurants as red bean soup.

1 1-pound bag Camellia red kidney beans (see appendix B)

2 tablespoons butter

1 onion, chopped

2 garlic cloves, chopped

2 tablespoons chopped celery

1 teaspoon dried thyme

3 tablespoons chopped fresh parsley

7 cups water

1 bay leaf

1 tablespoon salt

1 teaspoon pepper

4 tablespoons butter

Salt and pepper

4 cups cooked rice

Salt and pepper

1.  Rinse beans in cold water and set aside.

2.  In large Dutch oven over medium heat, melt butter and sauté onions, garlic, celery, and thyme for about 2 minutes. Add parsley and sauté to blend. Add beans, water, bay leaf, salt, and pepper, and stir. Bring to boil; then reduce heat to simmer. Cook covered for about 1 hour. Uncover, add butter. Scoop out 1 cup of beans. Mash beans and return to pot. Continue to simmer ½ hour or until the beans are tender and liquid is creamy. Adjust taste with salt and pepper. Discard bay leaf. Serve over rice.

Makes 6–8 servings.

# *Dear Rosemary*

Dear Rosemary—

I'm not stingy. It's just that you have so much already. Look at you. You're perfect. Your leaves are like paintings of nature's spring greens of olive, lime, and jade. When removed from your stem, your leaves do not part, and your fragrance is constantly intact. What can I, a common potato, give that is equal to your royal herbal life?

Now, thyme, I know she's most popular, and I do spend a lot of time with thyme, but she's young and flirtatious, and I admit she's delicately delicious. And if she ask of me my time, I must give, for my need for her is absolute.

But you, you're strong on your own. Not needing chumps like me to protect your honor and dress you with other herbal delights. Now basil, the Englishman, he will anoint you with a city life and prance you around Creole bay leaves, and both will take you to Mardi Gras. And that French tarragon, who brags of fine herb membership and his life with béarnaise, surely always impresses your delight. As for me, I'm a country boy living a country life. We can roast in a hot oven nearby. Invite Ms. Olive and Master Salt and deliver comfort with just us four. We can bring salad. She's always looking for something to do. And she doesn't cost much. Yes, I know, back to my stinginess. It's not that. It's that I have little. But all that I have to give this day, I give to you, Rosemary.

Yours truly,
*Flakey*

P.S. Please forgive me for not coming to your party last week. I was with French fries. She's a hoot.

## Roasted Rosemary Potatoes

Potatoes are like lovers who have stood the test of time. They are always available. They are flexible. They are comforting. They are truly accommodating. They will go with you anywhere. No fuss. But from time to time, indulge them as you would a new love. Sprinkle fragrant herbs over them. Massage them with luscious oil. Let them roast lazily to a golden brown.

Preheat oven to 325 degrees.

> 2 large baking potatoes, peeled, washed, dried, cut in half and
>     sliced in thirds
> ¼ cup virgin olive oil
> 2 rosemary sprig leaves, chopped
> 1 teaspoon salt

1. In medium bowl, mix potatoes, olive oil, rosemary, and salt, and toss thoroughly.
2. Pour all into an oiled cast-iron skillet. Spread potatoes out so they do not touch (to eliminate moisture), make sure rosemary leaves are on top of potatoes. Bake until golden brown on one side, about 30 minutes. Then turn potatoes over, and continue baking another 15 to 20 minutes until golden brown on that side. Remove from oven. Serve hot.

Makes 2 servings.

garlic

# Possessed

Possessed of your yolk
barely am I here
covered in your carnal care
lost am I to thee

Gladly in this state
though wishing differently
it's too late
for I'm in way too deep

'Cause you have folded me gently
and this I cherish endlessly
to be caressed with your softness
becoming one with thee

It's not your fault I know
love's passion consumes the knowing
drowning all in its path
unions of one are enthralled

But what of two
two loves equally measured
two loves equally desired
two loves equally served

No love survives equally

So you, you eggplant take hold
be grateful for thine egg
she has with your delight
joined you two just right

And look at you, you fool
how wonderfully delicious you are
not possible with you as one
you egghead eggplant you

*She brought beauty into your life*
*she brought continuity for you both*
*oh that you were yourself*
*you would be all alone*

*Still whole but not whole*
*still dark and oblong*
*hanging out with purple friends*
*who wish to be the chosen man*

*Consider yourself lucky*
*possessed and all consumed*
*love eats greedily*
*surrender and applaud love freely*

## Fried Eggplant Frittata

You say frittata . . . I say omelet. A frittata is an Italian omelet that has the eggs mixed well into the ingredients, unlike a French omelet whose ingredients are sprinkled over it and then folded in. A frittata is firmer than an omelet after cooking at low heat. An omelet is cooked quickly over moderately high heat. An omelet becomes a plump half-moon with ingredients folded into it. A frittata becomes a soft, fluffy pie with all its ingredients exposed in their glory.

1 large Chinese eggplant, sliced into ½-inch pieces
¼ teaspoon salt
¼ teaspoon white pepper
9 tablespoons olive oil, in all
2 tablespoons chopped shallots
2 tablespoons diced red pepper
4 eggs
¼ cup shredded Cheddar cheese
¼ teaspoon Creole seasoning (see appendix B)
1 tablespoon butter

Special equipment: Medium ovenproof skillet

1.  Season sliced eggplant with salt and pepper.

2.  Heat 2 tablespoons oil in the skillet over medium-high heat. When oil smokes slightly, brown eggplant slices cooking them in 2 batches, repeating with 2 tablespoons oil. Cook 2 minutes on one side and 1 minute on other side. Remove from skillet, and place on platter.

3.  Remove skillet from heat. Add 1 tablespoon oil in same skillet. Sauté shallots and red pepper about 30 seconds. Place shallots and peppers on platter with eggplants.

4.  In wide mixing bowl, lightly whisk eggs, cheese, and Creole seasoning. Fold in cooled eggplant mixture, making sure all the eggplant is covered. Remember, what you see now is what you will see once you remove the eggplant frittata from the pan, so make sure design is attractive.

5.  Wipe skillet clean. Heat 1 tablespoon remaining oil and 1 tablespoon butter in skillet over medium-high heat. When butter is melted, pour egg and eggplant mixture into skillet. Once slightly set, lift egg mixture edges with a rubber spatula to prevent sticking. Cook about 2 minutes. Place skillet under broiler to brown, about 30 to 50 seconds. Remove from oven. Place plate over skillet and turn frittata upside down. Slide frittata back into skillet, and let cook about 30 seconds over medium heat. Turn frittata back over with eggplants showing, and place on serving plate. Cut into wedges and serve.

Makes 2–4 servings.

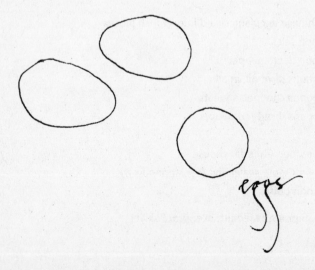

# *Let Everything Taste Good*

*Let everything taste good*

*So shall the crepe be moist and round*
*        and its circular edge be crisp*
*        and its buttery flavor pronounced*
*        and it welcomes each bit bite by bite*
*So shall the nipples be firm and in orbit*
*        and their grapelike tips invite kisses*
*        and their clean fresh skin be perfumed*
*        and they become more prominent lick by lick*
*So shall the spinach be cooked and well seasoned*
*        and it is not blanched and sautéed to death*
*        and it can be eaten alone with deep pleasure*
*        and it opens your palate even wider and wider*
*So shall the mouth be wet and soft*
*        and it be voluptuously vibrant*
*        and it be fragrant with mint or lavender*
*        and it be the prelude to succulent succulence*
*So shall the spinach ricotta mix be yummy*
*        and it fills out your crepes like a plump tummy*
*        and it is quite a treat uncovered*
*        and it is your imagination you must follow*
*So shall the breasts be like floating scoops of ice cream*
*        and they be soft yet firm as ripe mangoes*
*        and they are perfumed where they tenderly meet*
*        and they are so good that a mouthful just won't do*
*So shall the crepe be embodied with savory spinach and ricotta*
*        and it is filled to hold tight all within*
*        and it is folded where it sizzles in the oven*
*        and it is hot, well seasoned, and all good*

# Crepes with Spinach and Ricotta

Crepes are sweet or savory paper-thin pancakes made with a small amount of batter fried on both sides in a small skillet. The consistency of the batter must be thin enough to pour easily and spread evenly in the skillet. You should fry them to a golden hue and stack them until ready to fill. In France, crepes are served to celebrate hopes for good fortune and happiness in the future. Let everything taste good!

Preheat oven to 350 degrees.

FOR THE CREPES:

1 egg

2 ounces milk

3 teaspoon butter, melted

¼ teaspoon salt

¼ plus ⅛ cup flour

2 teaspoons butter

FOR THE SPINACH RICOTTA FILLING:

3 cups water

½ teaspoon salt

8 ounces fresh spinach, stems removed

1 bowl ice water

1 tablespoon butter

1 teaspoon diced onions

¼ teaspoon salt

¼ teaspoon pepper

2 tablespoons grated fresh Parmesan

⅓ cup ricotta

1 small egg

Pinch of cinnamon

1 medium plum tomato, diced

Pinch of salt

Special equipment: Small ovenproof skillet; parchment paper to line cookie sheet

1. *To prepare the crepes:* Whisk egg in bowl to blend. Add milk, 3 teaspoons melted butter, and salt, and whisk to blend. Gradually whisk in flour, whisk until smooth.

2. Over medium-low heat, place ½ teaspoon melted butter in small omelet skillet and immediately pour about 2 tablespoons crepe batter in skillet. Swirl pan to allow batter to thin out into circle. Cook 30 seconds or until edges lift easily, then turn over and cook 20 seconds. Remove and place on a cookie sheet. Repeat until you have cooked all crepe batter and used remaining butter. Makes about 4 crepes.

3. *To prepare spinach ricotta filling:* In medium pot, boil salted water, blanch spinach (see p. 212), and refresh in ice water. Drain and squeeze off as much liquid as you can and place in colander. Put butter in skillet over medium heat. When melted, add onions, and sauté about 1 minute. Add spinach and stir 1½ minutes. Season with salt and pepper. Remove from skillet and place in bowl. Add Parmesan and stir. Add ricotta, egg, and cinnamon, and blend well.

4. Place 2 to 3 tablespoons spinach mixture in a line down the center of crepe. Roll up and place on parchment-lined cookie sheet with seam down. Repeat to make 4 stuffed crepes.

5. Place in oven, and bake about 10 minutes or until crepes' edges are slightly brown. Remove from oven, and place crepes, seam side down, on serving plate. Top with tomatoes, and sprinkle with a pinch of salt.

Makes 2 servings.

onion, peppers

# *Many a Glorious Morning*

*Many a glorious morning have I turned to thee*
    *seeking comfort from your grains in me*
    *never forsaken by your hot hominy*
    *rejoiced am I to be close to thee*

*Many a glorious morning have I turned to thee*
    *warming my soul in dawn's early light*
    *full tears of joy falling endlessly*
    *caused by your swelling love having all of me*

*Many a glorious morning have I turned to thee*
    *gathering all loving parts as a servant for thee*
    *watch I do in full view your formation for me*
    *silenced moans of pleasure thrive in early morns with thee*

*Many a glorious morning have I turned to thee*
    *soothing wet sinks sweet deep in me*
    *embrace I thee by morn's early rise to comfort me*
    *readied by day and dateless nights for thee*

## Creamy Southern Grits

In the South, grits are to mornings what collard greens are to evenings. They are the soul-soothing breakfast food for many a glorious morning. Shrimp and grits, quail and grits, catfish and grits, or just eggs and grits, say, "I love you and I'm here to comfort you this morning and forevermore."

    4 cups water
    1 cup grits
    2 teaspoons salt
    4 tablespoons butter

1.  In large pot, bring water to boil. Add grits and salt, and stir vigorously. Turn heat to low, cover, and cook, stirring occasionally. Cook about 20 minutes or until grits are creamy. Remove from heat. Stir in butter and additional salt to taste.

Makes 4 servings.

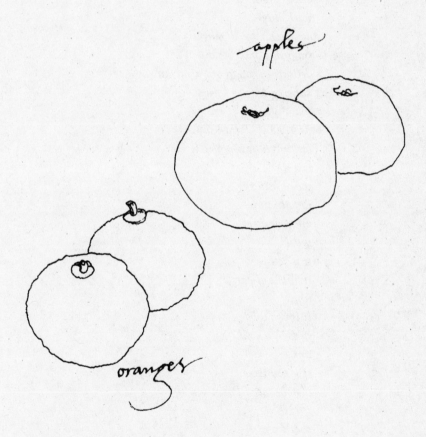

# Enter My Nakedness

*I was born naked*
*and so shall I be*
*naked*
*always with you*
*with only*
*affectionate grill marks*
*fragrance of olive's oil*
*delicate shavings of Parmesan*
*dancing parsley leaves*
*that's all*
*nearly naked did I say*
*for disrobing completely*
*is a sin*
*when seducing*
*imagination*
*must run free*
*until*
*it is you who*
*strip me of parsley*
*until*
*it is you who*
*sucketh my oil*
*until*
*it is you who*
*disrobe me of Parmesan*
*it is then*
*that I am*
*good and naked*
*for you*
*by your hands*
*the act will be done*

*the mystery will unfold*
*at the end*
*for now*
*to call your gaze*
*of my moist skin*
*to taste the bitter sweetness*
*of my balsamic*
*to wipe your lips*
*of my entrance*
*for now*
*nakedness*
*is no longer a sin*
*as you have uncovered me*
*provocatively*
*one layer at a time*
*allowing your hands*
*to disrobe me naturally*
*before you naked*
*I stand*
*ready to be devoured*
*naked*
*or*
*you can put*
*my Parmesan*
*back on*
*you can put*
*my parsley*
*back on*
*you can put*
*my balsamic*
*back on*
*and*
*only lift slightly the veil*
*of my adornment*
*to enter my nakedness*
*it's more fun.*

# Grilled Vegetables Sprinkled with Balsamic Vinegar and Parmesan Shavings

Grilling vegetables must be the cooking method veggies desire most, for their essence delivered full with flavor. Not only do you get those sexy grill marks, but you get to savor their true character. Portobellos are musky, meaty men. Asparagus are dainty, delicious darlings. Eggplants are versatile, vivacious victuals. Peppers are sweet, spirited swingers. Plum tomatoes are popular, plump perishables. Zucchinis are sexy-shaped specimens. Grill me, baby.

Preheat oven to 350 degrees.

4 asparagus spears, hard ends broken off

¼ teaspoon salt

1 medium eggplant, sliced diagonally into ½-inch-thick pieces

1 zucchini, sliced diagonally into ½-inch-thick pieces

1 small red bell pepper, seeded and sliced 3 inches thick

1 small yellow bell pepper, seeded and sliced 3 inches thick

2 Portobello mushrooms, stems removed, wiped dry

2 firm Italian plum tomatoes, sliced in half

Salt and pepper

½ cup olive oil

Can of cooking oil spray

2 tablespoons balsamic vinegar

½ cup Parmesan shavings

1.  Tie asparagus spears with kitchen twine so that they will stand up. Place in boiling salted water with spear tips up, and cook about 4 minutes. Drain and pat dry.

2.  Place eggplant, zucchini, red and yellow peppers, mushrooms, and tomatoes in large bowl, and generously coat with olive oil, salt, and pepper. Toss to coat vegetables well.

3.  Put grill pan over high heat and spray with light oil. Grill eggplants, zucchini, and asparagus about 2 minutes on each side to get those grill marks. Transfer to cookie sheet. Spray pan with light oil and grill peppers about 3 minutes on each side. Transfer to cookie sheet. Spray pan

with light oil and grill mushrooms, heads down, about 3 minutes; turn over and grill 2 minutes. Transfer to cookie sheet. Spray pan with light oil and grill tomatoes 1 minute on each side. Transfer to cookie sheet.

4.  Place cookie sheet in oven, and heat vegetables about 3 minutes. Remove from oven.

5.  Arrange vegetables attractively on large platter. Drizzle with balsamic vinegar; lay thin Parmesan shavings over vegetables. Serve immediately.

Makes 4 servings.

# *A Heavenly Love Is Thee*

*A heavenly love is thee*
*saffron threads wet and free*
*flowery fragrances of fine strains*
*flowing deliciously*
*pray tell how you came to me*
*For each thousands of you*
*tells the tale of one ounce or two*
*of your rich and glorious life*
*of pure essence*
*causing royal and peasant men alike*
*To risk their lives getting at your crocus*
*deep in your blossoming flower*
*only three stigmas to save*
*and some men misbehave*
*for they pinch more than they deserve*
*Overwhelmed by your perfumed essence*
*coming in the mist of dawn's heaven*
*autumn's breeze helps the squeeze*
*of many hands pulling leaves*
*of that tiny purple flower*
*Just saying your name—S a f f r o n—*
*flashes images of reigning queens*
*reclining in silk and satin*
*oh were you not spice*
*I would die too for your life*
*And pray for your total devotion*
*for you are a heavenly love*
*not often survived in this cruel world*
*but what little heaven sent*
*is worth lives spent*
*in heaven or hell for thee*

# Saffron Parmesan Risotto

This is a variation of the classic Italian Milanese Risotto and one of the most beautiful risotto combinations. Arborio rice is what I use to make risotto. It's a medium-grain rice from Italy that keeps its shape as it cooks to a creamy yet firm texture and welcomes the flavors and colors quite handsomely of most ingredients cooked with it in a slow-simmering stock. Risotto is a very sensual offering and a must for every culinary seductress's repertoire.

½ cup white wine
¼ teaspoon saffron threads
1 tablespoon olive oil
1 tablespoon butter
1 small onion, finely chopped
1 garlic clove, crushed
1 cup Arborio rice, uncooked
¼ teaspoon salt
¼ teaspoon white pepper
3 cups vegetable stock (see appendix A) or store-bought low-
    sodium vegetable broth
¼ cup heavy cream
½ cup grated fresh Parmesan

1.  Put wine in bowl and place saffron in to soak.

2.  Heat olive oil and butter in a wide, heavy-duty skillet over medium heat. Add onion and garlic, and sauté about 2 minutes. Stir constantly. Add rice, and stir to coat, about 1 minute. Add salt and pepper, and stir briefly to coat rice.

3.  Lower heat to medium-low. Add wine and saffron to rice, stirring until all the liquid has been absorbed. Stir in a cup of simmering stock, and cook, stirring occasionally. Shake pan back and forth often. When absorbed, stir in another cup. Continue this process for 20 minutes until all stock is added and rice is al dente (firm but not soft). Add cream and stir 30 seconds. Remove skillet from heat and stir in Parmesan.

Makes 2 servings.

# The Recipe

*Hold your asparagus and bend it where it naturally resists*
     *Forget that part and remember the rest*
*Simmer in a warm salt bath*
     *Then lift and hold up and wipe yourself dry*
*Now*
*Stroke my skillet with your wet butter and silky oil*
     *Fire up a sultry heat that penetrates our cheeks*
*Let us consummate our flavors inflamed by our passion*
     *A rendezvous of the willing delivered*
*Now*
*I burst out crying for my love of you, onion*
     *You are my master I am your mistress*
*You never forsake me you always satisfy me*
     *All is absent when sautéing you is forgotten*
*Now*
*You one single zucchini speak to me of your desire*
     *For your perfect resemblance causes me to tremble*
*'Cause slice you I must, yes slice you I must*
     *I'll buy another and keep you—I lust*
*Now*
*Yellow squash a not frequent lover adorned or admired*
     *Not much action there for either of us*
*Yet companionship of zucchini I know is your weakness*
     *I understand, yes I understand*
*Now*
*Mushroom penetrate me en masse with your pungent male musk*
     *The darker you become the deeper you enter*
*Into my skillet now full with fragrance*
     *Enchanted now with a male must I inhale*
*Now*
*Spinach I love you but stems I must discard you*

*Your bitterness is not welcome*
*Odd you attach to a leaf as lovely as this*
    *Though we all have attachments, 'tis, 'tis, remember this*
*Now*
*To all my seasonings holler if you hear me*
    *Sing your song of glory spray me with magic*
*Quite mysteriously at your bequest*
    *We all deliver the best*
*Now*
*Golden Parmesan you anointest my soul*
    *before, behind, between, below*
*God only knows how you flatter me so*
    *To transform my goodness into greatness*
*Now*
*Fresh herbs ha fresh herbs*
    *You're not forgotten*
*Don't repeat it but I love you the most*
    *And know your fragrance is our eternal memory*
*Now*
*Come, ricotta, cream cheese, and my dear eggs, come*
    *It is your turn to give up some*
*Fatten us with your rich cream and beaucoup calories*
    *Your love folding into us is worth all of that*

## Vegetable Torte

Tart or torte—what's the difference? A tart is a pastry crust with shallow sides, a sweet or savory filling, and no top crust. A torte is often a multilayered cake usually made with nuts or bread crumbs, eggs, sugar, flavorings and layered with buttercream or jam. When making these multilayer tortes, you seek to create an attractive presentation not only from its top layer but most especially from its assembled layers.

Preheat oven to 375 degrees.

8 medium-small asparagus spears

1 tablespoon olive oil

1 tablespoon butter

1 small onion, diced

2 garlic cloves, crushed

1 medium zucchini, sliced into 1-inch circles

1 small yellow squash, sliced into 1-inch circles

2 teaspoons Creole seasoning, in all

¾ teaspoon salt, in all

¾ teaspoon pepper, in all

1 cup sliced button mushrooms

¼ pound spinach, stems removed

1 tablespoon chopped fresh basil

1 tablespoon chopped fresh thyme

1 cup grated Parmesan cheese, in all

1 cup ricotta

¼ cup sour cream

4 eggs

Special equipment: 8-inch springform pan

1.  Snap off woody ends of asparagus and discard. Cut spear tips, and slice spears into 2-inch slices. Bring saucepan of salted water to boil, and cook asparagus spears for 3 minutes; then add tips and cook for 1 minute. Drain and set aside.

2.  Blanch spinach. Drain, squeeze dry with paper towel. Set aside.

3.  Place oil and butter in skillet over medium-high heat, and sauté onions and garlic about 1 minute. Season zucchini and squash with 1 teaspoon Creole seasoning, ½ teaspoon salt, and ½ teaspoon pepper. Add to onion and cook about 2 minutes. Add mushrooms and cook about 1 minute. Add spinach and stir about 1 minute.

4.  Remove from heat and add asparagus, basil, thyme, and ¾ cup Parmesan, and stir. Put vegetables in a colander to drain liquid. Set colander aside and let cool completely.

5.  In large bowl, whisk to blend well ricotta, sour cream, eggs, and remaining 1 teaspoon Creole seasoning, ¼ teaspoon salt, and ¼ teaspoon pepper. Gently fold cooled vegetable mixture into ricotta mixture.

6.  Butter springform pan and dust with Parmesan. Pour vegetable and cheese mixture into pan. Sprinkle top with remaining Parmesan. Place pan on hot baking sheet, and cook until torte is done, 30 to 35 minutes. Insert skewer into middle to test doneness. When it comes out dry, it is done. Place under broiler to brown about 15 seconds. Cool on rack. Serve warm.

Makes 6 servings.

*Note:* I use Tony Chachere's Creole seasoning (see appendix B).

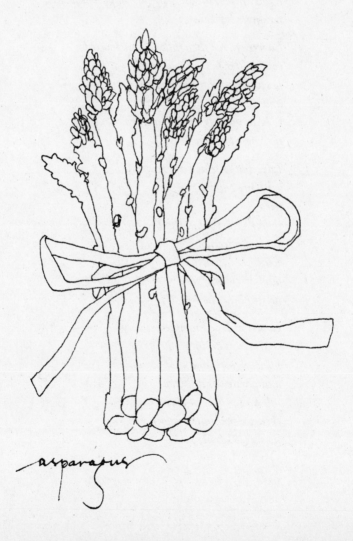

asparagus

# Layers of Love

Layers of love as I move in this world
are what I seek
topping each other, curving all corners
overlapping, flowing over, smothering layers
tightly fitted, precisely sized, compacted neatly
no single lay here

Layers of love thoughtfully constructed
good butter first and always
to sweetly smear the surface
and cause the endings
to be as good as the beginnings
no single lay here

Layers of love as I am reminded
with my tears
need
reflective determination
studied affection
watchful attention
adulterous diligence
no single lay here

Layers of love sprinkled evenly
with spices and fresh herbs
minced garlic and chopped onions
and parsley and thyme
salt and pepper of course
then we met butter again
no single lay here

*Layers of love held together*
*with care*
*with forgiveness*
*with thoughtfulness*
*with gratitude*
*no single lay here*

## Potato Cake

This dish is simple and elegant. And with each layer of seasoned potatoes and fresh herbs and hot butter, you get love and happiness, as Al Green would sing. There is no need for this preparation to be laborious. It is quick. It is delicious. Make this wonderful little delicious dish, and get gigantic praise for your efforts that supersedes the gratitude of love you are about to receive. Love is built a layer at a time.

Preheat oven to 325 degrees.

> 5 medium small white potatoes, peeled and thinly sliced
> 8 tablespoons butter, in all
> 1 small onion, finely chopped
> ½ cup chopped fresh parsley
> 2 garlic cloves, minced
> 2 tablespoons chopped fresh thyme
> Pinch salt and pepper
> 4 tablespoons grated Parmesan
> 10 tablespoons grated mozzarella
> 3 tablespoons milk
> Salt and pepper
>
> Special equipment: 9-inch tart pan

1. Peel and thinly slice potatoes, and place in water. Just before cooking onions, place potatoes on paper towels to dry.
2. Melt 4 tablespoons of the butter over medium heat. Add onions, parsley, garlic, and thyme, and sauté about 2 minutes. Put aside.

3. Melt remaining ½ stick butter in saucepan and pour into small bowl. Set aside to drizzle on layers of potatoes.

4. Coat 9-inch tart pan with ¼ teaspoon melted butter. Place first layer of sliced potatoes overlapping each other in pan. Spoon 2½ tablespoons onion mixture and spread over potatoes. Sprinkle with pinch of salt and pepper. Sprinkle 1 tablespoon Parmesan, 2 tablespoons mozzarella, and then 1 tablespoon butter. Repeat with 2 more layers. End with top layer of potatoes covered with pinch of salt and pepper to taste and remaining Parmesan, mozzarella, butter, then milk. Put tart pan on parchment-covered cookie sheet.

5. Bake in oven for 30 minutes; increase heat to 400 degrees, and bake 20 to 30 more minutes until potatoes and cheese are slightly browned. Let cool slightly before cutting into wedges to serve.

Makes 6 servings.

bananas

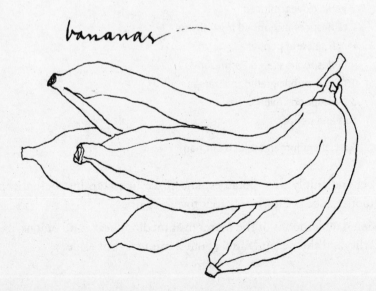

# *In My Skin*

*In my skin you are most gentle*
*where my flesh is moist and soft*
*now high heat has changed my inner firmness*
*to not give up but to give in*
*to your complete fullness*

*In my skin you are most gentle*
*where I am most expansive now*
*to beget most all of me easily*
*causing an exhilarating exodus*
*of pushes and pulls timed perfectly*

*In my skin you are most gentle*
*as you slice me once*
*you use your rod to gather my meat*
*while I sizzle and bounce about*
*on a hot cookie sheet*

*In my skin you are most gentle*
*stuffing me again and again*
*now causing me to overflow*
*with your lustful fillings*
*of roasted red peppers and mo'*

*In my skin you are most gentle*
*as you stir in juicy mushrooms*
*and crunchy rice*
*all sautéed with onions and garlic*
*in olive's oil so nice*

*In my skin you are most gentle*
*all lying in bed with me now*
*with flavors that make me better*
*adding herbs of oregano and parsley*
*I am now a seasoned woman I tell ya*

*In my skin you are most gentle*
*carefully consummating our union*
*with mozzarella and sprinklings of Parmesan*
*getting me but not getting me undone*
*I am whole again in my skin*

## Stuffed Roasted Eggplant

Even though eggplants are commonly thought to be vegetables, they are actually fruit! Eggplants range in color from deep purple to white and in length from 2 to 12 inches; they can be oblong to round. The eggplant I use most often, and use in this recipe, is the medium large, purple, pear-shaped eggplant. The most common eggplant found in the markets is this variety. But there are the Italian eggplants that look like miniature versions of the large pear shaped eggplant. Chinese eggplants are solid purple, long and curvy, with a sweeter flesh and are the most phallic. Hurray for eggplants!

Preheat oven to 400 degrees.

> 1 medium eggplant, roasted and cut in half lengthwise
> 2½ tablespoons olive oil, in all
> 1 small red bell pepper, roasted, seeded, and thinly sliced
> 2 tablespoons butter
> 1 garlic clove, minced
> ½ medium onion, chopped
> 1 cup sliced button mushrooms
> Pinch of salt
> 1 cup brown rice, cooked
> 1 tablespoon chopped fresh oregano
> ⅓ cup chopped fresh parsley
> 1 teaspoon salt
> ¼ teaspoon pepper
> ½ cup mozzarella
> ¼ cup grated Parmesan, in all

1. Rub eggplant with ½ tablespoon of the oil, and place on cookie sheet. Roast 25 to 35 minutes or until eggplant is soft. Turn eggplant over

once. Remove from oven. Remove eggplant from cookie sheet and let cool. Cut in half lengthwise. Carefully remove eggplant pulp. Chop pulp and set aside. Set aside eggplant skin to use later.

2. Roast pepper over high heat on top of gas stove or electric oven (see p. 16). Slice in half lengthwise and remove seeds. Slice thinly and set aside.

3. Place remaining 2 tablespoons olive oil and 2 tablespoons butter in large saucepan over medium heat. Sauté garlic and onions about 30 seconds. Stir constantly. Add mushrooms and pinch of salt, and sauté about 1½ minutes.

4. Add peppers, eggplant pulp, and cooked rice, and sauté 1 minute. Stir oregano and parsley into mixture. Sprinkle in salt and pepper. Stir and cook about 1½ minutes. Stir constantly. Remove from heat and stir in mozzarella and ½ of Parmesan.

5. Carefully place eggplant skins in small ovenproof skillet. Spoon eggplant stuffing into skins. Sprinkle remaining Parmesan on top and place under broiler 1 minute to melt Parmesan. Remove and serve.

Makes 2 servings.

mushrooms

# The Art of Being Loved

| THE ART OF BLANCHING SPINACH | THE ART OF BEING LOVED |
|---|---|
| Remove the stems. | Remove all pretensions. |
| Wash the spinach in lots of water. | Wash all suspicions away. |
| Heat a large pot of water slightly salted. | Heat your heart until it's wide open. |
| Boil briskly for 2 to 3 minutes, stirring. | Boil away thoughts of Mr. or Ms. Right. |
| Remove spinach from boiling water. | Remove obstacles to hope. |
| Dip into ice-cold water. | Dip into the world of possibilities. |
| Drain spinach in a large colander or sieve. | Drain suitors in abundance. |
| Take handfuls and squeeze hard, extracting all water. | Take that one hand outreached, extracting compassion and affection. |
| Lay on paper towel to rest. | Lay you upon him and rest. |
| Heat a little butter in skillet. | Heat up the action. |
| Add spinach and sauté briefly. | Add time and patience. |
| Season with salt and pepper. | Season with maturity and sincerity. |
| And that's it. | And that's it. |

# Sautéed Spinach

I have heard many women describe the lack of love in their lives. I have heard what they expect from relationships and all the goodies they expect from their beaux. I have heard them speak as if their mere presence was enough to demand all good things flow to them. But the art of being loved is the art of giving love equally, without expecting a reward for just being in the room.

1 pound fresh spinach, stems removed
½ stick butter
1 teaspoon salt
1 teaspoon pepper

1. Remove the spinach stems.
2. Wash the spinach in lots of water.
3. Heat a large pot of water, slightly salted.
4. Boil briskly 2 to 3 minutes, stirring.
5. Remove spinach from boiling water.
6. Dip into ice-cold water.
7. Drain spinach in a large colander or sieve.
8. Take handfuls and squeeze tight or wrap in clean towel and squeeze.
9. Extract all water.
10. Lay on paper towel to rest.
11. Heat a little butter in skillet.
12. Add spinach and sauté briefly.
13. Season with salt and pepper.
14. And that's it.

Makes 2 servings.

# *Magnum Opus Pour Ma Pus*

*Handsome meaty Portobello*
*dark chocolate shade*
*come to this solemn space*
*magnum opus pour ma pus*

*Handsome meaty Portobello*
*glisteningly mellow*
*let her with kisses*
*bind thee together*

*Handsome meaty Portobello*
*explicitly manly*
*arise and call upon her*
*leap into her deeply*

*Handsome meaty Portobello*
*loyal royal musk*
*find eternal scent in thee*
*endless pleasures of lust*

*Handsome meaty Portobello*
*copiously graced*
*bless the bed of thyme*
*nothing lasts in taste forever*

*Handsome meaty Portobello*
*last forever or not*
*life to live a love with thee*
*death to live without*

# Roasted Portobello Mushrooms

Purchasing individually picked mushrooms is advisable rather than buying them in a package. Their shelf life is short. Avoid buying mushrooms that are damp, blemished, darkening, or broken. Select those that are firm and evenly colored. Store them in the refrigerator covered with a slightly damp towel. Never soak in water to clean them. Only a damp cloth or brushing or two is needed to clean mushrooms.

Preheat oven to 375 degrees.

> 12 ounces Portobello mushrooms, cut into 3-inch-thick slices
> ½ cup extra-virgin olive oil
> 2 tablespoons butter, melted
> 1 tablespoon chopped fresh parsley
> 1 tablespoon chopped fresh thyme
> Salt and pepper

1. Snap off Portobello stems. Discard. Place sliced Portobellos in small ovenproof bowl and drizzle with olive oil and butter. Coat evenly. Toss parsley and thyme with pinch of salt and pepper.
2. Allow Portobellos to lie on top of each other.
3. Roast about 20 minutes. Toss to place bottom Portobellos on top; then continue to roast another 10 minutes. Remove from oven, and serve hot.

Makes 4 servings.

# *Each Time*

*Each time*
*it is with a deep desire to stay together*
*and I of you wish the same, slightly*
*but for me to consume*
*each time*
*your beauty*
*of red wine infused*
*balls*
*of clustered plump risotto*
*I must separate you*
*each time*
*so I penetrate your mound*
*and capture that musky wine flavor*
*and thin slivers of Parmesan*
*and thyme to spare*
*each time*
*I only look to separate you further*
*into my mouth*
*against my jaws*
*down my throat*
*each time*
*but I am graced by the tenderness*
*of staying together*
*and this truly I seek, I think,*
*for it brings*
*security and comfort*
*each time*
*though I am selfish I admit*
*I must separate you a bit*
*to eat your*
*balls*
*of clustered risotto*

*each time*
*and I do*
*now*

# Risotto with Red Wine and Parmesan

*When cooking, you must taste.* You want to combine all the layers of flavors as you cook. Your taste is different from anyone else's. You need to adjust your taste to any recipe you try. Make it your personal gift.

*When making love, you must taste.* Try different kisses in different places. Hold kisses long and tenderly in some places and loose or tight in others, then release quickly. Try different touches and see how your lover responds. Make it your personal gift.

> 2½ cups vegetable stock (see appendix A) or store-bought
>    low-sodium vegetable stock
> 4 tablespoons butter
> 2 shallots, chopped
> 1 large garlic clove, mashed
> ¼ teaspoon salt
> ¼ teaspoon pepper
> 1 tablespoon chopped fresh thyme
> 1 cup Arborio rice, uncooked
> 1 cup dry red wine
> ½ cup grated Parmesan, in all

1. In small pot, bring stock to slight boil. Lower heat and simmer.

2. Melt butter in medium saucepan over medium-low heat. Add shallots and garlic and cook until shallots are translucent but not browned, about 1 minute. Add thyme and stir to coat, about 10 seconds; then add rice and thoroughly stir to coat, about 1 minute. Add salt and pepper and stir.

3. Add half the wine. Stir constantly. Cook about 1 minute until wine is nearly absorbed.

4. Add ½ cup of the hot stock. Stir constantly. Simmer about 3 minutes. Cook until nearly all stock has been absorbed before more liquid is added.

5. Add remaining wine, and simmer about 3 minutes until wine is nearly all absorbed. Stir constantly.

6. Repeat with ½ cup stock added, and continue simmering another 3 minutes as you stir constantly. Repeat ½ cup stock additions until nearly all stock is absorbed and rice is al dente (firm but not soft) with total cook time of about 20 minutes. Remove saucepan from heat, and stir in ¼ cup of the Parmesan. Sprinkle remaining Parmesan over each serving.

Makes 2 servings.

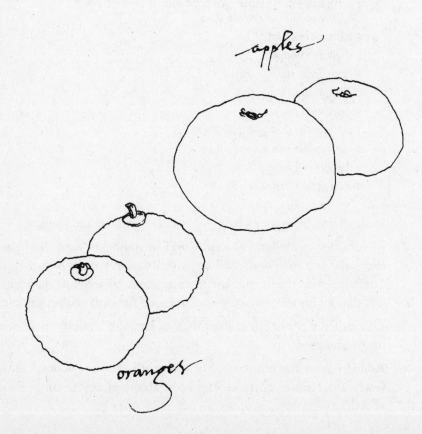

# I Fed Him

*I fed him*
*Sweet potatoes, corn, and collard greens*
*He has followed me ever since*
*Not did I think love would ensue*
*It was just a meal or two*
*But what developed in the years to come*
*Was not expected from the first come-on*
*It just got bigger, wider, and deeper*
*With each plate served weekly*

*I fed him*
*Sweet potatoes, corn and, collard greens*
*We ate in the kitchen, dining room, and bedroom*
*Each late afternoon on Sundays*
*For twenty years and one on Monday*
*He was always gracious, prompt, and with appetite*
*He shared in the cleaning of dishes and putting away of food*
*We often watched a little TV or caught a movie*
*But it was the meal that always brought him near me*

*I fed him*
*Sweet potatoes, corn, and collard greens*
*But one day he fed me a goose*
*And something called a merliton stuffed with*
*Crawfish, shrimp, and andouille*
*And then he fed me a bowl of turtle soup*
*After all these years*
*I did not know who this man was*
*Serving me food so unfamiliar to my nature*
*But this is what got me and kept me*
*Feeding him*
*Sweet potatoes, corn, and collard greens*

# Whipped Sweet Potatoes

I usually have my sweet potatoes in a pie, a soufflé, or julienned and sautéed in butter with cinnamon, nutmeg, and brown sugar, or just baked and finished with a little butter. Until recently, whipped potatoes meant white potatoes to me. But one day Ed and I had whipped sweet potatoes as a side vegetable in a trendy restaurant. We were delightfully surprised by the idea. So now whipped sweet potatoes are a part of my culinary repertoire.

Preheat oven to 400 degrees.

> 4 teaspoons vegetable oil
> 4 cups sweet potatoes (about 4 medium potatoes)
> ¾ cup brown sugar
> 2 tablespoons sugar
> ½ teaspoon nutmeg
> ½ teaspoon mace
> ¼ teaspoon cinnamon
> ¾ teaspoon salt
> 4 tablespoons butter, melted
> 4 tablespoons cream
> 1 tablespoon Grand Marnier

1. Rub oil over sweet potatoes. Wrap in aluminum foil and place on baking sheet. Bake 30 to 40 minutes or until potatoes are soft.
2. Remove potatoes from oven, let cool, and peel. Scoop out pulp and place in mixing bowl. Add sugars, nutmeg, mace, cinnamon, salt, butter, cream, and Grand Marnier. Whip with mixer until smooth.

Makes 4 servings.

# *Lovely*

*Lovely as four arms embrace*
  *with grace, harmony, and beauty*
*lovely as four eyes gaze*
  *with scorching passion igniting*
*lovely as two lips collide*
  *with open mouths locked in a kiss*
*lovely as two souls meet*
  *with eternal commitment to satisfy*
*lovely as two hearts join*
  *with red hot desire forever more*

## Sautéed French Beans

French beans are the young, thin, expensive green string beans commonly referred to as haricots verts. It has been reported that green beans were brought to France by Pope Clement VII to present to his niece, Catherine de Medici, at her wedding to the future Henri II. French beans properly prepared with a little butter and salt and pepper can truly be a gift of love.

  ½ pound fresh French beans, blanched
  1 bowl ice water
  4 tablespoons butter
  ⅛ teaspoon salt
  ⅛ teaspoon pepper

1. Snap off French beans' rough bottom tips and discard.
2. Blanch beans (see p. 57) in boiling salted water for 5 to 10 minutes or until beans are al dente (firm but not soft). Drain and then place imme-

diately in ice-cold water. Allow to cool, about 1 minute. Drain, then place on paper towels. Pat dry.

3.  Melt butter in large skillet, and add beans. Add salt and pepper, and stir. Sauté 3 minutes. Stir well. Remove from heat. Place beans on platter to serve.

Makes 2 servings.

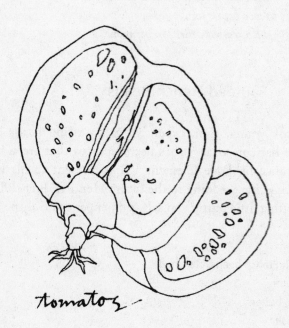

tomatos -

# If I Am Naked

If I am naked
will you cover me with
good oil
        will you comfort me with
spicy sauces
if I am naked

If I am naked
will you dust me with
seasoned breadcrumbs
        will you layer me with
memories
        if I am naked

        I am naked
revealed before you
washed of warm water
        I am naked
dipped in your yolk
coated with your crumbs
        I am naked
sizzling in your oil
layered with your love

Naked
I disrobe my purple coat
Naked
I take my bath
Naked
I slice my soft spot
Naked
I am yours

# Eggplant Parmesan

When cooking eggplant, I'm always torn between removing the skin or not. I believe flavor is abundant in every fiber of the eggplant. From habit, I often choose to undress the eggplants, leaving them naked and vulnerable. In an attempt to justify my action, I seek always to cover them with good stuff. Stuff that I know the eggplants would consider of equal epicurean value. Stuff that honors their uniqueness and only seeks to cover their nakedness sweetly. Stuff that will also keep too much oil from seeping into them, making them all soggy and unattractive. A good egg wash and the best-flavored bread crumbs give them the royal coating they deserve.

Preheat oven to 400 degrees.

> 1 large fancy eggplant, peeled and sliced into ½-inch-thick pieces
> Salt
>
> FOR THE HERB MIXTURE:
> 2 eggs
> 2 tablespoons finely grated fresh Parmesan
> 2 tablespoons chopped fresh parsley
> 2 tablespoons chopped fresh basil
> Pinch of salt and pepper
>
> FOR THE EGG WASH:
> 2 eggs and 2 tablespoons of water, mixed well
>
> FOR THE BREAD CRUMB MIXTURE:
> 1 cup bread crumbs
> 2 teaspoons fresh parsley
> ½ teaspoon dried oregano
> ½ teaspoon dried thyme
> 2 teaspoons grated fresh Parmesan
> Pinch of salt and pepper
> 8 tablespoons olive oil, in all
> 1 24-ounce can Italian tomato sauce

1 ½ cups Parmesan cheese shavings
½ cup julienned fresh basil leaves
½ pound sliced mozzarella cheese

**Special equipment: 8×8×2-inch Pyrex dish**

1. Generously salt eggplant slices and place in colander. Let sit about 30 minutes. This helps to eliminate a bitter taste from the eggplant. Rinse and then place slices on paper towels. Pat dry.

2. *To make herb mixture:* Mix eggs, Parmesan, parsley, basil, and pinch salt and pepper in medium bowl, and set aside.

3. *To make egg wash:* Mix beaten eggs and water in small bowl, and set aside.

4. *To make bread crumb mixture:* Mix bread crumbs, parsley, oregano, thyme, Parmesan, and pinch salt and pepper in medium bowl, and set aside.

5. Coat eggplant slices with herb mixture. Dip in egg wash, but do not turn over so as to keep herbs on slices. Remove and coat with bread crumb mixture.

6. In large skillet, heat 4 tablespoons of the oil over medium-high heat. When oil begins to smoke slightly, cook ½ batch of the eggplant slices until brown, about 1 to 1½ minutes, each side. Cook in batches to prevent overlapping of slices. When browned, place on paper towel to drain excess oil. With paper towel wipe pan of excess bread crumbs. Repeat with remaining eggplant and oil until all slices are cooked.

7. Coat Pyrex dish with ⅔ cup tomato sauce. Place single layer of eggplant slices over sauce. Top with ½ cup Parmesan. Sprinkle ⅛ cup of the basil over Parmesan. Top with single layer of mozzarella slices. Pour ⅔ of tomato sauce over mozzarella. Repeat with layers twice, but top the last layer with remaining mozzarella on top of sauce.

8. Bake approximately 30 minutes until dish is bubbly and mozzarella cheese is spottily brown.

Makes 4–6 servings.

# A Cloud of Dreams

a cloud of dreams floats by
　　as I yield my lips to thee
　　and I hold my neck slightly back
　　as I embrace heaven's gift to me
　　　　love's not promise
　　　　love's not sane
　　　　love's not sometimes
　　　　　　the real thing
　　but
a cloud of dreams floats by
　　as I feel your softness in me
　　and I know and like your taste
　　as I am tongue-tied by your pace
　　　　love conquers
　　　　love rules
　　　　love takes no
　　　　　　prisoners
　　but
a cloud of dreams floats by
　　as I am bewilderingly intoxicated
　　and I seek not to be freed
　　as I live in this maze with ease
　　　　love tramples
　　　　love commands
　　　　love transposes all of
　　　　　　rationality
　　but
a cloud of dreams floats by
　　as I sink further into thee
　　and I am calmed by this our repast
　　as I end this plea with thee
　　　　love is the beginning

*love is the end*
*love is the creator of*
*all things*
*that's why*
*a cloud of dreams floats by*

## Roasted Garlic Whipped Potatoes

"Ed," I said, "how are the potatoes?" "They're okay, but next time try roast garlic and sour cream." This is an example of how I've moved through my epicurean life. Ed, I believe, has perfect taste buds. With a teaspoon taste, he can instantly suggest to how to improve a dish. Like a wine connoisseur, he takes a sip, swirls the food around his mouth, and then provides a comprehensive food review. His cooking experience and love of cooking, I'm sure, have enabled him to achieve such expertise.

Preheat oven to 375 degrees.

> 3 large garlic cloves, unpeeled
> 2 tablespoons olive oil
> 6 medium russet potatoes
> 1 cup half-and-half
> ½ cup sour cream
> 1½ teaspoon salt
> ½ teaspoon white pepper
> 8 tablespoons butter, softened

1. Place garlic cloves on aluminum foil, pour olive oil over cloves, enclose in the foil, and roast until soft, 20 to 30 minutes. Remove from oven. When slightly cool, pop out garlic, and set aside. Discard husks.
2. Peel and cut potatoes, and place in medium pot. Cover potatoes with water and bring to a boil. Cook until potatoes are soft and slightly breaking apart, about 30 minutes. Drain potatoes and place in large mixing bowl. Add garlic, half-and-half, sour cream, and salt and pepper (to taste). Whip with an electric mixer until potatoes are smooth. Add butter. Add salt and pepper. Keep warm.

Makes 4–6 servings.

# 'Cause We Have Love That Well

*Sins of southern nouvelle cuisine*
*possesseth thy life*
    *flash fried*
      *sautéed in olive oil*
      *cooked al dente*
*by skinny young chefs*
*against my love of thee*

*Show me your leaves well cooked*
      *yet not over cooked*
*Show me a turkey leg*
      *wrapped in your mist*
*Show me your pot liquor*
      *readied for my lips*

*For I know you*

*'Cause you have loved that well*
      *every Sunday evening*
      *plus twice each week*
      *Thanksgiving*
      *Christmas*
      *Birthdays*
      *all*
      *you were there*

*'Cause you have loved that well*
      *with soulful juices*
      *of my desire*
      *with a bite*
      *of tender love*
      *with meat*
      *of flavors neat*

*They thinketh you*
*their new discovery*
> *with sundried tomatoes*
> *with capers*
> *with sesame seeds*

*Oh my!*

*But stay with me greens*
> *give not gourmet glory*

*not you*

*For I will keep you warm as you simmer*
*I'll keep you wet as a dream*
*I'll keep you wild and loose*

*'Cause we have loved that well*

## Collard Greens

A note on collard greens. Somehow our mamas got it right in determining how long to cook collards. Most of my contemporaries cook collards to death—until they are limp and tasteless. I have discovered in my "collard green testing kitchen" that somehow the essence of the green is captured at a point of 1 to 1¼ hours of simmering, depending on the size of the leaf of the green, but any more than 1¼ to 1½ hours is too much. When purchasing collards, get the smaller green leaves and thinner stalks. Select collards that are still attached to their stalks, and you can better determine if the collards are young and tender. Also, do not drown them. Use only enough water to cover the greens once they are cooked down.

    5 cups water
    4 large smoked turkey wings
    1 large onion, peeled and quartered
    1 bunch collard greens, leaves quartered, stems removed
        and discarded
    1 jalapeño pepper, seeded and diced
        (wear rubber gloves)
    2 teaspoons salt

**3 vegetable bouillon cubes**
**¼ teaspoon cayenne pepper**
**1 tablespoon apple cider vinegar**
**Salt**

1.  In large stockpot, bring water with turkey and onion to a boil. Simmer for 30 minutes.

2.  While turkey is cooking, remove stems from greens, cut leaves into 2-inch strips, and wash in cold water. Place greens, jalapeño, salt, bouillon cubes, cayenne, and apple cider vinegar in pot with turkey. Bring to a boil, then simmer 1 to 1½ hours or until greens are tender but not too soft. Stir and toss occasionally. Season with salt to taste.

Makes 4 servings.

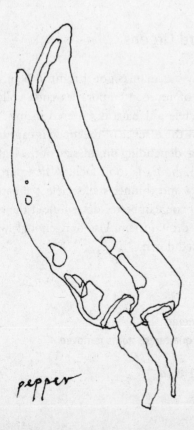

pepper

# A Plate Full of Love

*smell cornbread dressing*
*Thanksgiving aroma*
*a plateful of love*

## Cornbread Rice Dressing

In our family, cornbread dressing and Thanksgiving go together like fish and water. And if you host Thanksgiving, you prepare both the turkey and dressing. On one Thanksgiving celebration, when my sister was the host, she did not cook the dressing. She had a beautifully golden turkey but no dressing. When time came for all to feast upon the buffet of numerous food selections, there were blank stares of confusion. My daddy, in an attempt to break the ice, announced that he had cooked brownies, and we should all eat quickly to get to his sweeties. Everybody laughed and jumped into the feast.

Preheat oven to 350 degrees

> 8 cups crumbled cornbread
> 1 stick unsalted butter, in all, softened
> 1 cup chopped onions
> 1 cup chopped celery
> 1 cup chopped parsley
> 2 large shrimp, peeled, deveined, and mashed
> ½ pound chicken livers, cooked and mashed
> 2 tablespoons sage
> 1 tablespoon thyme
> 2 cups chicken stock (see appendix A) or low-sodium
>     store-bought chicken broth
> 2 cups white rice, cooked
> 1 teaspoon salt
> 1 teaspoon pepper

1. Place cornbread in large mixing bowl. Set aside.

2. Melt 2 tablespoons of the butter in saucepan over medium heat, and sauté onions, celery, and parsley, cooking about 2 minutes. Add shrimp, and sauté 2 minutes. Remove from heat and pour into cornbread. Add livers, sage and thyme, and stir well. Add stock, rice, and remaining butter, and mix well. Season with salt and pepper.

3. Pour cornbread mixture into greased medium sized baking pan. Bake until done, about 1 hour.

Makes 8–10 servings.

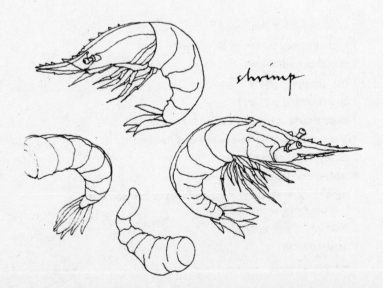

shrimp

# Wherefore Do You Lie upon Me

Wherefore do you lie upon me
when I seek warmth
a delicate embrace
a hot kiss
some satisfaction
and you bring a cold slaw
and dare not I question your intent
for you know I am a vex
and want always to be fixed
with that that you giveth me
your gum bo
your turtle
soup
your goose
how, I pray, can a cold slaw
engage my intimacy
of your spiced epicurean delights
catfish
you say catfish
I didn't see catfish
why didn't you tell me
catfish was here
is it cooked
is it hot
and mashed potatoes
you say
with lots of butter
and cream
you say
Wherefore do you lie upon me

# Southern Coleslaw

For me, most cold foods, like coleslaw, are not sexy. But when served next to hotties, like catfish, coleslaw takes on a totally new role. The accompaniment of the cool flavored coleslaw with the steamy hot fried catfish creates a yin-yang experience. The coleslaw has now moved into the arena of assisting in the potential seduction of anybody eating this food combination. Believe me.

> 1 small cabbage, shredded
> 2 medium carrots, shredded
> ¾ cup dill relish
> ⅛ cup chopped onions
> 1 cup mayonnaise
> ½ teaspoon salt
> ½ teaspoon pepper

1. Mix all ingredients in large mixing bowl, and keep covered in refrigerator until ready to serve.

Makes 4 servings.

onion, peppers

# In My Bowl

*In my bowl*
> *sauced and spiced tonight*
> *al dente to the bite*
> *a God gift mighty sight*
> *you come to me forthright*
> *ready to incite*
> *and stimulate me outright*
> *wetting my appetite*
> *increasing my Fahrenheit*

*In my bowl*
> *shaped just right*
> *quick to ignite*
> *to last all night*
> *pleasantly firm skintight*
> *quite right*
> *hug me tight*
> *you are my knight*
> *I'm ready to unite*

## Parmesan Penne Pasta

There are hundreds of shapes, sizes, thicknesses, and colors of pasta. Most can be cooked properly with this simple recipe. Remember always to pour a little oil and pinch of salt in your pot of boiling water to cook the pasta. This prevents pasta from sticking together. And when cooked, drain and toss with olive oil and Parmesan—do not rinse pasta. Imported dried pasta is made with semolina, a durum wheat flour. It is reported that pasta made of semolina does not absorb much water and therefore when cooked properly, achieves a pleasant, firm bite—al dente.

**TO MAKE PASTA:**
1 teaspoon salt, in all
4 tablespoons olive oil, in all
1 1-pound bag pasta
2 tablespoons grated Parmesan

1.  To a large pot of boiling water, add ½ teaspoon salt and 2 tablespoons of the olive oil. Add pasta and stir; cook until al dente, according to package directions. Drain, drizzle with remaining olive oil, and season with remaining salt to taste. Stir in Parmesan.

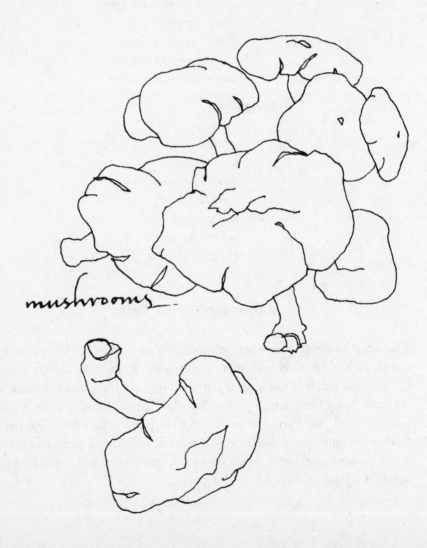

mushrooms

# *Nice*

My dear sweetheart—

I offer you all that may satisfy you at this time and pray you seek no further desires. Not that I wish your desires were not consummated. But I wish your desires were consummated with my offerings and me for now. I know that I cannot serve all your pleasures. I know that it is without malice that your cravings may turn elsewhere. For who wants a temperate love each day? Hot and wild, I know, is exciting and can surely offer dreams of seduction. I can even admit to having such dreams. I can admit to wanting such lust. Hot lust, yes, is most desirable, especially when you are without the heat of the heart. But I do have a heart. Not hearts of artichoke, but I do have devoted olives, irresistible capers, beloved tomatoes, and luscious tuna. I have all the makings of a warm heart, but it is just chilled. A chilled heart is good here. It is chilled for the worth of the moment with you. Yes, I am not a hottie. But I am Nice.

Loving you always,
*Nice*

Dear Nice—
You are.

Wanting you for now,
*Craving*

## Salad Niçoise

Niçoise, meaning "as prepared in Nice," is a French Riviera classic salad. Because of its numerous bold ingredients, it can be served as a main course on a nice summer day. This salad is even tastier when you season each ingredient as you assemble it. Don't rely on the vinaigrette to seep down into and around your salad to deliver the well-balanced flavoring this salad requires.

FOR THE VINAIGRETTE:

¼ cup lemon juice

¼ cup extra-virgin olive oil

1 small shallot, minced

1 teaspoon chopped fresh thyme

1 teaspoon chopped fresh parsley

½ teaspoon yellow mustard

Salt and pepper

FOR THE SALAD:

2 small russet potatoes, peeled

½ cup vinaigrette

Salt

14 French beans, blanched (see p. 57)

2 cups ice-cold water

1 head Boston lettuce, torn into bite-size pieces

1 4-ounce can tuna in olive oil, drained, separated into chunks

1 medium vine-ripened tomato, cored and cut into eighths

½ small red onion, thinly sliced

10 black olives, pitted

1 tablespoon capers

2 hard-boiled eggs, peeled and quartered lengthwise

1. *To prepare the vinaigrette:* Whisk together all ingredients in small bowl. Season with salt and pepper to taste. Set aside.

2. *To make the salad:* Cook potatoes in boiling salted water until tender and easily pierced with fork; about 10 minutes. Drain and then cut into bite-size pieces. Toss with 1 teaspoon of the vinaigrette, and salt to taste. Put aside.

3. Blanch beans in salted boiling water until al dente; then place in ice-cold water to cool. Drain and toss with 1 teaspoon vinaigrette, and salt to taste. Put aside.

4. Toss lettuce with 1 tablespoon vinaigrette. Salt to taste and place on serving platter. Attractively scatter tuna, potatoes, beans, tomatoes, onions, olives, and capers over lettuce. Pour remaining vinaigrette over salad and surround salad with egg wedges.

Makes 4 servings.

# *My Momma Told Me About You*

My mommy told me about you. She said you were the reliable one. She said you were the consistent one. She said. My mommy said you didn't need much to be appealing. She said you were happy all by yourself. My mommy likes you. He's good, she said. He's good for you, she said. I usually let my mommy talk. I let her go on and on. I'm not in it, I say. But I was young, then. Now I'm grown. My mommy, I have come to learn, was wise. My Sunday evenings aren't complete without you on my plate. When I see you, I know I'll be fed well. When I see you, I know I'll not long for much else. When I see you, I know you'll satisfy my hunger for something full and smooth in my mouth—something well seasoned, tasteful, and comforting. How would I reply to my momma now? With a smile.

## Potato Salad

When Hurricane Katrina hit, we had New Orleans friends come stay with us. We were so happy to provide them with food and some comfort. Kalamu's son, Tuta, his wife, Keisha, and their smart and delightful children, Logan, Amara, Hasani, and Tejan shared a meal of Ed's gumbo, potato salad, collard greens, sweet potatoes, roast chicken, corn, and cornbread with delicious lemonade prepared to perfection by the children. Upon coming to the table after placing all the food for a serve-yourself dinner, I noticed the children placing potato salad next to the rice on top of their gumbo. I ran to get salad plates for their potato salad. They looked at me, puzzled. I said, "I'm so sorry. Here is a plate for the potato salad." They smiled and said, "Oh no, this is the way we eat our potato salad with our gumbo, yeah."

> 6 medium russet potatoes, peeled and cut bite-size
> 4 eggs, boiled
> 1 celery stalk, diced
> ½ small green bell pepper, diced
> ¼ cup sliced green onions

1 8-ounce jar dill pickle relish
1 3-ounce jar pimientos, diced
½ cup mayonnaise
1 tablespoon yellow mustard
½ teaspoon cayenne pepper
½ teaspoon pepper
1 teaspoon salt

1. Boil potatoes and eggs until potatoes are tender but not broken, about 20 minutes. Drain and place in a large bowl. Peel eggs. Dice eggs and add to potatoes. Add remaining ingredients, and stir until well blended. Cover with plastic wrap, and refrigerate to chill completely before serving.

Makes 6 servings.

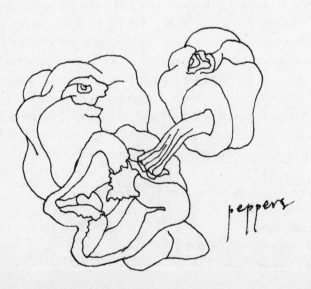

peppers

# CHAPTER SIX

# Delectable Desserts

*So smooth so firm*
*so direct and exact*
*that I quite openly blush*
*when near you appear*
*and come my dear*
*snugly into my tush*

—BANANA PUDDING,
"I KNOW THE SWEETNESS OF YOUR BANANA"

**RECIPES:**

"I Remembered You This Morning" / Chocolate Mousse

"I Know the Sweetness of Your Banana" / Banana Pudding

"It Is Night Again" / Coconut Pound Cake

"One Single Kiss" / Apple Tarte Tatin

"Sweet, Oh So Sweet" / Sweet Potato Pecan Pie

"You Were a Bit Chilly Last Night" / Lemon Mousse

"If I Could Separate the Head" / Pecan Praline Pound Cake

"You Perfumed My Lips" / Chocolate Walnut Pound Cake with
    Chocolate Ganache

"The Sounds of Pleasure" / New Orleans Bread Pudding with
    Brandy Sauce

"Beat Me Tenderly 'Til I'm Soft and Wet" / Cheesecake with Fresh
    Strawberries

"Gimmesome Mo'" / Very Berry Mascarpone Cream Tart
"You Red Velvet So-and-So" / Red Velvet Cake
"It's the Kiss" / Strawberries in Champagne Sabayon
"The Chocolate The Chocolate" / Chocolate Walnut Brownies
"Pursuit of Happiness" / Chocolate Chunk Pecan Cookies

# *I Remembered You This Morning*

Dear Moussey—

I remembered you this morning. You are still truly always on my mind. And I wish desperately for your return. For I know how wonderful life is with you. And I wonder why have I not come your way again. Can we flirt with the possibility again? Can we move toward that sweet love again? Miss you, yes, I miss you with all my yearning of pleasure, with all my moments of exodus missed. Imprisoned passion possesses me even now as I think of you. For though you were always cold, you were always sweet. I miss you dearly, but you have obviously chilled in my absence. I hope, though, that our love once cherished has not dissolved. Because I am most desirous of your praise and pray that time has not yet eroded your memory of me. For I remember your dark smooth round top expanding and then effortlessly melting in my mouth. I remember how you came into me and made me full with your chocolate froth. I remember how you enraptured me with your bittersweet flavors. I remember sucking the spoon you came on and how the first and last licks were most gratifying. Please, I beg of you, remember me, too.

*Yearningly yours*

Dear Yearning—

Each time the refrigerator door opens, I turn and hope to see you. For you were most gentle with me, and this I must have in order to survive. You indulged me. You shaved mounds of chocolate into my bowl. You folded me over with good butter in a warm water bath bed. You used the best vanilla extract with Madagascar Bourbon in my concoction. Remember you? How can I forget? I am me because of you. Were it not for you, I would be scattered about in egg cartons and butter sticks and chocolate wraps and sugar canisters. You brought me together. Through heat and high water, you whisked and you whipped and you folded me, giving form to my life. You increased my character. You restorest my froth. My soufflé cup runneth over. Surely, goodness and flavor shall follow me all the days of my life, and I shall dwell in full volume from your love forever and ever.

*Forever Moussey*

# Chocolate Mousse

This rich, airy, chocolate dish is simple, quick, and delightful. Because of its simplicity and elegance, it is one of the most popular desserts in the United States. Your more classic mousse calls for more egg yolks and whites. I worked against that because I do not like the thought of eating raw eggs in my desserts. So I developed this recipe with the minimum eggs necessary to create a mousse. I also cook the egg by stirring it in the hot chocolate mixture. And I use whipped cream instead of whipping egg whites to make it the moussey mousse it should be.

>   1 cup chopped semisweet chocolate
>   1 tablespoon butter
>   1 egg yolk
>   1 tablespoon Grand Marnier
>   1 cup heavy cream
>   2 tablespoons sugar
>   2 egg whites
>   Pinch of salt

1.  Soften chocolate in metal bowl over a saucepan of simmering water. Add butter and stir to melt chocolate and butter. Remove from heat and stir in egg yolk. Add Grand Marnier and stir. Set aside.

2.  Using electric mixer, whip cream until it forms soft peaks. Add sugar gradually and whip until stiff.

3.  In another bowl, beat egg whites until they form soft peaks. Fold egg whites into cream.

4.  Whisk ⅓ of cream mixture into chocolate mixture. Add pinch of salt. Fold in remaining cream mixture into chocolate until thoroughly mixed.

5.  Pour into dessert cups. Cover with plastic wrap and refrigerate at least 2 hours to set. Serve chilled.

Makes 2 servings.

# *I Know the Sweetness of Your Banana*

Oh how I know the sweetness
of your banana
when ripened from the bush
you peel so easily
with grace and speed
to reveal an oblong husk

So smooth so firm
so direct and exact
that I quite openly blush
when near you appear
and come my dear
snugly into my tush

wait wait
too soon
not this
not yet
I know the sweetness
to come

I wish to prolong
this sweet come-on
don't want to hear the hush
for if I enclose tight
my sweet honey fig might
surely turn you into mush

## Banana Pudding

Bananas are a perfect erotic fruit. I'm sure the apple story is wrong. It surely must have been the banana that Eve offered to Adam. Its shape arouses thoughts of sexual encounters. The unpeeling of a banana makes me sweat.

Its firm yet tender texture conjures up fantasies of full-mouth succulence. To ripen your banana, keep uncovered at room temperature. For speedy ripening, enclose it in a brown paper bag.

>   1 cup milk
>   1 8-ounce can condensed milk
>   ½ cup plus 1 tablespoon sugar, in all
>   3 egg yolks
>   1 tablespoon cornstarch
>   1 tablespoon flour
>   ¼ teaspoon vanilla extract
>   1 cup heavy cream
>   10 ripe bananas
>   1 12-ounce box of vanilla wafers

**TO PREPARE CUSTARD:**

1.  Over medium-low heat, scald the milk and condensed milk and ½ cup sugar in medium saucepan.

2.  In separate bowl, beat egg yolks until thick. Add 1 tablespoon sugar, cornstarch, and flour, and whisk until well blended.

3.  Pour ¼ of hot milk mixture into egg yolks, and whisk quickly to prevent eggs from cooking.

4.  Pour half of milk mixture into egg yolks, and whisk. Then pour all the egg mixture into the hot milk mixture, and add vanilla. Whisk briskly and constantly while bringing to boil. Cook until mixture becomes very thick, about 4 minutes. Remove from heat. Strain into clean bowl. Add cream and blend well.

**TO ASSEMBLE THE BANANA PUDDING:**

5.  In medium glass bowl, alternately layer sliced bananas and vanilla wafers. Cover each layer with custard and repeat to at least 3 to 4 layers, ending with custard. Allow to cool before covering with plastic wrap; refrigerate to cool completely before serving.

Makes 6 servings.

# It Is Night Again

It is night again
and the brightness of your
snow white coconut
is the only light I see.

It is night again
and the warm sweet milk
of your creation
is the only warmth I seek.

I find you
in the mist of my dreams
floating in coconut flakes
just above my brow.

I find you
in the dark, quiet, still moments
of the night
reaching for that last bite.

I find you
in very private moments of pleasure
eating your soft flakes
with crunchy sweetness

It is night again
as you bless me with your
presence of slow cream
cheese frosting
that oozes from your outer body.

It is night again
and I know that you have touched me
and awakened me to your
sweet love once again.

# Coconut Pound Cake

I really don't understand why some cake lovers dislike coconut. I have asked them why. They can't seem to articulate a clear reason. The closest I have heard is that it is the texture of coconut that they seem to dislike. I still don't quite understand. But I have turned some disbelievers into believers. Not to boast, but once they've eaten my coconut cake, their disillusions fade. One trick to making store-bought coconut flakes more palatable is to sprinkle and toss them with water until the flakes are moister and more flavorful.

Preheat oven to 325 degrees.

FOR THE POUND CAKE:

2½ cups sugar

16 tablespoons (2 sticks) unsalted butter

3 ounces good white chocolate, melted

6 eggs (place whole eggs in a bowl of warm water until use)

3 cups flour, all-purpose unbleached

½ teaspoon baking power

½ teaspoon salt

¾ cup milk, room temperature

1 teaspoon pure vanilla extract with Madagascar Bourbon
     (see note at end of recipe)

1 teaspoon coconut extract

⅛ teaspoon pure almond extract

½ cup fresh coconut flakes


FOR THE COCONUT FROSTING:

8 ounces cream cheese

5 cups powdered sugar

1 14-ounce bag coconut flakes, sweetened

1 tablespoon milk

2–3 tablespoons water to sprinkle on coconut flakes

Special equipment: 10-inch Bundt pan

1.  *To prepare the pound cake:* Combine sugar and butter in large mixing bowl, and mix in electric mixer until creamy, about 20 minutes. Add melted white chocolate and mix to blend. Mix in eggs one at a time.

2.  In a medium bowl, sift together flour, baking powder, and salt, and set aside.

3.  Alternately add portions of one quarter flour mixture and one third of milk to the sugar mixture. Start and end with flour. Repeat about 4 times. Mix well, but do not overmix. Overmixing makes the cake tough.

4.  Add vanilla, coconut, and almond extracts, and briefly mix. Remove mixing bowl from mixer, and fold in coconut flakes.

5.  Butter and lightly flour Bundt cake pan. Pour cake mixture into pan. Bake about 1 hour and 15 to 20 minutes. Test for doneness with a skewer inserted into cake. If it comes out clean, cake is done. Also, if cake begins to pull away from edges of pan, cake is done. Remove from oven, and place pan on rack to cool. After 10 minutes, remove cake from pan and turn cake upside down on rack, and continue to cool.

6.  Let cool completely before frosting.

7.  *To prepare the frosting:* In blender, mix cream cheese to soften. Add powdered sugar and mix until smooth. Add 1 tablespoon milk and mix.

8.  With a metal spatula, spread frosting over cooled cake.

9.  In separate bowl, mix coconut flakes with sprinkles of water, and, using hands, mix well. Using your hands, pat coconut over frosted cake to cover completely.

Makes 10–12 servings.

*Note:* I use Nielsen-Massey's Pure Vanilla Extract with Madagascar Bourbon (to order, see appendix B).

# One Single Kiss

They eloped, all of them, underneath a blanket of cinnamon
    piecrust, each comforting the other with overlapping embraces
    and smiles of complicity.
How many?
One dozen, plus two.
Breast-plump golden delicious apples sliced in crescent shapes.

"We're not going back," they said.
Hard core was not for them.
For now, they were soft as wet lips and light as a dream.
As the first to escape caramelized in a low simmer to a dark
    golden sweet glaze, the lucky ones lay on top to consummate
    the rendezvous by thickening and receiving the juice as
    it flowed upward and inward.

"We've had enough. Never will we be separated again," they said,
bringing with them fantasies that would not even let them sleep.
All of them tightly packed, hugging each other in a black cast-iron
    skillet
of sizzling butter and sparkles of crystallized sugar crying out,
"When we kissed, we but only kissed."

But with every sugary bubble between them, they would slide
    and steal yet another kiss
and who knows what else, as they continued to caramelize to seal
    their fate.
Their love's not secret now.
For once again, love shakes the skillet
and the near halves are now whole
and they are now but one single kiss.

# Apple Tarte Tatin

This upside-down tart was made famous by two French sisters named Tatin who ran a hotel-restaurant in Lamotte-Beuvron, France, in the early twentieth century. The juices of the apples caramelize when cooked in butter under a sweet pastry crust and are then served with the pastry underneath and overlapping caramelized apples on top. This recipe is delicious when served with a rich vanilla ice cream.

**FOR THE DOUGH:**
¾ cup flour
3 tablespoons cold unsalted butter, cut into 3 pieces
½ teaspoon sugar
⅛ teaspoon salt
¼ cup ice-cold water

**FOR THE FILLING:**
8 medium Golden Delicious apples, peeled and cored
¼ cup lemon juice
3 tablespoons unsalted butter
1 cup sugar
¾ teaspoon ground cinnamon
¼ cup powered sugar

1. *To make the dough:* Into food processor, put the flour, butter, sugar, and salt. Mix quickly until the mixture is the consistency of meal. Pour cold water through the tube while processor is on. Mix until dough rolls into a ball. Remove and pat briefly into round flat ball. Wrap in plastic wrap and refrigerate for at least 30 minutes. After first 15 minutes, preheat oven to 425 degrees.

2. *To make the filling:* Peel and core apples. Cut apples in half and then into 8 slices lengthwise. Place in bowl and toss in half the lemon juice.

3. Melt butter in 9-inch ovenproof skillet over low heat, and stir in sugar evenly. Remove from heat, and place half the apple slices in skillet, laying each slice tightly against the other in a spiral circle from the outer edge to the middle of the skillet.

4. Toss remaining apples with lemon juice, and repeat the placing of these slices on top of apples in the skillet. Return to heat, and simmer 30 minutes until juices are thickened and golden. Remove from pan and set aside 5 minutes. Sprinkle with cinnamon.

5. *To assemble the pie:* Remove dough from refrigerator. On lightly floured surface, roll dough into a 10-inch circle (1 inch wider than diameter of skillet).

6. Lay dough over apples in skillet. Press edges of dough down the inside sides of skillet. Use fork to prick 4 small holes into dough to allow cooking steam to escape.

7. Place skillet in oven and bake 25 minutes or until crust is golden brown. Remove from oven and let cool 5 minutes. Invert skillet onto an oven-proof dish, sprinkle with powdered sugar, and place tart 2 to 3 inches under a moderately hot broiler for about 3 minutes to caramelize top. Remove from oven.

Makes 6–8 servings.

# Sweet, Oh So Sweet

*You open me up when you press your nuts against my spoon*
*sweet, oh so sweet potato pecan pie.*
*Would you, could you press harder*
*sweet, oh so sweet potato pecan pie.*
*Press in slightly harder even more*
*sweet, oh so sweet potato pecan pie.*
*Sometimes I can't receive all of you at once*
*sweet, oh so sweet potato pecan pie.*
*As I scoop both the pecan topping and sweet potato filling*
*sweet, oh so sweet potato pecan pie.*
*For you are hot and hard and soft and wet*
*sweet, oh so sweet potato pecan pie.*
*Your flowing syrup now caramelized coats your head of dough*
*sweet, oh so sweet potato pecan pie.*
*While your soft moist sweet potatoes hug the lips of my mouth*
*sweet, oh so sweet potato pecan pie.*
*And your pecans float to the top, thinly veiled with a wet*
   *sugar skin*
*sweet, oh so sweet potato pecan pie.*
*Now cooked to a crisp head, now nuts of sweet gender*
*sweet, oh so sweet potato pecan pie.*
*No longer can I see you outside of me*
*sweet, oh so sweet potato pecan pie.*
*Inside, you, me,*
*sweet, oh so sweet potato pecan pie.*

## Sweet Potato Pecan Pie

The natural sweetness of sweet potatoes should never be overwhelmed by sugar or spices. You want to taste sweet potatoes, not nutmeg and sugar. So avoid overspicing and sweetening the sweet potato filling. Remember, also, the pecan topping is an overkill of sweetness with syrup and sugar. This will seep into the sweet potato filling to intensify further the sweetness of this most sweet pie.

Preheat oven to 450 degrees.

4 teaspoons vegetable oil
2 medium sweet potatoes, baked (yield about 2 cups)

FOR THE DOUGH:
¾ cup flour
3 tablespoons unsalted butter, cut into 3 pieces
½ teaspoon sugar
⅛ teaspoon salt
¼ cup ice-cold water

FOR THE SWEET POTATO FILING:
2 cups sweet potatoes, prepared
1 small egg, beaten well
⅓ cup light brown sugar
1 tablespoon sugar
¼ teaspoon salt
2 tablespoons heavy cream
2 tablespoons butter, melted
1 teaspoon pure vanilla extract with Madagascar Bourbon (see
    note at end of recipe)
½ teaspoon cinnamon
⅛ teaspoon ground nutmeg

FOR THE PECAN PIE SYRUP:
½ cup sugar
½ cup light corn syrup
2 tablespoons unsalted butter, melted
1 teaspoon pure vanilla extract
⅛ teaspoon cinnamon
Pinch of salt
1 small egg
1 cup pecan halves

Special equipment: Parchment paper; dry beans as pie weights

1. Rub sweet potatoes with oil, and bake them for 30–40 minutes or until they are soft.

2. Remove potatoes from oven, let cool. Cut lengthwise and scoop out pulp, place in bowl, and set aside.

3. *To prepare the dough:* In food processor, put flour, butter, sugar, and salt. Mix dough quickly until it is the consistency of meal. Pour cold water through the tube while processor is on. Mix until dough rolls into a ball. Remove and pat briefly into a round. Wrap in plastic wrap and refrigerate for at least 20 minutes. Remove dough from refrigerator, and roll on flour-dusted surface into a 10-inch circle. Place in 9-inch pie pan and shape dough to pan. Let rest 15 minutes in refrigerator. Lower heat to 325 degrees. Remove from refrigerator. Blind bake dough. Cover inside of pan with parchment paper, and fill with dry beans. Bake about 10 to 15 minutes. Remove parchment with beans and continue to bake dough 5 minutes.

4. *To prepare the sweet potato filling:* Mix all sweet potato filling ingredients in an electric mixer, and beat at medium speed about 5 minutes or until mixture is smooth.

5. *To prepare the pecan pie syrup:* Combine sugar, corn syrup, and butter in medium mixing bowl, and mix slowly, about 3 minutes. Remove from mixer; add vanilla, cinnamon, and salt, and stir. In another bowl, briefly whisk egg. Slowly add syrup mixture into egg, stirring constantly. Fold in pecans.

6. Spoon sweet potato filling into slightly cooked piecrust pan. Pour pecan syrup on top of sweet potatoes. Bake about 1 hour and 20 minutes. Let cool. Slice to serve.

Makes 1 9-inch pie.

*Note:* I use Nielsen-Massey's Pure Vanilla Extract with Madagascar Bourbon (to order see appendix B).

# *You Were a Bit Chilly Last Night*

My Dearest Moussey—

You were a bit chilly last night. I didn't mean to overwhip you. Was that the reason? Or did I leave you alone too long to chill? I had hoped to meet with you sooner. Maybe your stiffness would never have been created if I had but stepped away sooner. I thought my absence would have caused a longing that I desired and hoped for from you, for I do indeed desire you, even though you are a bit bitter with your lemony tang. You woo me. You soothe me. I admit. But your bitter side frightens me, for I fear you will forsake me. Please write.

Forever yours,
*Whippier*

My Dear Whippier—

I'll never be warm to you again. You have whipped me much too long. Your whipping technique is inept and boring and causes me to lose my glossy full body. If you ever want me to swell and become full and smooth for you, you'll have to learn the true loving whipping method, and while you're at it, learn to fold.

Once was yours,
*Moussey*

P.S. Don't be so cheap. Buy a copper bowl.

## Lemon Mousse

Fluffy, foamy, frothy, let me be there. Love must be close by. I can even see it in the air floating like sweet clouds just above me. Mousse—just saying it creates a kiss. All you need is a partner to say it with you. But unlike the desire for a warm-hearted lover, cool is cool for whipping cream. Chill your mixing bowl and beaters in freezer at least 20 minutes before whipping the cream. This helps to bring your cream to a smooth, thick, glossy foam and stabilize its peaks. You have overwhipped if its shine becomes dull. The same goes for any warmhearted lover.

> ½ tablespoon lemon zest
> ½ cup fresh lemon juice (about 4 large lemons)
> 1 cup sugar
> 4 egg yolks
> 1 whole egg
> Pinch of salt
> 8 tablespoons unsalted butter, cut into pieces
> 1 large bowl ice and water
> 1 cup heavy cream, chilled

1. Place lemon zest and juice, sugar, yolks, whole egg, and pinch of salt in glass bowl, and whisk to combine. Pour into a nonreactive saucepan. Add butter and cook over medium-low heat. Stir constantly with wooden spoon. Cook until lemon curd thickens, about 10 minutes.

2. Strain curd into glass bowl. Set bowl in an ice bath to cool, about 15 minutes. Stir occasionally. Remove glass bowl from ice bath. Cover curd with plastic wrap. Refrigerate 1 hour.

3. Pour cream into a chilled mixing bowl. With electric mixer, whip cream to soft but firm peaks. Fold curd into cream. Pour into wine glasses. Cover and refrigerate at least 4 hours.

Makes 4 servings.

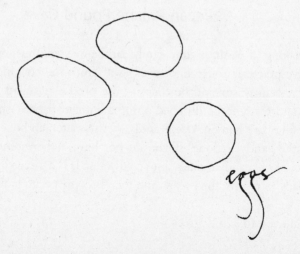

eggs

# *If I Could Separate the Head*

*Your head keeps me coming back*
*It's hard and good and that's a fact*
*No reason to justify the rest of the cake*
*Just let me at your head for god sake*

*Your nuts are nice, too*
*Too few but they'll do*
*I love nuts in clusters not few*
*But I'll take your nuts and that head, oh god, too*

*The cake, oh the cake it's OK*
*The perfect cake to share with two*
*All sweet and moist and texture tender*
*But I've passed it up every time for that gender*

*Sweet no sweeter delicious praline candy*
*Lay hard on his cake making it worth the wait*
*If I could separate the sweet candy head and walk away*
*That's exactly what I'd do every day*

## Pecan Praline Pound Cake

The making of pecan praline candy can be mastered by anyone. It just takes attentive practice. You cannot walk away from the cooking of pralines. You must constantly stir and be there at the precise moment when it becomes candy and ready to be dropped onto parchment paper—spoonfuls at a time just before they harden. Use a candy thermometer, and once it reads 240 degrees, the candy is done. If you do not have a thermometer, drop a small amount of the candy mixture into cold water. If it hardens into a ball, it's done and ready to receive the pecans and then become pecan pralines.

Preheat oven to 325 degrees.

FOR THE PECAN PRALINE CANDY:

2 cups sugar

1 cup brown sugar

3 tablespoons light syrup

1 cup condensed milk

2 tablespoons unsalted butter, in all

1 teaspoon pure vanilla extract

2 cups pecan halves

FOR THE CAKE:

2½ cups sugar

2 sticks unsalted butter

6 eggs (place whole eggs in bowl of warm water to remove chill)

3 cups flour, all-purpose unbleached flour

½ teaspoon baking powder

½ teaspoon salt

¾ cup milk, at room temperature

1 teaspoon pure vanilla extract with Madagascar Bourbon
(see note end of recipe)

Special equipment: 10-inch Bundt pan; parchment paper

1. *To prepare the pecan praline candy:* Stir white and brown sugars, syrup, and milk in a medium heavy-duty saucepan over high heat, stirring constantly until you begin to see boiling bubbles, 1–2 minutes.

2. Add 1 tablespoon of the butter and continue stirring. Cook about 8 minutes, or until candy thermometer reads 240 degrees.

3. Remove from heat. Add remaining 1 tablespoon butter, and stir rapidly, counting to 100. Quickly add vanilla extract and pecans, and continue to stir.

4. Quickly pour onto parchment paper on a cookie sheet, and spread out to a thin layer. Let cool to harden.

5. *To prepare the cake:* Butter and lightly flour a Bundt pan. Line bottom of pan with parchment paper. Set aside. Mix sugar and butter for 20 minutes in large mixing bowl with electric mixer. Add eggs one at a time while mixer is running.

6. Sift flour with baking powder and salt into a medium bowl. Alternately add about ¼ of flour mixture, and mix well. Add ⅓ of milk, mix well, beginning and ending with flour. Add vanilla and mix briefly. Remove mixing bowl from stand.

7. Place single layer of praline candy pieces on top of parchment in prepared pan.

8. Pour cake batter on top of pecan praline candy in pan.

9. Bake for 1 hour and 20 minutes. Test doneness with skewer inserted in middle of cake after 1 hour and 20 minutes. If skewer comes out dry, cake is done. Also, if cake pulls away from edges of pan, cake is done. Remove from oven, and place on wire rack to cool, about 20 minutes.

10. Set cake on countertop with cake pan tube up. Use knife to release candy from edge of the pan. Slide knife between bottom of tube and bottom of body of pan. When loosened, remove tube from body of pan. With bottom of tube sitting on a wooden board, slide knife between parchment paper and bottom of tube. When loosened, place plate on top of cake and turn cake upside down. Parchment paper will be on top of cake. Allow to cool.

11. Gently remove the parchment from candy on top of cake. When ready to slice cake, turn cake upside down onto serving plate with praline candy on bottom, and slice to keep candy from cracking. When serving, have praline candy on top.

Makes 10 servings.

*Note:* I use Nielsen-Massey Pure Vanilla Extract with Madagascar Bourbon (to order see appendix B).

# You Perfumed My Lips

*You perfumed my lips*
*with your deep dark ganache*
*with smears of thick glossy chocolate*
*dripping down the corners of my mouth.*

*You expand there*
*as I gather all parts of you*
*that suddenly spread beneath my tongue*
*then over to coat me completely.*

*You sweeten me always*
*with your moist texture*
*saturated with cocoa,*
*chocolate, sugar, and butter.*

*You move still, oh so still*
*within me*
*like milk flowing*
*through a black hole*
*as I endlessly consume your pleasure.*

*You arouse me*
*with your abundant nuts*
*that replenish my desire*
*for a craving that aches hard.*

*You relax me*
*as in an opium moment*
*causing me to be intoxicated by you*
*and see the world disappear*
*with your taste only remaining.*

# Chocolate Walnut Pound Cake with Chocolate Ganache

As a cake baker, I have sold cakes to many coffeehouses, restaurants, law offices, and other businesses in Atlanta. A lawyer at one of the law firms often ordered cakes for her bond closings and for her home. She called me one morning to report how satisfying the cakes were and that she had some left over and had taken it home. Upon returning home the next day, she saw pieces of cake on the floor and walked into her kitchen to see her dog devouring the remains of the cake. She said she felt so ashamed that her thoughts were not with getting her dog away from the cake, but with thinking that there was no more cake.

Preheat oven to 325 degrees.

**FOR THE POUND CAKE:**

1½ sticks unsalted butter

3½ cups sugar

¾ cup vegetable oil

2 ounces good bittersweet dark chocolate, melted

2 teaspoons pure vanilla extract

5 eggs

3 cups flour, all-purpose unbleached flour

1 teaspoon baking powder

1 teaspoon salt

½ teaspoon baking soda

1 cup Dutch-processed cocoa powder

1¼ cups buttermilk plus ¼ cup water (at room temperature)

1 cup chopped walnuts

**FOR THE CHOCOLATE GANACHE:**

1 cup heavy cream

8 ounces chocolate, chopped

Special equipment: 10-inch Bundt pan

1. *To prepare the pound cake:* Butter and lightly flour cake pan. In large electric mixing bowl, mix butter and sugar 10 minutes. Gradually pour in oil

and beat until light and fluffy. Continue to mix 10 minutes, scraping down the sides twice.

2. In microwave, melt chocolate (about 1 minute and make sure it does not burn). Pour into butter mixture. Continue mixing and add vanilla. Add eggs, one at a time.

3. In large bowl, sift together flour, baking powder, salt, baking soda, and cocoa. Combine buttermilk and water. With mixer on low speed, alternately add one-quarter flour mixture and one-third buttermilk water mixture to the batter, combining each before adding next ingredient. Start and end with flour mixture. Repeat three times.

4. Remove mixing bowl from mixer. With spatula, fold walnuts into batter. Pour batter into prepared cake pan. Bake until cake begins to separate from sides of pan or until cake is done, about 1½ hours. Test for doneness with skewer inserted in middle of cake. If it comes out dry, it's done.

5. Transfer cake pan to wire rack to cool for one hour. Turn pan upside down onto cake platter. Allow cake to cool completely before frosting.

6. *To prepare the chocolate ganache:* Heat cream to bring to boil over medium heat. Remove from heat. Pour over chocolate. Let set 5 minutes. Whisk to smooth. Pour ganache over completely cooled cake.

Makes 12 servings.

bananas

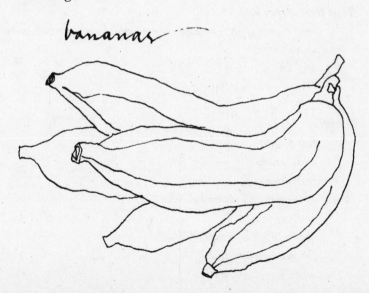

# The Sounds of Pleasure

*The sounds of pleasure at my table are*
    *"Yummmmmmm"*
    *or "ump, ump, ump"*
    *or a long dragged out melodic "g . . . i . . . r . . . l"*
    *or if he can free his mouth long enough, "Girl this some*
        *good."*
*The motions might be*
    *a slow shaking of the head from left to right*
    *head down,*
    *eyes closed,*
    *and a simultaneous scooping up of that which is being*
        *eaten,*
    *and then*
    *slowly removing the hat and placing it softly on the table.*
*Or that universal motion of*
    *shaking a foot back and forth*
    *to what must be a Stevie Wonder love song.*
*Then there is that look*
    *head turned slightly toward the food and slightly toward me*
    *at an angle*
    *and I might hear*
    *"Why you do me this way?"*
    *I like that.*
*Sometimes I get*
    *just a smile*
    *and I know*
    *it is a smile*
    *of comfort and joy and delight*
    *at being fed*
    *that which has brought pleasure*
    *for that moment in his life*
    *and that—I really like.*

## New Orleans Bread Pudding with Brandy Sauce

The key to this bread pudding is to get a good-tasting loaf of French bread. It does not have to be stale. It can be fresh. Slice the loaf down the middle lengthwise and then slice the halves again down the middle lengthwise. Then slice across to create bite-size cubes. Another key is to add condensed milk to the milk mixture. It adds a sweeter taste to the custard. Just before you pour the warm milk mixture over the cubed bread with raisins and pecans, make sure the top layer is the brown crust of the french bread. Also make sure enough raisins and pecans are in sight. After you allow it to soak thoroughly, pour the mixture into the pan keeping the top brown crust in sight on the top. When it is cooked and you remove it from the oven, it will have a beautiful interwoven golden design.

Preheat oven to 350 degrees.

FOR THE BREAD PUDDING:

1 8-ounce can condensed milk

3 cups milk

8 tablespoons unsalted butter

1 cup sugar

1 teaspoon cinnamon

½ teaspoon nutmeg

¼ teaspoon salt

2 teaspoons pure vanilla extract with Madagascar Bourbon (see note end of recipe)

1 loaf French bread with crust, cubed (about 12 ounces)

1 cup raisins

1 cup pecan halves

4 eggs

FOR THE BRANDY SAUCE:

8 ounces cream cheese

4 cups powdered sugar

⅓ cup milk

¼ cup good brandy

Special equipment: 9×2-inch round cake pan; parchment paper to line cake pan

1. *To prepare the bread pudding:* Butter and lightly flour the cake pan, and line with parchment paper.

2. Over medium heat in saucepan, mix milk, condensed milk, butter, and sugar to soft boil, then remove from heat. Stir occasionally. Whisk in cinnamon, nutmeg, salt, and vanilla.

3. Cut bread into 1-inch cubes, and place in large bowl. Turn cubes with crust side up. Sprinkle raisins and pecans on top. Set aside 3 tablespoons milk mixture and pour remaining over bread mixture.

4. In small bowl, slightly stir eggs and then whisk with 3 tablespoons hot milk mixture to temper eggs (see note 2 at end of recipe). Pour tempered eggs over bread. Use your hands to push bread down into milk mixture. Let bread and milk mixture soak for 20 minutes, pushing down occasionally.

5. Pour bread mixture into the pan so that the top crust stays on the top. Put bread pudding in 350-degree oven, and immediately raise heat to 400 degrees. Cook 10 minutes at 400 degrees, then turn oven down to 350 degrees and bake 30 minutes. Turn oven to 400 degrees for last 5 minutes. Remove from oven.

6. Transfer pan to wire rack to cool completely. Turn pudding out by placing flat plate on top of pudding and turning upside down. Remove parchment from bottom of pudding, and turn right side up to place on serving platter.

7. *To prepare the brandy sauce:* With electric mixer, beat cream cheese until smooth. Add powdered sugar and continue mixing until smooth. Add milk and mix well. Remove mixing bowl from mixer and stir in brandy. Pour about 3 tablespoons over warm slice of bread pudding.

Makes 10 servings.

*Notes:* 1. I use Nielsen-Massey's Pure Vanilla Extract with Madagascar Bourbon (to order, see appendix B).

2. Tempering eggs blends uncooked eggs with hot liquid to prevent a scrambled-egg consistency when stirred into remaining hot mixture.

# *Beat Me Tenderly 'Til I'm Soft and Wet*

Beat me tenderly 'til I'm soft and wet
yes there yes I have no regrets
press please harder sink you into me
enter my caresses and be lost with thee

Mix 'til cream flows from my secret nest
kiss quick kiss need not make a mess
rich luscious cream swells into a dream
voluptuous waves of lust yea I do beam

Pour don't rush coat all of thee
hold me tight close 'til you lay down me
gently in your bed of a bain-marie
watch me close don't let eyes off me

I promise to stay whole if you comfort me
I promise to be sweet if you sweeten me
I promise to not split if you indulge me
just beat me tenderly 'til I'm soft and wet

## Cheesecake with Fresh Strawberries

I found that using aluminum foil to cup the pan and then placing the pan in a bain-marie helps prevent cheesecakes from splitting. A bain marie is a cooking technique, whereby you place a pan of food into a large shallow pan of warm water before cooking the food in an oven. This creates a gentle heat for delicate foods like cheesecakes.

Preheat oven to 325 degrees.

2 cups graham cracker crumbs
4 tablespoons butter, melted
2 pounds cream cheese, at room temperature

2 cups sugar

6 eggs

1 cup heavy cream

½ cup plus 1 tablespoon flour

¼ teaspoon salt

1 teaspoon pure vanilla extract with Madagascar Bourbon
(see note at end of recipe)

1 pint large fresh strawberries

¼ cup apricot preserves

Special equipment: 12-inch springform pan; large shallow pan

1. Mix graham cracker crumbs and melted butter, and press mixture into bottom of 12-inch springform pan. Cover and seal outside, bottom, and sides of pan with aluminum foil to prevent leakage, and place pan in large shallow pan containing hot water that comes about 1 inch up the sides of the cake pan. Set aside.

2. In food processor with metal blade, slice cream cheese and mix until smooth and well blended. With processor on, add sugar and mix well. Add eggs one at a time. Add cream. Add flour, salt, and vanilla, and continue processing until filling is smooth.

3. Pour filling into pan with graham cracker crumbs. Bake 1½ hours. Do not open oven door while cooking. Turn oven off, and let cheesecake remain in oven another 30 minutes. Remove from oven, and run knife around sides of pan to help cake separate from pan. Gently take pan out of water, and remove aluminum foil from pan. Place pan on wire rack to cool completely. Cover with plastic wrap without plastic touching top of cheesecake. Refrigerate overnight.

4. Remove sides of springform pan. Slide cake off bottom of pan onto a serving plate.

5. Slice large strawberries in half and place on edges of cheesecake. Warm apricot preserves to melt. Strain preserves. With baker's brush, glaze strawberries with strained preserves.

Makes 12 servings.

*Note:* I use Nielsen-Massey's Pure Vanilla Extract with Madagascar Bourbon (to order, see appendix B).

# Gimmesome Mo'

*The Dough*
> Why am I crying here
> as I knead you
> over into yourself
> pushing you back and forth
> patting you where you're roundest?
> Is it that our intimacy is but for a brief moment?
> Is it that you will depart from me at your best?
>
> Why am I crying here
> as I knead you
> into perfection
> constantly rolling and comforting you
> sprinkling flour where bubbles surface?
> Is it that you enjoy the cold marble more than my warm
>     hands?
> Is it that you have risen but must rise yet again?
>
> Why am I crying here
> as I knead you
> I soften your firmness
> slowly allowing you to enter
> my oven?
> Is it that I now have no purpose?
> Is it that you have now fully formed?
> As I knead you,
> I need you.

*The Berries*
> You leave me bruised with your seduction
> as you bear your bosomy berries
> of red, black, and blue.
> I first eat a small bite of you

*but immediately realize that you have scarred me and*
*crazily I eat more and more and more of you*
*until red, black, and blue am I*
*covered by your very berries.*
*I pause.*
*I look upon you*
*and am saturated by your delicious sweetness.*
*Berry by berry I am chained.*
*I know this*
*and seek to be locked deep in your nectar*
*for it is worth any price, any consequence.*
*'Cause the reward is oh so great*
*when love eats you.*

*The Sweet Mascarpone Cream*
*ohmygodohmygodohmygodohmygodohmygodohmygodohmygodoh*
*mygodohmygodohmy*
*ohmygodohmygodohmygodohmygodohmygodohmygodoh*
*mygodohmygodoh*
*mygodohmygodgimmesome mo'*

## Very Berry Mascarpone Cream Tart

This is a knockout luscious dessert. Watch eyes widen and smiles broaden when you bring this tart out. Always present it whole so it can be seen all dressed up piled high and lovely. Then allow your lover to slice into it and serve you. The mascarpone cream cheese underneath is so sensual, it's exciting all by itself.

Adapted from *Gourmet*, July 1998, p. 91.

FOR THE SWEET PASTRY DOUGH:
¼ cup plus 1 tablespoon butter, softened
¼ teaspoon salt
1 cup flour
¼ cup ground blanched almonds
     (see note at end of recipe)

⅓ cup powdered sugar

1 small egg

FOR THE TART FILLING:

8 ounces mascarpone cheese

4 ounces cream cheese

¼ cup heavy cream

⅓ cup sugar

1 cup small strawberries, halved

1 cup raspberries

1 cup blackberries

1 cup blueberries

1 cup green grapes

1½ tablespoons apricot preserves

1 tablespoon Grand Marnier

Special equipment: 8-inch tart pan; dry beans or rice
    as pie weights

1. *To prepare the pastry dough:* In food processor with metal blade, combine butter, salt, ¼ cup flour, ground almonds, and powdered sugar. Mix just to combine.

2. Add egg and mix briefly; then add remaining flour and mix just until dough comes together in a ball. Remove from processor and flatten into a round disk. Wrap in plastic. Chill for 1 hour.

3. Butter 8-inch tart pan. Roll pastry on well-floured surface. Roll a circle wide enough to cover tart pan. Gently fold pastry in half, lift dough into prepared pan, and unfold. Dough is fragile and may tear. Use fingers to press back together, and press into bottom and up sides of pan. Chill 30 minutes. Halfway through chilling, preheat oven to 375 degrees.

4. Remove pan from refrigerator. Place parchment paper on top of pastry, and cover with dry beans or rice to fill the pan. Bake 20 minutes. Remove parchment with beans or rice. Bake an additional 10 minutes until golden, piercing any bulges with a fork. Cool completely while preparing filling.

5. *To prepare the tart filling:* Mix mascarpone, cream cheese, heavy cream, and sugar in electric mixer until mixture holds stiff peaks. Spread evenly over cooked, cooled pie dough in pan.

6.  Combine strawberries, raspberries, blackberries, blueberries, and green grapes in bowl. In small saucepan, simmer apricot preserves and Grand Marnier about 2 minutes, then strain and allow to cool slightly. When slightly cooled, pour over fruit. Strain juice from fruit. Mound fruit on top of cream cheese in pie pan. Refrigerate 30 minutes before serving.

Makes 1 8-inch pie (6 servings).

*Note:* Put shelled almonds in a saucepan. Cover with cold water and bring to a boil. As soon as water boils, remove from heat and drain. Put almonds in bowl and cover with cold water to cool. Drain again, pat dry with paper towels, and slip skins off between thumb and forefinger. Dry almonds on paper towels. Or you can purchase blanched almonds from most grocery stores.

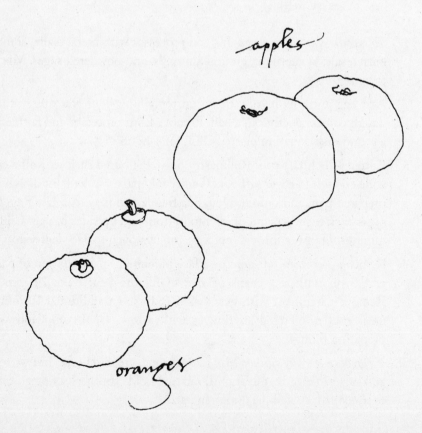

# *You Red Velvet So-and-So*

*You red velvet so–and-so*
*You come to these parties and take over.*
*everyone embraces you and*
*swarms to your plate,*
*praising your radiance,*
*reaching out for you,*
*crowding, pushing, grabbing you,*
*and you like it.*

*You strut your stuff*
*with your snow white coat of cream cheese frosting*
*that promotes your flamboyant fiery body*
*and nutty meat of pecans*
*that further induces a myth of crowning glory,*
*and you like it.*

*You think you're the queen of the South,*
*the one every Southerner knows well,*
*the one every Northerner wishes to know.*
*women and men alike think you're fabulous*
*and boast of your "oh so moist" texture,*
*and you like it.*

*I tried to put you in your place,*
*putting out other cakes that are just as worthy,*
*like the chocolate walnut with his slick dark chocolate body and*
*    heavy nuts,*
*or the cute little coconut cake with her coconut flake dimples,*
*but no, they love you.*
*leaving all others way behind*
*to gather and re-box,*
*and you like it.*

*You evoke such arousal.*
*like a hopeful sexual encounter,*
*you create excitement in the air.*
*you make dry lips wet,*
*nipples hard,*
*things spring into action,*
*and you like it.*
*We like it, too.*

## Red Velvet Cake

My sister Sylvia is a femme fatale. She wears nine-inch high heels and has Tina Turner legs that she proudly exposes in short, tight miniskirts. My younger sister, Bea, and I can't compete. During our youthful, carefree years, we frequented nightclubs as a threesome and enjoyed the single's life of sisters out to dance the night away. And even though Bea and I had a respectable number of requests to dance, it was Sylvia who had the choice to either dance or turn down every man in the club. They all approached her first and last, leaving us on the sidelines to watch and laugh at the rejects who most often turned to us as the second choice to get that quick swing on the floor. My red velvet cake at my catering events is the Sylvia of our young nightclub excursions. My catering company, Valinda's Gourmet Pounds, specialized in pound cakes, and though all my cakes were loved by all, it was the red velvet cake that was never re-boxed to return home. She was always totally devoured—with love.

Preheat oven to 350 degrees.

FOR THE CAKE:

8 tablespoons unsalted butter

3 cups sugar

1½ cups vegetable oil

2 ounces red food coloring

2 teaspoons Dutch-processed cocoa powder

2 teaspoons pure vanilla extract with Madagascar Bourbon
     (see note at end of recipe)

6 eggs (place whole eggs in a bowl of warm water until use)

3 cups flour, all-purpose unbleached

2 teaspoons baking powder

½ teaspoon salt

½ teaspoon baking soda

1 ½ cups buttermilk, room temperature

1 ½ teaspoons white vinegar

FOR THE CREAM CHEESE FROSTING:

12 ounces cream cheese

5–6 cups powdered sugar

1 teaspoon pure vanilla extract

1 to 2 tablespoons milk plus more for desired frosting consistency

1 cup chopped pecans

Special equipment: 3 10-inch round cake pans; parchment paper to line pans

1. *To prepare the cake:* Butter and lightly flour 3 12-inch round cake pans. Line with parchment.

2. In large mixing bowl, cream butter and sugar, mixing about 10 minutes. Gradually pour in oil, and beat until light and fluffy, 10 minutes, scraping down sides twice.

3. Mix red food coloring and cocoa powder in glass bowl (see note at end of recipe). Pour into butter mixture. Add vanilla. Add eggs, one at a time.

4. In large bowl, sift together flour, baking powder, salt, and baking soda. With mixer on low speed, alternately add one quarter of flour mixture and one third of buttermilk. Start and end with flour mixture. Repeat four times.

5. Remove mixing bowl from stand and fold in vinegar.

6. Divide batter evenly among the three prepared cake pans. Bake until cake begins to separate from sides of pan, about 20 to 25 minutes. Remove from oven.

7. Place pans on wire racks to cool completely, 1–1½ hours. To remove from pan, place plate over cake and turn pan upside down. Remove parchment. Turn plate right side up and place cake on flat surface to cool.

8. *To prepare the cream cheese frosting:* In bowl of electric mixer fitted with paddle attachment (or use handheld mixer), beat cream cheese on medium speed until smooth, about 3 minutes.

9. Reduce speed to low and add powdered sugar and vanilla. Beat until mixture is smooth and fluffy, about 3 minutes. Add 1 to 2 tablespoons milk and mix to make fluffy. Scrape down sides of bowl and mix another 2 minutes.

10. Reserve most attractive layer for top of cake. Clean off loose crumbs. Place one cake layer on serving platter. Spread top with about 5 ounces cream cheese frosting. Repeat with second layer. Cover top and sides with thin layer of frosting. Refrigerate cake about 10 minutes. Remove cake from refrigerator and add second layer of frosting to cover cake generously. Sprinkle top center of cake with chopped pecans.

Makes 1 12-inch 3-layer cake (12 servings).

*Notes:* 1. I use Nielsen-Massey's Pure Vanilla Extract with Madagascar Bourbon (to order, see appendix B)

2. Red food coloring stains. If possible, use glass rather than plastic utensils.

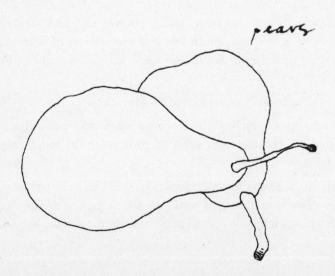

pears

# It's the Kiss

It's the kiss that leads me back to you
It's silky smooth as I remember
your kiss the good kiss
is a slow deliberate smooch
first
dry no tongue
Protruding full lips only
to meet and greet and press first
to feel me
then flatten against each lip
you release the kiss to
open mouths
still no tongue
our lips glide from side to side
to hold each other's lips at
the edge of our mouths
to then push one lip
the bottom one
slightly open
not to receive the tongue
but to feel the heat of our breath
and you pause there
then you press against my mouth
open
to drag your lip across mine
and further on across my cheeks
and take your hand and place it
softly between our mouths
to touch our full yearning lips
and appreciate the contrast between
the dry skin of our lips
and wetness of plump ready tongues

*you pull away*
*quickly*
*for a moment*
*you look at me with affection*
*you smile*
*and reach again*
*this time*
*with a voracious tongue*
*colliding*
*madly for*
*the kiss*

## Strawberries in Champagne Sabayon

Called zabaglione in its land of origin, Italy, this most sensuous dessert is called sabayon in France. The major difference, I'm told, is in the choice of wines. Italians traditionally use Marsala wine. The French use champagne. The light frothy cloud of custard draws smiles of kisses from anyone served this glorious dessert. It's simple to make and most impressive.

    1 bowl ice cubes
    2 egg yolks
    ¼ cup sugar
    ⅛ cup champagne
    1 tablespoon raspberry liqueur
    ½ cup heavy cream
    ½ pint fresh large strawberries, sliced and quartered

1.  Fill large bowl with ice, and set aside.
2.  *To prepare the sabayon:* Mix yolks and sugar in large metal bowl. Place bowl over saucepan of simmering water, and whisk until foamy about 1 minute. Add champagne and liqueur. Continue to whisk until mixture is thick and creamy, 4–6 minutes. Remove from heat. Strain into a clean bowl. Place bowl over bowl of ice, and let cool completely.

3.  In separate metal bowl, pour cream and with electric mixer at medium high beat until stiff about 1 minute. Fold into egg yolk mixture.

4.  Place strawberries equally into two fluted glasses. Pour sabayon over strawberries.

Makes 2 servings.

bananas

# The Chocolate The Chocolate

*A silky penetration you enter*
*All dark and deep you appear*
*A marvelous threshold you beget*
*All moist and sweet you hex*

*Crazy fool am I*
*Crazy love you create*
*Can't go on much longer*
*Can go on forever*

*All your nuts are good*
*All hard, and dark, and crunchy*
*A texture of perfection*
*A sweet, dense concoction*

*All I have is yours*
*All I shall ever have is yours*
*All I need is you*
*All I shall ever need is you*

*I can't sleep*
*I can't think*
*I'm moving too fast*
*I'm moving too slow*

*No light*
*No direction*
*No reason*
*I have*
*to live*
*without you*

*I'm falling in love again*
*Now*
*All this makes sense.*

# Chocolate Walnut Brownies

Brownie defined: A small, chewy chocolate cake. As I reviewed the definition, I thought how it is that love comes in the smallness of giving. The acts of thoughtfulness, graciousness, and tenderness are small things when you acknowledge that they don't cost anything and they don't take much of your time. But the spiritual and emotional foundations you create with these small acts are enormous and long-lasting.

Preheat oven to 350 degrees.

½ tablespoon butter, melted

4 ounces good bittersweet chocolate, chopped

½ tablespoon plus 2¼ cups sugar

8 tablespoons unsalted butter

3 eggs

1 teaspoon vanilla extract

⅛ teaspoon almond extract

¾ cup flour, all-purpose unbleached

¼ cup Dutch-processed cocoa

⅛ teaspoon baking soda

⅛ teaspoon salt

1 cup walnut halves

Special equipment: 8×8-inch pan; aluminum foil to line pan

1. Place aluminum foil in pan. Press into corners and shape foil to pan. Remove excess foil. Melt ½ tablespoon butter, and pour into pan. With your fingers, coat pan with butter.

2. Place chocolate in small metal bowl, and place over a pan with 2 inches of simmering water. Stir until chocolate is smooth. Remove bowl from heat. Set aside to slightly cool.

3. With electric mixer, blend sugar and butter in mixing bowl, about 5 minutes. Add eggs one at a time, and beat until creamy, about 5 minutes more. Add vanilla and almond extracts to butter mixture. Add chocolate and mix just to blend. Sift flour, cocoa, baking soda, and salt, and fold into chocolate mixture until well blended. Fold walnuts into batter.

4.  Pour batter into pan, and bake about 25 minutes. Top of brownie should have a crust. Brownie will be fudgy and still slightly wet inside. This is okay. Do not overcook. Place pan on rack to cool; refrigerate overnight before cutting.

5.  Use serrated bread knife to cut into squares. Store in plastic wrap or airtight container in refrigerator.

Makes 8–10 servings.

*Note:* I use Nielsen-Massey's Pure Vanilla Extract with Madagascar Bourbon (to order, see appendix B).

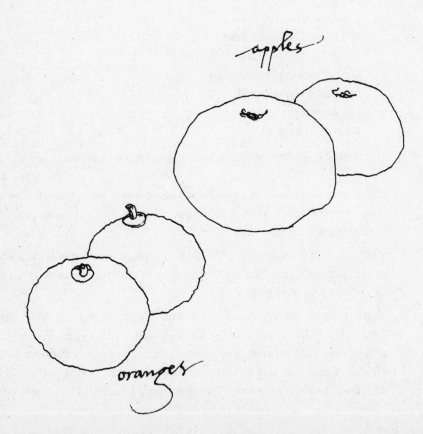

apples

oranges

# Pursuit of Happiness

*Memories are strong in our pursuit of happiness*
*Like having cookies and milk*
*brings instant thoughts of unconditional love*
*from moms who left them on the kitchen table*
*waiting for you after school days*
*Or shrimp and grits for me brings sandy beaches*
*relaxing in the sun dabbling in the ocean*
*reading at my leisure or just having fun*
*with friends, family, and loved ones*
*What of your memories how do they come for you*
*Open your mind for thoughts of pleasure at will*
*Pause for the cause and relax*
*Let thoughts of pleasure flood your mind*
*Stop what you're doing and sit or recline*
*Drink your favorite coffee, tea, or glass of wine*
*Close your eyes and reflect on the past*
*Remember foods that have tingled your libido*
*Contemplate your future pleasures and they will come*

## Chocolate Chunk Pecan Cookies

I first baked these cookies with my grandchildren one Sunday afternoon. Aliyah was in charge of scooping the dough for each cookie, rounding them, and placing them on the cookie sheet. Tyler was in charge of patting the cookies down. We baked them and pulled them out of the oven to cool. The cookies were delicious, and, of course, after eating only one, the children wanted more. I said that we would eat another after dinner. Alexis said, "Well, let's have dinner."

8 tablespoons unsalted butter

½ teaspoon vanilla extract

½ cup sugar

½ cup light brown sugar, packed

1 egg

1 ¼ cups unbleached flour

½ teaspoon salt

¼ teaspoon baking soda

½ teaspoon baking powder

1 cup good bittersweet chocolate, cut into half-inch pieces

1 cup coarsely chopped pecans

Special equipment: Parchment paper to cover cookie sheet

1. In large mixer, mix butter until creamy, about 2 minutes. Add vanilla, sugar, and light brown sugar, and mix well. Add egg and mix just until blended.

2. Whisk together flour, salt, baking soda, and baking powder in a bowl. Add to butter mixture, and beat until just combined, scraping down sides with rubber spatula. Do not overmix.

3. Remove mixing bowl from mixer, and fold in chunks of chocolate and pecans. Cover with plastic wrap, and refrigerate for at least 30 minutes. After 15 minutes, preheat oven to 350 degrees.

4. Remove cookie dough from refrigerator, and scoop 2-inch rounds of dough. Place on parchment-covered cookie sheet. Pat cookie rounds down once. Bake about 6 minutes. Turn cookie sheet around, and bake 5 minutes more, until cookies are golden brown on edges.

5. Remove from oven. Use metal spatula to remove cookies and place on wire rack. Let stand 2 to 3 minutes. Serve warm with cold milk.

Makes 15 3-inch cookies.

# CHAPTER SEVEN

# Creating Romantic Evenings

## MENUS AND TIPS FOR SPECIAL OCCASIONS

**ROMANTIC EVENINGS:**

Valentine's "Let's Make Love All Day" Dinner

New Year's Eve "Eternally Yours" Supper

Sunday "Seduce Me" Brunch

Birthday "Born to Love You" Bash

First Day of Spring "Spring into My Arms" Dinner

"Cook in Advance/Seduce at Your Leisure" Dinners

I don't want to miss this opportunity that is unfolding before me—the opportunity to share what I know about food and love and passion with you. I don't want to look the other way and say, oh, it's nothing, this food thing, this food-love thing—I want you to have it, taste it, touch it, feel it.

I have learned to be aware of, accept, and enjoy food erotica as another layer of love in my life. Everyday love is good in itself, but if you dig more deeply, you will learn that discovering extra love in our lives is restricted only by our lack of imagination. It is in our hearts and our hands. It is free but for the price of food, and it is undemanding but for the efforts necessary to make it a part of our lives. It is a chance to develop a culinary indulgence in our kitchens and in our bedrooms with those we love through the sharing of scrumptious foods and reading of poetic food erotica to live in a romantic mist.

We can control and share this love with the simple gesture of turning on the oven, by chopping vegetables and by creating a sensual, succulent meals for those we love. If you embrace this, you'll find that every aspect of the preparation brings forth erotic sensations and is much like falling in love again.

Deciding on the menu and the atmosphere for the occasion is the tease of a new love affair. Touching, smelling, and selecting the firmest clear-eyed fish, the shapeliest purple eggplant, and the freshest red strawberries is the foreplay. Getting your ingredients lined up on the kitchen counter to mix and season and then sauté and simmer are the simple kisses of love's interplay. Sitting at the table to share a well-planned romantic evening with delicious foods and erotic food poetry and then to receive a kiss, an embrace, and all that unfolds from this interlude is the consummation of this other layer of love.

Sharing food should always be an event—and it's not always simple. Some energy is required. Some planning is necessary. But the reward is so great, who cares? Envision the scene for romance. What to wear? What to cook? What music to play? How to act? These questions must be answered with a strong determination to please and to receive pleasure. Inhibitions must vanish. Imagination must bloom. I offer some suggestions as starters to create romantic evenings through the foods and poetry of *Succulent Tales*.

# Adorning the Table

An attractive dining table is to the gastronomical sensors what a rumpled bed is to an active libido. The sense of sight reveals one's affection without anyone ever saying a single word. Sight is the most ethereal of all the senses and has remarkable powers. Take care to dress your table. You will know that you are loved when you are invited to share a table that has been well dressed. The domain of the sensual senses will be extended far beyond your table to greet your lover on sight of your delicious effort. A good-looking table creates a confidence of affection toward the one who has so thoughtfully labored to introduce beauty into the other's life. A dressed table says, "I love you dearly." It is separate and in itself an intimate gift of love.

So it is with total surrender that one should create a loving, seductive, and engaging dining environment, a table that complements the menu as well as the evening. Visit linen shops and discover the many different table coverings and settings available. Classic embroidered white linen is always a good choice. You can always dress it up without complicating the patterns of sensual moods you are working toward. White linen is also a good choice because it exudes elegance. However, colorful, flowered, art decor or complex patterned table coverings can be just as engaging and should be used interchangeably with different menus. Always consider good taste, simple elegance, sensuality, and attractiveness as your measuring rod, but especially, be aware of the table dressing that best increases the chance of the most ecstatic loving reflection from your lover. Yeah, get that one. Menu planning and planned food consumption are the blueprint to a successful evening of food seduction. Take care not to overdo anything. The quantity of food offered is not what we seek, but the quality and complementary grouping of foods are what make a good menu. I have created menus based on my taste, so they are specific to my culinary delights. However, there are general rules that all of us must abide by. As Jean Anthelme Brillat-Savarin, the nineteenth-century French food writer, told his readers in *The Physiology of Taste*, I offer some general rules to my contemporary culinary seducers in hopes that they hear me as "clearly as an oracle":

- Let the performance of the meal always start on time.

- Let the fragrance of the air be light and mysteriously charming.

- Let the temperature be pleasantly mild.

- Let the surroundings be clean and uncluttered.

- Let the dining room be romantically lit with strategically placed candles or dim lighting.

- Let the music complement the mood of your planned seduction.

- Let the table covering be attractively pleasant and uncomplicated.

- Let the menu be one of complementary foods that are distinctively different and not within the same food family throughout the meal.

- Let the menu not allow you to overeat.

- Let the food on the plate taste good.

- Let the food on the plate look good.

- Let hot food be hot when served.

- Let cold food be cold when served.

- Let the wine you cook with and eat with be good wine.

- Let the passage of time not escape you.

- Let the charm of your company be enjoyed by your companion.

- Let the meal be accompanied by an attractive goblet of cold spring water.

- Let the coffee be hot and excellent and available.

- Let the sexual drama build up as the evening unfolds.

- Let the passage to your more erotic planned moments be not too late.

- Let the passage to your drawing room, bedroom, or any other room of seduction be the anticipation of more to come of your lover's desires.

When "supper is well and truly over," as Brillat-Savarin would say, the acknowledgment of the culinary love you've shared will be abundantly appreciated.

# Thirty Unforgettable Menus

Always remember that he who eats well is capable of performing incredible feats. This is what we want in the world of food eroticism—a thoughtful meal and good sex. One who reflects on the nature and longevity of seduction for an evening of food erotica must consider the selections and consumption of a well-planned menu. Above all, we want to avoid exhaustion. So, if, for example, you choose Braised Oxtails in Red Wine Sauce for an evening of seduction, do not combine this with macaroni and cheese, collards, cornbread, and two servings of dessert. For a seductive menu that includes braised oxtails, choose only one additional vegetable or carb—I suggest creamy whipped potatoes with a light dessert simply to sweeten the mouth. Not much else is needed. Heavy meals induce sleep, not sex. And we want to enjoy food eroticism without fatigue and diminished pleasure. We want to go to that mysterious place in food eroticism, where, when thoughtfully planned and executed, only climactic satisfaction and happiness are felt. And with that in mind, I offer the following menus.

## Valentine's "Let's Make Love All Day" Dinner

Valentine lovers can reach their optimum passion simply with a wink and a smile. Not much else is needed, for everyone knows what's expected, and besides, love and sex are in the air. But if we've the opportunity to throw just a tad bit more into the mix to achieve nirvana, who's gonna turn away from that? Thoughtful and uninhibited planning is the key to achieve a fun-loving memorable evening of wine, food, poetry, and sex. Imagine your lover's welcome-home as you extend a glass of wine and he extends roses and a kiss. Now let's just expand that moment of sincere love into intense passion for the evening.

> *The Setting:* Plan to share your evening of food erotica in your bedroom. Create a highway of red rosebuds to your chamber. Have heart-shaped candles on your nightstand. Cover your bed with a fluffy white down comforter with lots of plump red and purple pillows tossed about. At a glance, rumpled comforters suggest playful eroticism. Have a table for two, near your bed, dressed with a white linen tablecloth, matching napkins, crystal

wine and water goblets, clear plates, and red roses in a crystal vase as the centerpiece.

*The Music:* Romance, romance, romance—whatever music ignites your flame is the music to choose. Remember, though, the rythmn you choose will meter your lovemaking. The sultry rythmns of jazz and seductive sounds of R&B create an intercourse of love for me. My favorites are Miles Davis's classic, *Kind of Blue*, a forever winner; Jon Lucien's *By Request*; D'Angelo's *Voodoo*; or repeatedly playing Al Green's *Simply Beautiful*, and they can sustain an evening of fabulous love-making. However, all music is good. Choosing you and your lover's favorite music is key to achieve your musical interlude.

*The Foreplay:* A box of sex toys that include long-stem fluffy feathers, fragrant massage oil, perfume-scented dustings, and attractive silk scarves to accompany poetry readings during your meal is an extraordinary sensual creation of eroticism. Just before the soup is served and you have sipped your wine and relaxed for the coming of love and a meal, recite the poetry of the soup selected and follow with each entrée. After dessert, as you both go toward your inviting bed, have your lover recite the dessert poem as you pull out your toys to play with deep into the night.

## Menu Options

**MENU #1**

Soup:       Crawfish and Corn Bisque (see p. 9)
Entrée:     Salmon in Puff Pastry (see p. 84)
            Sautéed French Beans (see p. 221)
Dessert:    Very Berry Mascarpone Cream Tart (see p. 270)

**MENU #2**

Soup:       Tomato Basil Soup (see p. 25)
Entrée:     Crawfish Risotto (see p. 48)
            Sautéed Spinach (see p. 213)
Dessert:    Cheesecake with Fresh Strawberries

**MENU #3**

| | |
|---|---|
| Soup: | Roasted Peppers and Pear Soup (see p. 31) |
| Entrée: | Duck à l'Orange (see p. 136) |
| | Whipped Sweet Potatoes (see p. 220) |
| | Grilled Vegetables (see p. 198) |
| Dessert: | Strawberries in Champagne Sabayon (see p. 278) |

**MENU #4**

| | |
|---|---|
| Soup: | Brie and Smoked Salmon Soup (see p. 7) |
| Entrée: | Chicken Chasseur (see p. 142) |
| | Roasted Portobello Mushrooms (see p. 215) |
| | Whipped Potatoes (see p. 74) |
| Dessert: | Red Velvet Cake (see p. 274) |

**MENU #5**

| | |
|---|---|
| Soup: | Potato Leek Soup (see p. 20) |
| Entrée: | Quail with Cherries (see p. 162) |
| | Risotto with Red Wine and Parmesan (see p. 217) |
| Dessert: | Chocolate Mousse (see p. 244) |

# New Year's Eve "Eternally Yours" Supper

It's midnight and the dawn of a new year. A new opportunity to love and be loved. A moment to witness the birth of a new year and to share that moment with someone you love. In planning your New Year's Eve "Eternally Yours" Supper, a light meal is essential, and it must be easy to prepare, present, and devour. Remember, this is a midnight celebration; the entire evening should be planned out to savor deliciously each hour before we get to the celebratory midnight hour. A menu selection with foods cooked in advance to warm and serve easily is ideal. It can be a substantial soup, say gumbo; or a light entrée of crawfish risotto; or sirloin steaks with shallot brandy sauce served with French bread and a dessert. Overeating dulls the seductive senses, and most, if not all, of the evening's lovemaking will occur after midnight. So, at midnight, we don't want to fall asleep; we want to fall in love again.

*The Setting:* After selecting your menu, you've got to create the drama before and after supper. It won't be too difficult, for it's New Year's Eve. The drama is there, but how do you interweave the "Big Kiss" at midnight into your plan for supper and sex? Plan each hour to lead into the kiss. At 9 o'clock, the sparkles from a table full of slender white candles on a white-and-gold dressed dining room table should be the only light your lover sees as he enters your home and you greet him with a glass of champagne and a lovely tray of assorted cheeses, grapes, and olives.

*The Music:* The early-evening music should be joyous frolicking dance music. The plan is to dance with your lover before supper, and on your lover after supper. I suggest your favorite rock 'n' roll, R&B, rap, country, reggae, whatever gets you on the dance floor.

*The Foreplay:* Good food, erotic poetry, and a lap dance is the prelude to bring in the new year. At 9:30 you share supper and poetry, as you read to each other. At 11:00 you sit your lover in your living room to relax with more champagne while you go to change into layers of sensuality. Wear something light and airy. Top layer: try a cocoa chiffon wrap with wide sleeves. Come out dancing around him. Let him inhale your air, touch your wrap, and see that there's more, but less beneath. Second layer: wear a bone-colored stretch-lace chemise, low cut, barely covering your nipples, with a deep v-shaped back. Begin a gentle massage around his neck, around his shoulders, and down his back as you press your body hard against his. Last layer: cocoa lace-bun panties that allow the bottom of your derriere to peek out, and a matching cami that pushes your breasts slightly upward. This is the layer he sees as you come to him with your New Year's Eve lap dance. Facing him, you sit between his legs. It is now midnight, and time for the "Big Kiss." Happy New Year!

# Menu Options

**MENU #1**

Starter:    Assorted cheeses, grapes, and olives
Entrée:    Ed's Gumbo (see p. 3)
            Hot Buttery French Bread
Dessert:    Apple Tarte Tatin (see p. 251)

**MENU #2**

Starter:    Assorted cheeses, grapes, and olives
Entrée:    Crawfish Risotto (see p. 48)
            Hot Buttery French Bread
Dessert:    Chocolate Walnut Brownies (see p. 281)

**MENU #3**

Starter:    Assorted cheeses, grapes, and olives
Entrée:    Sirloin Steak with Shallot Brandy Sauce (see p. 129)
            Hot Buttery French Bread
Dessert:    New Orleans Bread Pudding with Brandy Sauce
            (see p. 265)

**MENU #4**

Starter:    Assorted cheeses, grapes, and olives
Entrée:    Parmesan Penne Pasta with Chicken and Andouille
            Sausage (see p. 234)
            Hot Buttery French Bread
Dessert:    Lemon Mousse (see p. 256)

**MENU #5**

Starter:    Assorted cheeses, grapes, and olives
Entrée:    Vegetable Paella (see p. 182)
            Hot Buttery French Bread
Dessert:    Coconut Pound Cake (see p. 248)

# Sunday "Seduce Me" Brunch

Lazy Sunday mornings are excellent times to seduce. Purchase a Sunday *New York Times,* have a mimosa, and both of you dress leisurely in nothing but white terrycloth robes. Plan to eat, play, and love in your bed. Have large attractive food trays, layered with lace doilies, whereupon your casual sunflower dinnerware rests. Have a table nearby to place your tray on once you've completed your brunch so that you can then move easily into making love, taking a nap, then starting over again with another mimosa, reading yet another section of the *Times,* kissing and loving, and so on and so forth. Shrimp and Grits have always been a hit for brunch. It is absolutely delicious and marvelous to look at. It is quite seductive with the creaminess of the grits and the golden sauce of the shrimp and various red, yellow, and orange peppers sauntering about. Or try the Salmon with Mozzarella and Asiago Quiche and a small bowl of berries with crème fraiche. Whatever you choose, it should be bright, colorful, and cheerful, and I hope it brings out a smile and a sharp passion pain below your navel.

*The Setting:* But before all this happens, whether he greets you at the door at noon or turns to you, awakening with a kiss and a smile, both of you should gather with a mimosa in a warm bath of perfume-scented bubble-bath water with candlelight and burning incense surrounding the bath.

*The Music:* Slow and lazy Sunday afternoon music, such as *Levee Low Moan: Soul Gestures in Southern Blue* by Wynton Marsalis or John Coltrane's *A Love Supreme*, should be softly heard in the background. Any music selected should offer an absolutely relaxing escape into a sensual Sunday fantasy.

*The Foreplay:* You both step out of the tub, maybe after 30 minutes to an hour of bath drama, into the soft white terrycloth robes and then lie across the bed and begin a soothing massage and poetry reading. You go first. As you rub and press and stroke him with a strategic, relaxing, intimate massage, recite "Swim Upstream with Me," of Salmon with Mozzarella and Asiago Quiche. Then turn him over to begin the cycle of loving and eating and loving and eating during your Sunday "Seduce Me" Brunch.

# Menu Options

**MENU #1**

Entrée:    Shrimp and Grits (see p. 81)
                 Mini-croissants
                 Scrambled Eggs
                 Sliced Summer Red Tomatoes
Dessert:   Chocolate Chunk Pecan Cookies (see p. 283)
                 Mimosas and Good Hot Coffee

**MENU #2**

Entrée:    Salmon with Mozzarella and Asiago Quiche (see p. 78)
                 Bowl of strawberries, blueberries, and raspberries
Dessert:   Coconut Pound Cake (see p. 248) and Vanilla Ice
                 Cream
                 Mimosas and Good Hot Coffee

**MENU #3:**

Entrée:    Southern Fried Chicken (see p. 156) and Grits (see p. 194)
                 Scrabbled Eggs
                 Sliced Summer Tomatoes
                 Biscuits
Dessert:   Very Berry Mascarpone Cream Tart (see p. 270)
                 Mimosas and Good Hot Coffee

**MENU #4**

Entrée:    Crepes with Spinach and Ricotta (see p. 192)
                 Salad of Mixed Greens with Grilled Figs
Dessert:   Chocolate Walnut Pound Cake with Chocolate
                 Ganache (see p. 262)
                 Mimosas and Good Hot Coffee

**MENU #5**

Entrée:    Fried Eggplant Frittata (see p. 189)
                 Assortment of Fresh Fruit
Dessert:   Sweet Potato Pecan Pie (see p. 253) with Vanilla Ice
                 Cream
                 Mimosas and Good Hot Coffee

# Birthday "Born to Love You" Bash

For a Birthday "Born to Love You" Bash, drop your ego and think only of your lover. Reflect on what has made him happy. What foods and activities have most excited the one you love and transported you both to seduction? This is what you want to embrace. You want to seduce and be seduced. What food was the spark that lit the way? Surely you will come up with a previous repast that caused your lover's thighs to bounce open. My husband loves oxtails. Just the mention of them brings a smile. What do you share that causes such a reaction? Allow that to carry you to the menu for the Birthday "Born to Love You" Bash.

*The Setting:* Invite two or three couples to share this birthday celebration. Hire someone to serve as you entertain at the dinner table. Make the table setting elegant yet comfortable with fragrant flowers as your centerpiece. Create a scrapbook of baby pictures and eventful moments of your lover's life (nothing to embarrass) and pass it around. Lively conversation will be centered on the birthday boy. After dinner, play slow music only to keep couples embraced on the dance floor.

*The Music:* Slow, slow, slow moves into love is the music to choose. Any of Barry White's music will do. Cassandra Wilson's *Belly of the Sun* will keep you hot and sweaty—this is good sweat.

*The Foreplay:* After an evening of dinner with friends, vibrant conversation, laughter, and slow dancing, you thank your friends for coming and you say good-bye. You turn to your lover and pull out erotic poems and sex videos. Read "Succulent Tails" of Braised Oxtails in Red Wine Sauce or "Sonnet to a Leg of Lamb" from Leg of Lamb Stuffed with Spinach and Mint, then turn on the videos.

# Menu Options

**MENU #1**

Soup:       French Onion Soup (see p. 26)
Entrée:     Braised Oxtails in Red Wine Sauce (see p. 89)
            Whipped Potatoes (see p. 74)
            Sautéed Spinach (see p. 213)
Dessert:    Banana Pudding

**MENU #2**

Soup:       Ed's Turtle Soup (see p. 33)
Entrée:     Eggplant Parmesan (see p. 224)
            Roasted Rosemary Potatoes (see p. 186)
Dessert:    New Orleans Bread Pudding with Brandy Sauce
            (see p. 265)

**MENU #3**

Soup:       Sweet Corn Soup and Roasted Red Pepper Soup
            (see p. 14)
Entrée:     Leg of Lamb Stuffed with Spinach and Mint
            (see p. 92)
            Sautéed French Beans (see p. 221)
            Potato Cake (see p. 207)
Dessert:    Chocolate Walnut Pound Cake with Chocolate
            Ganache (see page 262)

**MENU #4**

Soup:       Butternut Squash Soup (see p. 29)
Entrée:     Stuffed Peppers and Collard Greens (see p. 101)
            Cornbread Rice Dressing (see p. 231)
Dessert:    Apple Tarte Tatin (see p. 251) with Vanilla Ice Cream

**MENU #5**

Soup:       Spinach Soup (see p. 22)
Entrée:     Stuffed Roasted Eggplant (see p. 210)
            Potato Cake (see p. 207)
Dessert:    Pecan Praline Pound Cake (see p. 258)

# First Day of Spring "Spring into My Arms" Dinner

This dinner should be eaten in the early evening and outside. It should be enjoyed while the birds are still singing their twilight songs. Design a romantic exit from inside your home to your balcony, porch, or lawn where dinner and more will be served. Wrapping sheer, colorful fabrics into a tunnel-shaped passage leading from the inside of your home to your outside setting creates a sensual passage to move from one location to another. And if you plan to make love outside, make sure your needs for security and comfort are met.

> *The Setting:* Hang wind chimes just outside your balcony, allowing a cool breeze to ring sounds of pleasure. Have a bunch of sunflowers in a wide flower vase as your centerpiece. Encircle scented candles on your balcony and place oversized colorful pillows on its floor for the two of you to lie against as you recite poetry and feed each other your spring dinner.

> *The Music:* Love sounds are important. So along with the bird songs and chimes, offer music of nature and romance. Bobby McFerrin's *Medicine Music* is a perfect choice.

> *The Foreplay:* The coming together of spring, love, food, and poetry is the beginning and the ending to this spring dinner. For all the evening, you will exchange victuals, drink wine, and recite poetry to each other as you lie under the stars of twilight in each other's arms.

## Menu Options

**MENU #1**

Soup:     Shrimp Bisque (see p. 11)
Entrée:   Seared Duck Breasts with Fig Sauce
          (see p. 139)
          Risotto with Wild Mushrooms (see p. 180)
Dessert:  Chocolate Walnut Pound Cake (see p. 262)
          with Vanilla Ice Cream

**MENU #2**

Soup:     French Onion Soup (see p. 26)
Entrée:   Seared Salmon with Shiitake Mushrooms,
          French Beans, and Tomatoes (see p. 55)
Dessert:  Chocolate Mousse (see p. 244)

**MENU #3**

Entrée:   Braised Rainbow Trout with Crawfish Potato
          Hash (see p. 59)
          Sautéed Spinach (see p. 213)
Dessert:  Lemon Mousse (see p. 256)

**MENU #4**

Soup:     Potato Leak Soup (see p. 220)
Entrée:   Salmon in Puff Pastry (see p. 84)
          Grilled Vegetables Sprinkled with Vinegar
          and Parmesan Shavings (see p. 198)
Dessert:  Cheesecake with Fresh Strawberries (see p. 267)

**MENU #5**

Entrée:   Grilled T-bone Steak (see p. 130)
          Roasted Garlic Whipped Potatoes (see p. 227)
Dessert:  Sweet Potato Pecan Pie (see p. 253) and Vanilla
          Ice Cream

# "Cook in Advance/Seduce at Your Leisure" Dinners

I have cooked meals immediately before an evening of romance. I have seduced with foods cooked in advance of the evening's seduction. Most foods
in my cookbook can be cooked hours or days ahead and refrigerated. The
choice to cook ahead depends on the menu you chose and the overall plan
for the romantic encounter. Because I have always worked outside the home,
I know how tiring it is to come home after an eight-hour workday and then
to be faced with cooking and cleaning. So it is advisable to plan out your
evening's menu to realize what is required to have a successful, relaxing, and
deliciously erotic evening.

*The Setting:* With "Cook in Advance/Seduce at Your Leisure" Dinners, you have time to go to the movies, catch a play, view an art exhibition, or just sit in the park with your lover, before you engage in your culinary adventure. Your dinner is cooked. Your table is set. Your bedroom is clean. Your new nightie is *mise en place* (put in place) just over your bed covering that is folded back. It is 5 o'clock on a Saturday evening, and you're ready to go out and enjoy pre-dinner plans—not that sometimes you might want to just eat out, but this is a cookbook, so come back home to that lovely dinner you have prepared. Once you return home, share a glass of chilled wine and relax before you prepare for dinner.

*The Music:* Put your lover in charge of the musical selections while you warm the food to display on attractive serving platters. Make sure your CD player needs only to be turned on when CDs have been chosen to play.

*The Foreplay:* Slip into something seductive: a floor-length, semitransparent, black lace negligee with undies of a black lace g-strap and low-cut bra; or a short, elaborately designed kimono with extra wide sleeves and hem barely above your derriere with nothing underneath. Just before each entrée, stand before your lover and read the poems. The mere titles of the menu for Wild Mushroom Soup, "Your Musk Entered the Room" or Osso Buco, "Tie Me Up, You Say" or Apple Tarte Tatin, "One Single Kiss" inspire a sensual stream of eroticism. Watching a reading performance of a lover dressed so provocatively, and then sharing the foods just read, is a delicious enticement to prolonging pleasure.

# Menu Options

**MENU #1**

Soup:      Spinach Soup (see p. 22)
Entrée:    Eggplant Parmesan (see p. 224)
           Salad
Dessert:   Sweet Potato Pecan Pie (see p. 253) with Vanilla
           Ice Cream

**MENU #2**

Soup:      Roasted Sweet Potatoes with Andouille Sausage
           Soup (see p. 39)
Entrée:    Braised Lamb Shanks over Saffron Parmesan Risotto
           (see p. 201)
Dessert:   Coconut Pound Cake (see p. 248)

**MENU #3**

Soup:      Wild Mushroom Soup (see p. 17)
Entrée:    Osso Buco (see p. 122)
           Sautéed French Beans (see p. 221)
           Whipped Sweet Potatoes (see p. 220)
Dessert:   Apple Tarte Tatin

**MENU #4**

Soup:      Butternut Squash Soup (see p. 29)
Entrée:    Braised Roast Chuck with Caramelized Onion Po'
           Boy (see p. 104)
Dessert:   Chocolate Mousse (see p. 244)

**MENU #5**

Entrée:    Ed's Gumbo
           Hot French bread
Dessert:   New Orleans Bread Pudding with Brandy Sauce
           (see p. 265)

# Stocks and Roux

IMPORTANT COOKING NOTE: *Mise en place* (literally, put in place) means line up all your ingredients. I swear to this process. It ensures that you will not leave out an ingredient, and it helps prevent overcooking if you have everything ready to cook before you start.

## Beef Stock

Preheat oven to 425 degrees

> 3 pounds beef bones
> 2 tablespoons olive oil
> 1 cup tomato paste
> 2 stalks celery, quartered
> 1 large onion, quartered
> 1 carrot, peeled and quartered
> 4 garlic cloves, halved
> 5 quarts cold water
> 4 bay leaves
> 6 whole black peppercorns
> 1 teaspoon dried thyme
> 1 teaspoon dried basil
> 1 teaspoon salt

1. Drizzle oil over bones and roast 15 minutes.
2. Brush tomato paste over bones and add celery, onion, carrot, and garlic. Continue to roast 25 minutes.
3. Place bones and vegetables in a large stockpot. Add water, bay leaves, peppercorns, thyme, basil, and salt. Bring to boil; then simmer 3 hours. Strain, discard bay leaves, and keep warm for immediate use, or refrigerate, tightly covered, up to one week for use later.

Makes 3 quarts.

# Chicken Stock

2 pounds chicken bones (see note at end of recipe)
4 quarts cold water
2 stalks celery, quartered
1 large onion, quartered
4 bay leaves
4 garlic cloves, halved
10 whole black peppercorns
1 teaspoon dried thyme
1 teaspoon dried basil
1 teaspoon salt

1. Bring all ingredients to boil; then simmer for 2 hours.
2. Strain and keep warm for immediate use, or refrigerate, tightly covered, up to one week for use later.

Makes 3 quarts.

*Note:* You can obtain chicken bones from a butcher if you do not have frozen or fresh leftover bones.

# Shrimp Stock

2 pounds shrimp shells
4 quarts cold water
2 stalks celery, quartered
1 large onion, quartered
2 bay leaves
10 whole black peppercorns
1 teaspoon dried thyme
1 teaspoon dried basil
1 teaspoon salt

1. Bring all ingredients to boil; then simmer for 30 minutes.
2. Strain and keep warm for immediate use, or refrigerate, tightly covered, up to one week for use later.

Makes 3 quarts.

# Fish Stock

        2 pounds assorted fish carcasses
        4 quarts cold water
        2 stalks celery, quartered
        1 large onion, quartered
        2 bay leaves
        10 whole black peppercorns
        1 teaspoon dried thyme
        1 teaspoon dried basil
        1 teaspoon salt

1.  Bring all ingredients to boil; then simmer for 30 minutes.
2.  Strain and keep warm for immediate use, or refrigerate, tightly covered, up to one week for use later.

Makes 3 quarts.

# Vegetable Stock

        2 tablespoons olive oil
        2 medium carrots, scrubbed and sliced
        2 cups chopped cabbage
        2 stalks celery, quartered
        1 large onion, quartered
        4 bay leaves
        4 garlic cloves, halved
        10 whole black peppercorns
        2–3 thyme sprigs
        1 tablespoon chopped basil
        5 parsley sprigs
        2 tomatoes, chopped
        1 potato, sliced
        1 teaspoon salt
        4 quarts cold water

1.  Heat oil in large stockpot over high heat. Sautée all ingredients except potato and tomatoes, about 5 minutes. Add water, potato, and tomatoes.

2. Bring all ingredients to a boil; then cover and simmer 1 hour.

3. Strain and keep warm for immediate use, or refrigerate, tightly covered, up to one week for use later.

Makes 3 quarts.

# Roux

**Vegetable oil**
**Flour**
**1 cup stock or water**

1. *To prepare the roux:* The proportion of oil to flour is 1 to 1. The key to a good roux is to get it dark brown (for a dark roux) but not burned. If you burn the roux, you will see dark specks and it will taste bitter. So just start over.

2. *To prepare a dark roux:* Heat vegetable oil in a cast-iron skillet over medium heat. When oil begins to smoke, stir in flour, using a wooden spoon. Stir constantly, making sure to stir all areas of skillet. Stir until you reach a deep dark brown or near-black color. Then stir in stock. Remove from heat. And you have a roux to add to your gumbos, stews, or étouffées.

3. *To prepare a blond roux:* Use low heat and stir less, using the same steps as in the dark roux, but cook only until you get to a beige color. Usually, a blond roux is used in lighter seafood dishes.

# Mail Orders and Online Food Appendix

Tony's Seafood, Inc., 5215 Plank Road, Baton Rouge, LA 70805
800-356-2905
www.tonyseafood.com
   Will ship live seafood (crawfish, shrimp, crabmeat, crabs, red snapper, trout); dried shrimp; cooking pots; turtle meat; andouille sausage; and pecan pralines.

Tony Chachere's Creole Foods of Opelousas, Inc., PO Box 1639
Opelousas, LA 70571-1639
800-551-9066
www.tonychachere.com
   Will ship its famous Creole seasoning.

Fisherman's Cove, 3201 Williams Blvd., Kenner, LA 70065
800-443-3474
www.fishermanscovela.com
   Will ship live seafood (crawfish, shrimp, crabmeat, crabs, red snapper, trout); liquid crab boil.

L. H. Hayward & Co LLC, Haraham, LA 70183-0751
504-733-8480
www.camelliabrand.com
   Will ship Camellia Red Beans.

Nielsen-Massey Vanillas, Inc., 1550 Shields Drive,
Waukegan, IL 60085-8307
800-525-7873
www.NielsenMassey.com
  For Pure Vanilla Extract with Madagascar Bourbon.

Savoie's Sausage & Food Products, Opelousas, LA 70570
318-942-7241
www.realcajun.com
  Will ship andouille sausage.

Magic Seasoning Blends, New Orleans, LA 70123
800-457-2858
www.chefpaul.com
  Sells herbs and spices, andouille sausages, dried and ground chiles.

New Orleans School of Cooking and Louisiana General Store,
524 St. Louis Street, New Orleans, LA 70130
800-237-4841
www.nosoc.com
  Sells indigenous products such as Zatarain's products, crab and shrimp
boils, coffees, spice blends, and filé powder.

# Index